Image-based Se›

MW00779621

This book investigates the causes and consequences of image-based sexual abuse in a digital era. Image-based sexual abuse refers to the taking or sharing of nude or sexual photographs or videos of another person without their consent. It includes a diversity of behaviours beyond that of "revenge porn", such as the secret trading of nude or sexual images online; "upskirting", "downblousing" and other "creepshots"; blackmail or "sextortion" scams; the use of artificial intelligence to construct "deepfake" pornographic videos; threats to distribute photographs or videos without consent; and the taking or sharing of sexual assault imagery. This book investigates the pervasiveness and experiences of these harms, as well as the raft of legal and non-legal measures that have been introduced to better respond to and prevent image-based sexual abuse.

The book draws on groundbreaking empirical research, including surveys in three countries with over 6,000 respondents and over 100 victim-survivor and stakeholder interviews. Guided by theoretical frameworks from gender studies, sociology, criminology, law and psychology, the authors argue that image-based sexual abuse is more commonly perpetrated by men than women, and that perpetration is higher among some groups, including younger and sexual minority men. Although the motivations of perpetrators vary, a dominant theme to emerge was that of power and control. The gendered nature of the abuse means that it is best understood as a being on a "continuum of sexual violence" because victim-survivors often experience it as part of a broader pattern of gendered harassment, violence and abuse.

Written in a clear and direct style, this book will appeal to students and scholars of criminology, sociology, law and psychology. *Image-based Sexual Abuse* is also an essential resource for activists, legal and policy practitioners, technology companies and victim-survivors seeking to understand the deeply complex nature of intimate-image sharing in a digital era.

Nicola Henry is an Associate Professor and Vice-Chancellor's Principal Research Fellow in the Social and Global Studies Centre at RMIT University (Melbourne, Australia). She has published widely in the sexual field, and is the author of *War and Rape: Law, Memory and Justice* (2011) and *Sexual Violence in a Digital Age* (2017, co-authored with Anastasia Powell).

Clare McGlynn QC (Hon) is a Professor of Law at Durham University (UK), whose research and collaborations with politicians, policymakers and the voluntary sector has shaped new laws relating to pornography, sexual violence and image-based sexual abuse.

Asher Flynn is an Associate Professor of Criminology at Monash University (Melbourne, Australia). She has written on a wide range of issues and is lead researcher on several research projects examining gendered violence, AI-facilitated abuse, technology-facilitated sexual violence and image-based sexual abuse.

Kelly Johnson is an Assistant Professor of Criminology at Durham University (UK). Her research focuses on sexual and domestic violence, particularly in areas related to image-based sexual abuse and policing.

Anastasia Powell is an Associate Professor of Criminology & Justice Studies at RMIT University (Melbourne, Australia). She is the author of several books addressing both technology and sexual violence, including: *Digital Criminology* (2019, co-authored with Gregory Stratton and Robin Cameron), *Sexual Violence in a Digital Age* (2017, co-authored with Nicola Henry), and *Sex, Power and Consent* (2010).

Adrian J. Scott is a Senior Lecturer at Goldsmiths, University of London (UK), where he is a member of the Forensic Psychology Unit and the Co-Director of an accredited MSc programme in Forensic Psychology. He has a broad interest in forensic psychology, specialising in the areas of stalking and image-based sexual abuse.

"This book is essential reading for students, researchers, teachers, practitioners, and policy makers seeking a rich social scientific understanding of image-based sexual abuse. It is destined to become a classic piece of scholarship that significantly advances the study of the ways in which new technologies are used by men to abuse women."

Professor Walter S. DeKeseredy,
West Virginia University

"This book draws on original survey and interview data to provide a compelling account of how 'new' forms of abuse confront us yet again with the familiar challenges stemming from living in a world still shaped by gendered and patriarchal legacies."

Professor Jan Jordan,
Victoria University of Wellington

Routledge Critical Studies in Crime, Diversity and Criminal Justice

*Edited by Patricia Faraldo Cabana, University of A Coruña, Spain;
Nancy A Wonders, Northern Arizona University, USA*

The works in this series strive to generate new conceptual and theoretical frameworks to address the legal, organisational and normative responses to the challenges that diversity and intersectionality present to criminal justice systems. This series aims to present cutting edge empirically informed theoretical works from both new and established scholars around the world.

Drawing upon a range of disciplines including sociology, law, history, economics and social work, the series encourages different approaches to questions of mobility and exclusion with a cross section of theorists, empiricists and critical policy researchers. It will be key reading for scholars who are working on criminal justice, criminology, criminal law and human rights, as well as those in the fields of gender and LGBTQI studies, migration studies, anthropology, refugee studies and post-colonial studies.

The Political Economy of Punishment Today
Visions, Debates and Challenges
Edited by Dario Melossi, Máximo Sozzo and José Brandariz García

Gendered Injustice
Uncovering the Lived Experience of Detained Girls
Anastasia Tosouni

Image-based Sexual Abuse
A Study on the Causes and Consequences of Non-consensual Nude or Sexual Imagery
Nicola Henry, Clare McGlynn, Asher Flynn, Kelly Johnson, Anastasia Powell, and Adrian J. Scott

For more information about this series, please visit: https://www.routledge.com/criminology/series/CDCJ

Image-based Sexual Abuse

A Study on the Causes and Consequences of Non-consensual Nude or Sexual Imagery

Nicola Henry, Clare McGlynn, Asher Flynn, Kelly Johnson, Anastasia Powell, and Adrian J. Scott

Routledge
Taylor & Francis Group

LONDON AND NEW YORK

First published 2021
by Routledge
2 Park Square, Milton Park, Abingdon, Oxon OX14 4RN

and by Routledge
605 Third Avenue, New York, NY 10017

First issued in paperback 2022

Routledge is an imprint of the Taylor & Francis Group, an informa business

Publisher's Note
The publisher has gone to great lengths to ensure the quality of this reprint but points out that some imperfections in the original copies may be apparent.

British Library Cataloguing-in-Publication Data
A catalogue record for this book is available from the British Library

Library of Congress Cataloging-in-Publication Data
A catalog record has been requested for this book

ISBN 13: 978-0-367-52440-1 (pbk)
ISBN 13: 978-0-8153-5383-6 (hbk)
ISBN 13: 978-1-351-13515-3 (ebk)

DOI: 10.4324/9781351135153

Typeset in Times New Roman
by codeMantra

This book is dedicated to victim-survivors of image-based sexual abuse and their supporters.

Contents

Tables

Acknowledgements

This research was funded by an Australian Research Council Discovery project. The views expressed in the book are our own and not those of the funding agency or the Australian Government. We are grateful to the incredible support of the Australian Research Council and the institutions in which we work: RMIT University, Monash University, Durham University, University of Kent, University of Auckland, and Goldsmiths, University of London.

We would like to express our deep gratitude to our partner investigators on the project, Erika Rackley (University of Kent) and Nicola Gavey (University of Auckland). Their collegiality, support and wisdom has been inspirational and formative to both the project and the book. Many of the ideas, concepts and arguments originate from them and we gratefully acknowledge their significant contribution.

We would also like to thank the team of hard-working and dedicated research assistants who have completed an endless list of mundane and arduous tasks with gracious humility. Thank you to Jessamy Gleeson, Magdalena Furgalska, Stefani Vasil, Georgina Dimopoulos and Alice Witt for your incredible work and support on the project and the book.

Our thanks also to Thomas Sutton, Jake Rainbow and Jessica Phillips from Routledge for supporting this book and for your enthusiasm, patience and understanding. Thank you also to the anonymous reviewers who gave us the support we needed from the start.

We are enormously grateful to the victim-survivors who generously gave us their time and talked to us about their experiences of image-based sexual abuse. This book is dedicated to you and we hope that we have faithfully represented your stories in this book. We are also grateful to all the stakeholders who shared their expertise and insights and for the incredible work they do in helping make the world a better place.

Nicola: My deep gratitude is first to my loving family: Mum, Dad, Justine, Emma, Matt, Alex, Mike, Emily, Isabel, Maya, Esther, Owen, Sylvie, Claire and Ava, as well as my extended Henry, Cavanagh and Collett families. Thank you to my wonderful friends, colleagues, yoga/meditation teachers and mentors for their support and care, especially Angelica, Felicity, Ascelin, Harriet, Kirstie, Rachel, Lea, Megan, Duncan, Sharyn, Jackie, Nesam, Ceridwen, Catherine, Peta, Katherine, Suellen and Kerry. I would also like to thank Clare McGlynn and Nicola Gavey for their wonderful collegiality and mentorship. Last but not least, I want to thank, from the bottom of my heart, Brent, Frederick, Silky, Shadow and my beautiful chickens for the joy and lightness that you bring into my life.

Clare: I would particularly like to thank Erika Rackley for her ongoing personal and intellectual inspiration and support throughout this and many other projects.

Asher: I would like to start by thanking my co-authors and project team members for their contributions and the many hours we have spent working collaboratively on this research. To my wonderful colleagues and postgraduate students at Monash University, thank-you. In particular, to my mentor and head of Criminology, Rebecca Wickes, and to the ladies who lunch – Kate Burns and Robyn Oxley – thank-you for your support, friendship and endless messages. Thanks also to my Criminology friends and colleagues who provide guidance, motivation and many, many laughs – special mention here to David Bright, Greg Stratton, Anastasia Powell, Mary Iliadis and Rachael Burgin. Finally, a huge thank-you to my incredible family and to my beautiful son Henry – you make me smile and remember what is truly important every day.

Kelly: I particularly want to thank and acknowledge the victim-survivors and practitioners who gave their invaluable input into this research – so many of who participated in this project – to engender a better understanding of image-based sexual abuse, as well as to be part of a movement for positive social change.

Anastasia: I would like to thank the wonderful support of colleagues at RMIT University, including my Head of Department, Associate Professor Michele Ruyters and Professor Stuart Thomas, who have been so generous in their guidance and advice over the years. I would also like to acknowledge and thank my many criminologist friends and feminist allies, in particular Ruth Liston, Rebecca Hiscock, Lisa Sugiura, Cassandra Cross, Gregory Stratton, Robin Cameron, Adrian Scott, Asher Flynn and Nicola Henry, and many others who have been a source of much appreciated support and generosity in some difficult times. Last, I would like to thank my family, in particular my sisters Desiree and Kathleen, and my son Alexander. Your love means the world to me and I cannot imagine maintaining the resilience to do this work without it.

Adrian: I would like to start by expressing my thanks to Sofia for her love, support, patience and unwavering belief in me. I dread to think how many times Sofia has heard me say "I've got this" and I thank her for not rolling her eyes on every occasion. I would also like to thank Greg for introducing me to Anastasia, to Anastasia for introducing me to Nicola and Asher, and to Anastasia, Nicola and Asher for inviting me to be involved in this wonderful collaboration. I thoroughly enjoy working with you on our various collaborations, and it has been a pleasure to work with, and learn from, the broader team involved in this research project.

The order of authors after Henry and McGlynn is alphabetical and does not reflect the order of contribution to the book.

Chapter I

Image-based sexual abuse
Beyond "revenge pornography"

Introduction

In the 1980s, *Hustler* magazine ran a long-running feature entitled "Beaver Hunt" which invited readers to submit photographs of women's vaginas for publication. Several women sued *Hustler* for libel and an invasion of privacy for publishing the photographs without their consent. In one case, a man and a woman stole photographs of another woman at a party and then sent the photographs to *Hustler* which later appeared in the magazine. The woman sued *Hustler,* claiming that the magazine was negligent in falsely representing that she had consented to the publication of the images and in falsely attributing "lewd sexual fantasies to her" (*Ashby v. Hustler Magazine, Inc.*, 1986).

Back in 1986 when this case was before the courts, terms such as "revenge porn", "sextortion", "image-based sexual abuse" and "deepfakes" had not yet been coined. Camera-enabled smart-phones, social media and the World Wide Web had not yet been invented, and few could have predicted the ways in which new digital technologies would be used to perpetrate a range of harmful acts against children and adults alike. What the *Hustler* case shows is that the non-consensual taking or sharing of nude or sexual images – also known as "revenge pornography", "non-consensual pornography" or "image-based sexual abuse" – is not a new phenomenon. Indeed, since the invention of the camera over 200 years ago, people have long been engaged in the illicit taking or sharing of intimate images without the consent of the person depicted in the image. It is only recently that such practices have been given explicit labels and specific laws have been introduced to render these behaviours either criminal or unlawful. Up until the early 2000s, most attention to these hitherto unnamed phenomena was focused on leaked celebrity sex tapes or nude images of celebrities in exotic holiday destinations (Hayward & Rahn, 2015; Hillyer, 2004). Photographs were published or disseminated in women's and men's magazines, and videotapes sold or borrowed in R-rated sex shops or video stores, occasionally leading to a legal case for defamation or invasion of privacy by those who were wealthy enough to pursue their claims in the civil courts (Chard & Litherland, 2019).

Since the more recent advances in computer technology, including the World Wide Web, search engines, peer-to-peer file sharing, social networking, smart phone technologies, mobile phone apps and artificial intelligence, the dissemination of non-consensual nude or sexual imagery to potentially millions of people worldwide has become a significant global issue.

The term "revenge pornography" was coined in the mid-2000s in response to reports from victim-survivors whose images were being shared online without their consent, and the growing popularity of revenge-oriented websites hosting non-consensual nude or sexual imagery, often accompanied by the personal details of the victim. The non-consensual sharing of nude or sexual images has been further facilitated through a wide range of platforms and devices which enable users to create, upload, download and share nude or sexual images quickly and easily. As this book will explore, broader social and cultural trends also play a significant role, such as the proliferation of amateur pornography, the shifting nature of privacy, new patterns of voyeurism and exhibitionism, the over-saturation of visual imagery, as well as the pervasive inequalities relating to gender, sexuality, age, disability, race and ethnicity.

This book investigates the phenomenon of image-based sexual abuse – the non-consensual taking or sharing of nude or sexual images. The book has two key aims. The first is to investigate the pervasiveness, nature and impacts of image-based sexual abuse. The second is to consider the legal and non-legal responses to this problem in a global context. Building on collaborative, interdisciplinary and mixed-methods research, the book reports on the empirical findings of the most comprehensive study to date of image-based sexual abuse among adults and young people. This includes national surveys with 6,109 respondents, 75 victim-survivor interviews and 41 stakeholder interviews across Australia, New Zealand and the United Kingdom.

The book conceptualises and positions image-based sexual abuse within an understanding of gender, sexuality and inequality, drawing on a range of theoretical frameworks, including feminist legal theory, digital criminology, as well as gender and phenomenological theories. Our analysis is also informed by actor-network theory (Latour, 1991, 2005), which views artefacts, human actors and organisations as interacting in complex, interconnected ways. As such, we eschew the dichotomies often made between agency and structure, nature and society, actor and object, and online and offline (Henry, Flynn, & Powell, in press). We instead prefer to view technology not simply as a tool for motivated perpetrators to engage in egregious acts, but as part of an *overarching system of inequality and discrimination*, whereby societal norms, such as economic profit, excessive individualism, hypersexuality, heterosexuality and hegemonic masculinity, drive and shape behaviours, including those that are harmful, as well as those that are resistive, subversive and non-conformist.

In this first chapter, we begin by introducing the key terms used in this book, such as "revenge porn" and "image-based sexual abuse". The second section summarises the key findings of the survey and victim-survivor interviews. The third and final section provides a summary of each chapter of the book.

From "revenge pornography" to "image-based sexual abuse"

The problem with the term "revenge porn"

The term "revenge porn" was added to the Merriam-Webster dictionary in April 2016. It was defined as "sexually explicit images of a person posted online without that person's consent especially as a form of revenge or harassment". A combined ProQuest, Google Scholar and Factiva search of media and scholarly articles shows that the term "revenge porn" was first used over 20 years earlier in a film review about a group of friends on the run from a gang of drug dealers (Goodard, 1993). It was not until July 2002 that "revenge porn" was used for the first time to describe the actions of a man who posted non-consensual sexual photographs of his ex-girlfriend on a dumpster in retribution for her breaking up with him (Henry & Flynn, 2019). Then in 2005, the term was used again in a New Zealand *Sunday Star* article to describe the practice of former partners sharing non-consensual intimate images on purpose-built websites to "get back at their ex" (Hume, 2005). Around the same time, "sexting" first appeared in media reports after Australian cricketer Shane Warne sent a series of sexually explicit text messages to different women in different continents (Henry & Powell, 2015). Although "sexting" originally referred to the sending of explicit *text* messages, it has since evolved to describe the sending or receiving of nude, semi-nude or sexual images, and text and is often used interchangeably to refer to either consensual or non-consensual behaviours (see Crofts, Lee, McGovern, & Milivojevic, 2015).

In 2011, "revenge porn" came into popular usage after growing attention was given to the non-consensual sharing of nude or sexual images of musicians and sportspersons on the website IsAnyoneUp.com and the subsequent criminal trial of its founder Hunter Moore (Martens, 2011). Since then, the term has been popularised and widely used in media articles, public discourse and scholarly contexts, though not without extensive criticism.

While this salacious term has helped to draw attention to the problem of sharing non-consensual nude or sexual images over the past decade, many victim-survivors, victim support advocates, policymakers and scholars find it objectionable on a number of grounds. First, using the term "revenge porn" to describe all non-consensual sharing is a misnomer because not all perpetrators are motivated by revenge when they share nude or sexual images without consent, but rather may have other motives, such as sexual gratification, monetary gain, social status building or a desire for power and control (Citron & Franks, 2014). Second, by focusing only on the non-consensual sharing of images by ex-partners, the term "revenge porn" ignores other forms of image-based sexual abuse by known and unknown persons, such as the surreptitious or non-consensual filming in public or private places (e.g., "upskirting", "downblousing" or "creepshots"), or threats being made to share intimate imagery (see McGlynn & Rackley, 2017; McGlynn, Rackley, & Houghton, 2017; Powell & Henry, 2017; Powell, Henry, & Flynn, 2018). Third, the term arguably has victim-blaming connotations because it implies that the victim has done something to provoke the ire of the offender. Fourth, the use of the term "pornography" likens non-consensual nude or sexual imagery to the production of commercial pornography, which misrecognises the harms of image-based sexual abuse and fails to capture the diversity of images, many of which are neither pornographic nor sexually explicit (Powell & Henry, 2017). Finally, the term focuses attention on the *content of the image*, rather than on the *abusive actions of perpetrators* who engage in these behaviours (Rackley & McGlynn, 2014).

Defining image-based sexual abuse

To address the problems associated with the term "revenge porn", scholars have developed a range of other labels to describe these behaviours (see Maddocks, 2018), including "non-consensual pornography" (Citron & Franks, 2014; Franks, 2017), "involuntary porn" (Burns, 2015), "non-consensual sexting" (Henry & Powell, 2015) or "image-based sexual abuse" (McGlynn & Rackley, 2017; McGlynn et al., 2017; Powell & Henry, 2017; Powell et al., 2018). While no terminology is perfect, we prefer "image-based sexual abuse" because it better captures the nature and harms experienced by many victim-survivors, the diversity of behaviours, a much broader array of motivations, as well as a range of digital devices and platforms.

We use the term "image-based sexual abuse" to refer to three principal behaviours: First, the non-consensual *taking* of nude or sexual images; second, the non-consensual *sharing* of nude or sexual images; and third, *threats to share* nude or sexual images. We define "taking" to include the photographing or recording of a still or moving image, as well as altering images (digitally or through other means) to make it look as if the person depicted in the image is posing in a nude or sexual way or performing a sexual act. We define "sharing" to mean giving others access to images, which includes showing images to another person or persons, or circulating or distributing images via mobile phone or uploading onto a website for others to view and access. And, finally, we define *images* to include both photographs and videos, thus excluding text and written forms of speech.

Essentially, we treat "image-based sexual abuse" as an umbrella term for a diverse range of abusive behaviours involving non-consensually taken or shared nude or sexual images. These behaviours include (but are not limited to): the use of artificial intelligence or other digital manipulation techniques to construct fake pornographic videos that realistically depict the victim's face onto a body performing a sexual act (also known as "deepfakes" or "fakeporn"); the sharing of nude or sexual images on "revenge porn" websites that have been purposefully designed to entice users to "get back at" a partner, ex-partner or any other known person; the non-consensual taking and/or sharing of nude or sexual images via mobile phone or internet sites for revenge, sexual gratification, voyeurism, social status building or other motives; threats made by strangers online, or by intimate partners, to coerce victim-survivors into sharing more nude or sexual images, to pay money, or to engage in any unwanted act (also known as "sextortion"); and images taken and/or shared of sexual assaults and rape. We do not include pornographic images that are created or disseminated among consenting adults, although we acknowledge that what counts as "consent" in this context is the subject of much feminist debate (Tyler, 2016).

We restrict our focus to *nude or sexual images*. Such images might be pornographic or sexually explicit, or alternatively might depict a person's private sexual parts, including female breasts and/or genitalia, whether exposed or covered by underwear or a swimming costume. While we recognise that what counts as "nude" or "sexual" is open to much debate, particularly in different cultural contexts, our concept does not include images of atrocity, injury or death. We do, however, acknowledge the harmful consequences that may follow from the taking or disclosure of these other types of intimate images and urge other researchers to explore this in further detail.[1]

Furthermore, we use the term *abuse* as opposed to "exploitation" or "violence" as it better captures behaviours that do not necessarily involve acts of physical aggression. While we do not view violence as restricted to physical acts, we recognise that many victim-survivors, victim support advocates and others (including the community more generally) do in fact understand "violence" more narrowly in physical terms. Thus, using the language of violence can in practice result in underreporting and the trivialisation of experiences that do not fit into existing paradigms (see also Boyle, 2019).

The term "image-based sexual abuse" is also consistent with how many victim-survivors describe their experiences. For example, in 2014, actor Jennifer Lawrence referred to the hacking of her iCloud account and the extensive distribution of her nude images as a "sex crime" ("Jennifer Lawrence calls", 2014). Since then, other celebrity victim-survivors have made similar arguments in public debates, with YouTuber Chrissy Chambers describing her experiences as a "sexual assault" (Avila, 2016). In the interviews we conducted with victim-survivors, many shared this perspective. Lucy (UK), for example, commented that: "It's an abuse of me and my body. It feels like it's sexual abuse. I feel like it's on a par with sexual abuse". This was echoed by another of our participants, Deborah (UK), who described her experiences as "a type of rape, it's just the digital version" (discussed further in McGlynn et al., 2019).

Nonetheless, one of the challenges with using the term "image-based sexual abuse" is that some people whose images have been taken or shared without their consent may not recognise or identify themselves as "abuse victims". This may be because they have not been adversely affected by the experience. Nonetheless, our justification for labelling the non-consensual taking or sharing of nude or sexual images as "abuse" (regardless of perpetrator motive or victim impact) is to draw attention to the lack of consent in the act of taking or sharing images, and the significant harms that can ensue for many victim-survivors.

It is important to note, however, that we do not suggest that all acts of image-based sexual abuse are equally pernicious, nor do we suggest all acts should be treated in the same way. For example, criminal penalties for children or adolescents who engage in these behaviours should be a last resort (although of course there will be exceptions for more extreme cases). There might also be differences in punitive consequences for those who merely show images to others compared to those who share and circulate images online or via mobile devices, or for those who share sexually explicit images with friends or family members in order to seek support after being "cyberflashed".

As we hope to highlight in this book, experiences of image-based sexual abuse are by no means uniform. This is clearly demonstrated by the findings of our survey and interviews with people who had experienced image-based sexual abuse. Our aim then is to examine those diverse experiences in order to highlight the complexity of image-based sexual abuse, and to locate it within a broader discursive sociocultural system where gender and sexuality inequality in intimate relationships remains normalised and widespread. Moreover, we contextualise the non-consensual taking or sharing of intimate images as a common practice that sits within a much broader digital culture that is saturated with visual imagery and visual communications (Katz & Crocker, 2015).

Summary of findings: image-based sexual abuse victimisation and perpetration study

Throughout the book we report on the key findings of an interdisciplinary, multi-jurisdictional, mixed-methods project using qualitative interviews and quantitative surveys to examine the pervasiveness, nature and impacts of image-based sexual abuse. The project used a feminist methodology (Collins, 2000; Harding, 2004) appropriate for addressing social justice issues that are not only "gendered", but also shaped by interlocking systems of oppression and inequality on the basis of gender, sexuality, race, ethnicity, age, class and ability (referred to as "intersectionality" – see e.g., Collins,

2019; Crenshaw, 1991; May, 2015). The methodology allowed for acknowledgement of the importance of "subjugated knowledge" and the "complexities of differences of experiences" (Letherby, 2011: 75). The subsections below describe the methods used for the qualitative and quantitative data, respectively.

Victim-survivor interviews

Participants for victim-survivor interviews were required to be 18 years of age or older, live in Australia, New Zealand or the United Kingdom, and have experienced at least one form of image-based sexual abuse. Participants were recruited using a variety of methods. Through paid Facebook advertising we sought to recruit participants across a range of genders, ages, economic statuses, culturally diverse groups and geographic locations in Australia, New Zealand and the United Kingdom (see also Ramo, Rodriguez, Chavez, Sommer, & Prochaska, 2014; Robards, 2013). Other participants were recruited through private Facebook groups and Twitter. We also combined social media advertising with more traditional methods of recruitment, including snowball sampling to reach informal networks of victim-survivors of image-based sexual abuse, as well as the electronic and hard copy distribution of advertisements. A small number of participants were recruited through victim-support organisations and networks.

In total, 75 participants were recruited for semi-structured interviews in person, by telephone or via Skype, with 25 from each country (Australia, New Zealand and the United Kingdom). Of our 75 participants, the majority were younger adults. This included 68.0% (n=51) who were aged 18–29 years, followed by 20.0% (n=15) aged 30–39 years, and 12.0% (n=9) aged over 40 years. Participants also predominantly identified as women (89.3%, n=67), compared with men (8.0%, n=6), trans (1.3%, n=1) and self-identified "other" (1.3%, n=1). The majority of participants identified as heterosexual/straight (62.7%, n=47), followed by bisexual (18.7%, n=14), lesbian (2.7%, n=2), gay (2.7%, n=2), queer (2.7%, n=2), "other" (8.0%, n=6) and "unsure" (2.7%, n=2). In terms of race and ethnicity, 81.3% (n=61) identified as either White, European or Pākehā,[2] while the remaining respondents (18.7%, n=14) selected other indigenous or Black, Asian and Minority Ethnic (BAME) backgrounds, including New Zealand Māori (2.7%, n=2) and Black British (1.3%, n=1). Finally, 24.0% (n=18) of our participants identified as having a disability.

While this study is the largest study to have been conducted on image-based sexual abuse to date, it is important to note the specificities and limitations of our method. We were not able to recruit evenly across certain categories when compared to the broader population demographics according to age, gender, sexuality, race, ethnicity and ability. Nonetheless, that the majority of participants were younger should not be a surprise given that previous studies have shown that young adults are disproportionately affected by various forms of online abuse and harassment (e.g., Gámez-Guadix, Almendros, Borrajo, & Calvete, 2015; Pew Research Center, 2014; Powell & Henry, 2019). In relation to gender, while both women and men can experience significant harms from image-based sexual abuse, women may be more likely than men to identify as victim-survivors which may explain why we recruited more women than men. We were also unable to investigate in-depth the ways in which other vectors of marginalisation intersect with gender. Further targeted qualitative research on image-based sexual abuse among specific groups, such as minoritised, indigenous, migrant and refugee people, gender and sexual minorities, sex workers and those with a disability, is vital to explore diverse experiences of image-based sexual abuse in more detail.

We removed potentially identifying information regarding participant experiences (such as their race, ethnicity, age and sexuality), and all participants were assigned a pseudonym to protect their confidentiality and anonymity. Throughout the book, we provide the allocated pseudonym of our participants for longer quotes, however, for shorter or one-word quotations we have not included participant pseudonyms because many of the words were used by multiple participants (as many as n=15 in some cases). We have adopted this approach to avoid creating a hierarchy between participants and/or quotes in the depiction of short phrases. To protect participants' identities, we have only indicated, alongside their pseudonym, what country they are from and have not provided further information about them, such as their gender, age, sexuality, race or ethnicity.

Stakeholder participants were also recruited in New Zealand and the United Kingdom through snowball sampling within professional networks, as well as targeted approaches, in order to address potential gaps in our victim-survivor interview data. As part of a previous project completed in 2017, we conducted 52 interviews with stakeholders in Australia. As a result of the close proximity of time between completing these Australian interviews and undertaking additional stakeholder interviews, we decided against conducting further interviews in Australia. Instead, we spoke to representatives from a range of organisations in England, Wales, Scotland, Northern Ireland and New Zealand, who work with women and men survivors of sexual abuse and/or image-based sexual abuse, as well as with Māori and BAME women. We also interviewed stakeholders from law enforcement and government (police officers, lawyers, legal advice and support workers, policymakers), and charities focused on internet safety. The interviews typically lasted around an hour. As with the victim-survivor interviews, the questions were semi-structured and the interviews were recorded and later transcribed. For all interviews, appropriate consents were obtained, as well as an agreement to individual and institutional anonymity.

Key findings from the victim-survivor interviews

Overall, our victim-survivor participants reported a diverse range of experiences of image-based sexual abuse. A significant majority reported having had nude or sexual images of them shared without their consent. This included those who had initially shared the nude or sexual images consensually, those who had consented (or had not consented) to others taking images of them, and those who had not known they were being photographed or filmed. Many participants described how images of them were shown to groups of friends or colleagues via mobile phones or mobile apps, or posted on pornographic websites, social media sites, chatrooms or imageboard sites. Many also experienced someone threatening to share nude or sexual images of them, sometimes with the purpose of control and/or coercion into an unwanted act, such as paying money, performing a sexual act, sending more images or controlling the victim-survivor within the context of an ongoing or past intimate relationship.

Participants also reported that the perpetrator had taken nude or sexual images of them without their consent. In some cases, participants were photographed or filmed without their knowledge when they were asleep or drug- or alcohol-affected, or with the aid of a secret camera. For a very small number of participants, images of them were digitally altered to make them nude or sexual. Others described being pressured or coerced into either having photos or videos taken of them, for example, being groomed or coerced into sharing sexual images when they were children by predators online, or as adults by intimate partners. This abuse was not limited by location. Victim-survivors spoke about their images being taken or shared at home, work, school and parties, as well as more widely online and offline. Most of the reported abuse had taken place within the past five years, but, for some, the experiences had taken place a decade or so ago, with the effects still continuing.

Some participants reported multiple experiences by the same perpetrator or by multiple perpetrators, as well as image-based sexual abuse occurring in conjunction with, or alongside, previous experiences of other forms of sexual violence, domestic violence, stalking and sexual harassment – both online and offline. In the broader literature, multiple experiences of different kinds of victimisation and their cumulative impacts is known as "poly-victimisation" (see e.g., Finkelhor, Ormrod, Turner, & Hamby, 2005; Hamby et al., 2018). This has also been discussed more recently in relation to online forms of violence (see DeKeseredy et al., 2019; DeKeseredy, Schwartz, Nolan, Mastron, & Hall-Sanchez, 2019). Poly-victimisation was also a key finding in our study with just under one-third of our victim-survivor participants having had experiences of image-based sexual abuse alongside, or in the context of, other experiences of domestic violence. Notably, the harms described by this group did not differ to any great extent compared with participants whose perpetrator was a casual sexual partner, friend, colleague, housemate or stranger.

A striking finding from our interviews across all three countries was the way in which many victim-survivors talked holistically about the detrimental impacts of their experiences, beyond the commonly expressed trauma-based discourses. These descriptions of harms spanned victim-survivors' narratives, traversing geographical location, age, sexuality, race, ethnicity or a specific experience of image-based sexual abuse.

The survey

In 2019, we conducted a multi-country survey of 6,109 respondents aged 16–64 years in Australia, New Zealand and the United Kingdom (n=2,054: Australia; n=2,027: New Zealand; n=2,028: the United Kingdom). Drawing on previous quantitative research into image-based sexual abuse (Powell & Henry, 2019; Powell et al., 2018; Powell, Henry, Flynn, & Scott, 2019), our survey instrument comprised a range of items including those pertaining to: (1) demographic characteristics; (2) sexual image-based abuse myth acceptance; (3) online dating behaviours; (4) sexual self-image behaviours; (5) image-based sexual abuse victimisation; and (6) image-based sexual abuse perpetration. All respondents were recruited by Qualtrics Panels, an online panel provider, and informed that the purpose of the research was to examine attitudes and experiences of sex, technology and relationships.

Overall, women represented 52.1% (n=3,181) of respondents while men comprised the remaining 47.9% (n=2,928). In relation to sexuality, a majority of respondents (88.9%, n=5,430) identified as heterosexual, while 11.1% (n=679) identified as Lesbian, Gay or Bisexual plus (LGB+).[3] With regard to age, 6.1% (n=373) of respondents were 16–19 years, 23.1% (n=1,411) were 20–29 years, 25.9% (n=1,583) were 30–39 years, 18.6% (n=1,134) were 40–49 years and 26.3% (n=1,608) were 50–64 years. Finally, 73.6% (n=4,498) of respondents identified as White, European or Pākehā, while 26.4% (n=1,611) identified as either from indigenous or BAME communities.

As with all survey research, there were limitations to the study. The sample is a non-probability sample and, as such, is not representative of the populations, though quota sampling was used according to census data on age and gender for the different countries to approximate the population and provide additional confidence in the findings. The robustness of these findings is further enhanced by the large sample size, which in turn has also allowed for comparative analyses to be made for many population subgroups. Notably though, there were not sufficient transgender, intersex and non-binary gender respondents to facilitate comparable analyses for these groups, a problem common in much quantitative research and one that highlights the need for accompanying qualitative work to be inclusive of these groups (see Powell, Scott, & Henry, 2018). Another limitation is that the victimisation data on image-based sexual abuse may in fact represent an under-count of the true prevalence of these harms, since these data rely on victim-survivors knowing that their images have been taken or shared without their consent. Similarly, self-disclosed perpetration of image-based sexual abuse may represent an under-count, as individuals may be reluctant to identify themselves as having engaged in what are increasingly recognised as criminal behaviours.

Key findings from the survey

Overall, we found that image-based sexual abuse is pervasive, particularly among young adults. One in three respondents had experienced at least one form of image-based sexual abuse victimisation (37.7%, n=2,306), which included: One in three respondents who reported that someone had taken a nude or sexual image of them without their consent (33.2%, n=2,029); one in five who had experienced a nude or sexual image of them shared without their consent (20.9%, n=1,278); and almost one in five who reported experiencing someone threatening to share a nude or sexual image of them (18.7%, n=1,142). Moreover, we found that one in seven respondents had experienced all three forms of image-based sexual abuse (14.1%, n=862).

As discussed throughout the book, far from its popular characterisation as typically an act of "revenge" perpetrated by men against their women ex-partners, our survey indicates that image-based sexual abuse encompasses a diverse set of relational contexts and harms, as well as an array of differential victim impacts. Notably, the survey found that overall victimisation rates are not markedly different according to gender, with men and women reporting similar overall frequency of victimisation. However, when contexts, harms and impacts are considered, there are significant differences according to gender and other characteristics of inequality and/ or privilege. In particular, there are distinct ways in which women experience image-based sexual abuse in the context of multiple experiences of interpersonal harm and victimisation, including stalking, sexual violence or intimate partner abuse situations. Patterns of image-based sexual abuse victimisation also differ: For younger as compared with older respondents; for sexuality-diverse as compared with heterosexual respondents; and for those from indigenous, or racial or minority ethnic groups.

When it comes to perpetration, our multi-country survey found remarkably high self-reported engagement in image-based sexual abuse behaviours. One in six respondents had engaged in at least one form of image-based sexual abuse perpetration (17.5%, n=1,070), including: One in seven respondents who reported having taken a nude or sexual image of another person without their consent (15.8%, n=967); one in ten who reported having shared a nude or sexual image of another person without their consent (10.6%, n=648); and one in twelve who said they had threatened to share a nude or sexual image of another person with others (8.8%, n=536). Approximately one in thirteen respondents had engaged in all three forms of image-based sexual abuse perpetration (7.8%, n=479). Unlike victimisation, the self-reported engagement in image-based sexual abuse perpetration behaviours was markedly different by gender, with male respondents disclosing perpetration at approximately twice the rate of female respondents. Furthermore, although many perpetrators appear to minimise or fail to understand the potentially serious impact of their behaviour on victim-survivors, many others self-disclosed engaging in image-based sexual abuse in order to control their victim, to embarrass them or to "get back" at them.

In summary, the findings across both the qualitative and quantitative datasets point to a troubling trend where digital technologies are being used not only as a form of control, abuse and harassment, but as a further expression and consolidation of masculine entitlement and privilege, and as a tactic of sexuality-shaming women, women of colour or those identifying as lesbian, gay, bisexual, transgender, intersex or a non-binary gender. We argue that rather than viewing image-based sexual abuse as something qualitatively "new" in the digital age, it can instead be understood as an extension, elaboration and amplification of existing harmful structures and practices (see Powell & Henry, 2017). But, as we also highlight in this book, not all acts of image-based sexual abuse necessarily reflect these patterns of abuse, and not all victim-survivors of image-based sexual abuse are necessarily significantly affected by their experiences.

Structure of the book

In Chapter 2 we investigate a spectrum of image-based sexual abuse behaviours as experienced and articulated by victim-survivors in our study. We narrate those experiences through reference to three key behavioural categories: The non-consensual taking of nude or sexual images (including the creation of digitally altered images); the non-consensual sharing of nude or sexual images; and threats made to share nude or sexual images. To further understand and contextualise victim-survivor experiences, we describe the key findings of our cross-country survey, demonstrating the pervasiveness of image-based sexual abuse among marginalised groups, including women, as well as sexuality, racial and ethnic minorities. In the second half of the chapter, we argue that image-based sexual abuse is part of a "continuum of sexual violence", which includes other forms of violence, abuse and harassment used to control women and to reinforce gender inequality and legitimate gendered violence (Kelly, 1988; see also McGlynn et al., 2017; Powell & Henry, 2017). Finally, we argue that "continuum thinking" should be used to examine the intersectionality of structural systems of oppression to examine gender alongside other markers of difference, such as race, ethnicity, age, sexuality and ability (Boyle, 2019). In particular, exploring the relationship between gender and sexuality helps to uncover the underlying drivers of image-based sexual abuse, including perpetrator performances of celebrated forms of masculinity, and culturally specific and heteronormative expectations around gender roles, sexuality and sexual practice (which we discuss further in Chapters 4 and 5).

Chapter 3 (co-written with Erika Rackley and Nicola Gavey) explores the harms and impacts of image-based sexual abuse. Our survey results indicate that while the impacts of image-based sexual abuse can vary considerably, there are significant harms for many victim-survivors. To further explore the complexity of harms and impacts, we describe the key findings of our victim-survivor interviews. For some victim-survivors, the abuse is experienced as a form of "social rupture" because it leads them to divide their lives into two phases – before and after the image-based sexual abuse. Many victim-survivors described the totality of harms they experienced across their social, economic, digital, sexual and political lives. Victim-survivors also described the harms as continuous and ongoing. This "constancy" not only amplifies the harms, but it makes recovery and pursuing justice all the more elusive. The chapter also explores the themes of isolation, existential threat and violated trust, as well as considering the parallels with harms experienced by sexual assault victim-survivors.

While Chapters 2 and 3 focus on victimisation experiences, Chapters 4 and 5 explore the perpetration of image-based sexual abuse. In Chapter 4, we describe the key findings of our survey and victim-survivor interviews to investigate the motivations behind image-based sexual abuse. While we found that there were divergent, multifaceted and often overlapping motivations for engaging in these behaviours, including revenge, sexual gratification, social status building or financial gain, an overarching theme across these different motivations was power and control. Our survey and interview data revealed that men were significantly more likely than women to engage in image-based sexual abuse perpetration. Our interviews with victim-survivors also demonstrated that image-based sexual abuse is often perpetrated as part of a pattern of domestic violence or intimate partner abuse. As such, we argue that it is important not to lose sight of the gendered nature of these behaviours, and the connections to masculine entitlement and privilege. Furthermore, we argue that the non-consensual taking or sharing of nude or sexual images has become a normalised practice, constituting a form of "social currency" and a conduit in which to engage in "impression management" and build social status among groups of peers. These findings are significant because they can help shape the design and implementation of more effective criminal or civil laws, as well as other interventions for responding to and preventing image-based sexual abuse.

Although our survey findings indicate that men and women report image-based sexual abuse victimisation at similar rates, qualitative research shows that most digital platforms hosting image-based sexual abuse content are designed for heterosexual male pleasure and the objectification of women (see Hearn & Hall, 2018; Henry & Flynn, 2019; Uhl, Rhyner, Terrance, & Lugo, 2018). One explanation for this discrepancy is that survey research may underestimate the true prevalence of image-based sexual abuse because many victims will simply not know that images are being taken or shared of them online or via digital devices. In Chapter 5, we further examine the relationship between gender and sexuality with a focus on the micro and macro context that underpins the pervasiveness, nature and perpetration of image-based sexual abuse. The chapter draws on theories from within sociology, criminology, psychology and philosophy disciplines to investigate the "cultural scaffolding" of sexual violence (Gavey, 2019). We argue that image-based sexual abuse needs to be understood using an ecological framework of gendered violence that examines individual, community, cultural and structural factors underlying the perpetration of behaviours. We argue that within an ecological model of image-based sexual abuse, we need to also consider the broader social context of contemporary digital society, including the cultural obsession with visuality and realism, the proliferation of user-generated content (including amateur pornography) and the commodification of both content and users.

There is little doubt that image-based sexual abuse is being used as a tool or strategy by perpetrators to carry out harassment, sexual violence or intimate partner abuse in ways which both facilitate and extend the harms of that abuse. Yet, not all image-based sexual abuse fits within this broader and familiar pattern of gender-based violence. In Chapter 6, we seek to disentangle the complexity of image-based sexual abuse behaviours which are, in many instances, a tool of very serious and harmful forms of abuse, whilst in others, a behaviour which is not always perceived as overtly harmful. In order to navigate the complex spectrum of behaviours that constitute image-based sexual abuse, this chapter engages with the shifting social norms in relation to the taking and sharing of intimate images.

The introduction of specific criminal and/or civil laws is often considered a necessary first step in tackling image-based sexual abuse. A multiplicity of new (and proposed) laws aimed at addressing image-based sexual abuse sit alongside existing common law and statutory legal avenues: Privacy, harassment, copyright, data protection, voyeurism, blackmail, as well as specific laws prohibiting the non-consensual sharing of nude or sexual images. New government-funded and empowered agencies are currently working together with the police, lawyers, judges, support organisations and digital platforms to smooth and facilitate their operation. At the same time, it is clear from our interviews with victim-survivors that the law is not working as well as it could. Chapter 7 (co-written with Erika Rackley) examines victim-survivors' experiences of engaging with the law and legal systems and explores their ideas as to what would constitute "justice". Our participants identified a variety of justice needs, moving beyond a focus on the conventional criminal justice system, and towards education, prevention, recognition and more transformative justice approaches. In this chapter, we suggest the need for a multifaceted approach, one that encompasses comprehensive criminal and civil remedies, as well as regulatory and support mechanisms.

Chapter 8 investigates the different strategies and programs beyond the law that are designed to address and prevent image-based sexual abuse. In the chapter, we focus on education and digital platforms. In relation to education, we critically examine different anti-sexting campaigns and identify their shortcomings in terms of failing to capture the complexity of image-based sexual abuse, blaming the victim and failing to target potential perpetrators who remain visible or peripheral to these campaigns. In the second section, we focus our attention on the policies and practices of digital platforms and the extent to which these interventions can help in both responding to and preventing image-based sexual abuse. We argue that prevention interventions across these different community and educational sectors should deliver content which: Identifies and challenges the gender- and sexuality-based social norms and cultural practices that drive gendered violence; redirects the responsibility onto the perpetrators of image-based sexual abuse; and encourages and provides tools for people to take action as bystanders to report content for removal and call-out victim-blaming and shaming where they encounter the image-based sexual abuse of others. We argue that prevention interventions must, above all, be guided by a sexual ethics approach that prioritises affirmative consent, reciprocity, bodily integrity and sexual freedom.

The final chapter, Chapter 9, presents an overview of the book and makes suggestions for future research in this area.

Conclusion

This book contextualises the problem of image-based sexual abuse within a rapidly changing global community that is increasingly spatially, as well as territorially, demarcated, within which existing structural and systemic inequalities of gender, sexuality, age, ability and race and ethnicity continue to shape social relations. As we demonstrate, image-based sexual abuse is far more complex than the colloquial terminology "revenge porn" suggests. Advances in digital technologies make it easier for motivated perpetrators to engage in abusive behaviours, often anonymously and with impunity. And yet, the greatest challenge in many ways is actually "non-technological". We argue that the problem of image-based sexual abuse stems from deeply embedded norms around gender and sexuality that not only objectify and commodify bodies (especially female, feminine or non-conforming bodies), but are also used as a vehicle for harassment, abuse and violence.

Notes

1   Intermittently throughout the book, when we are discussing victim-survivor experiences, we sometimes use the term "intimate images" instead of "nude or sexual images". The reason for this is that some participants were more comfortable with the former term rather than the latter, although they were essentially referring to images that were nude or sexual.

2   Pākehā is a Māori term for New Zealanders who are primarily of White European descent. In the Australian context, the majority racial or ethnic background is White European, influenced heavily by British colonisation with many White Australians being of Anglo heritage. In the British context, "White British" is typically used to refer to the majority White racial group. For consistency, we have used the term "White, European or Pākehā" to refer to these majority racial groups across all the different countries, however we acknowledge that the terminology may in fact be used differently in different contexts.

3   Respondents were provided with multiple response options, including heterosexual, lesbian, gay, bisexual and a free text response for preferred sexuality identity. Small sample sizes prevent reliable separate analyses for some sexuality identities, and as such lesbian, gay, bisexual and the remaining preferred sexuality descriptors have been analysed as one Lesbian, Gay and Bisexual Plus (LGB+) group, and then analysed by key demographics within that larger group.

References

Ashby v. Hustler Magazine, Inc., 802 F.2d 856 (6th Cir. 1986).

Avila, T. (2016, June 29). YouTube star asks Hillary Clinton how she'll help stop revenge porn. *The Cut*. Retrieved from www.thecut.com/2016/06/hillary-asked-how-shell-help-stop-revenge-porn.html.

Boyle, K. (2019). What's in a name? Theorising the inter-relationships of gender and violence. *Feminist Theory, 20*(1), 19–36.

Burns, A. (2015). In full view: Involuntary porn and the postfeminist rhetoric of choice. In C. Nally & A. Smith (eds.), *Twenty-first century feminism* (pp. 93–118). London: Palgrave Macmillan.

Chard, H., & Litherland, B. (2019). "Hollywood" Hulk Hogan: Stardom, synergy and field migration. *Cinema Journal, 58*(4), 21–44.

Citron, D. K., & Franks, M. A. (2014). Criminalizing revenge porn. *Wake Forest Law Review, 49*(2), 345–391.

Collins, P. H. (2000). *Black feminist thought: Knowledge, consciousness, and the politics of empowerment*. New York; London: Routledge.

Collins, P. H. (2019). *Intersectionality as critical social theory*. Durham; London: Duke University Press.

Crenshaw, K. (1991). Mapping the margins: Intersectionality, identity politics, and violence against women of color. *Stanford Law Review, 43*(6), 1241–1299.

Crofts, T., Lee, M., McGovern, A., & Milivojevic, S. (2015). *Sexting and young people*. Basingstoke: Palgrave Macmillan.

DeKeseredy, W. S., Schwartz, M. D., Harris, B., Woodlock, D., Nolan, J., & Hall-Sanchez, A. (2019). Technology-facilitated stalking and unwanted sexual messages/images in a college campus community: The role of negative peer support. *Sage Open*, January–March, 1–12.

DeKeseredy, W. S., Schwartz, M. D., Nolan, J., Mastron, N., & Hall-Sanchez, A. (2019). Polyvicitmization and the continuum of sexual abuse at a college campus:

Does negative peer support increase the likelihood of multiple victimizations? *The British Journal of Criminology, 59*(2), 276–295.

Finkelhor, D., Ormrod, R. K., Turner, H. A., & Hamby, S. L. (2005). Measuring poly-victimization using the juvenile victimization questionnaire. *Child Abuse & Neglect, 29*(11), 1297–1312.

Franks, M. A. (2017). "Revenge porn" reform: A view from the front lines. *Florida Law Review, 69*, 1251–1337.

Gámez-Guadix, M., Almendros, C., Borrajo, E., & Calvete, E. (2015). Prevalence and association of sexting and online sexual victimization among Spanish adults. *Sexuality Research and Social Policy, 12*(2), 145–154.

Goodard, P. (1993, October 15). Stagecoach gets lost in city. *Toronto Star.*

Hamby, S., Taylor, E., Jones, L., Mitchell, K. J., Turner, H. A., & Newlin, C. (2018). From poly-victimization to poly-strengths: Understanding the web of violence can transform research on youth violence and illuminate the path to prevention and resilience. *Journal of Interpersonal Violence, 33*(5), 719–739.

Harding, S. G. (ed.). (2004). *The feminist standpoint theory reader: Intellectual and political controversies.* New York; London: Routledge.

Hayward, P., & Rahn, A. (2015). Opening Pandora's box: Pleasure, consent and consequence in the production and circulation of celebrity sex videos. *Porn Studies, 2*(1), 49–61.

Hearn, J., & Hall, M. (2018). "This is my cheating ex": Gender and sexuality in revenge porn. *Sexualities, 22*(5–6), 860–882.

Henry, N., & Flynn, A. (2019). Image-based sexual abuse: Online distribution channels and illicit communities of support. *Violence Against Women, 25*(16), 1932–1955.

Henry, N., Flynn, A., & Powell, A. (in press). Technology-facilitated sexual violence: A review. *Violence Against Women.*

Henry, N., & Powell, A. (2015). Beyond the "sext": Technology-facilitated sexual violence and harassment against adult women. *Australian & New Zealand Journal of Criminology, 48*(1), 104–118.

Hillyer, M. (2004). Sex in the suburban: Porn, home movies and the live action performance of love in Pam and Tommy Lee: Hardcore and Uncensored. In L. Williams (ed.), *Porn studies* (pp. 50–77). Durham, NC: Duke University Press.

Hume, T. (2005, June 5). Ex's set up with porn PXTs. *Sunday Star Times.*

Kashner, S. (2014, October 7). Jennifer Lawrence calls photo hacking a "sex crime". *Vanity Fair.* Retrieved from www.vanityfair.com/hollywood/2014/10/jennifer-lawrence-cover.

Katz, J. E., & Crocker, E. T. (2015). Selfies and photo messaging as visual conversation: Reports from the United States, United Kingdom and China. *International Journal of Communication, 9*(12), 1861–1872.

Kelly, L. (1988). *Surviving sexual violence.* Cambridge, UK: Polity Press.

Latour, B. (1991). Technology is society made durable. In J. Law (ed.), *A sociology of monsters: Essays on power, technology, and domination* (pp. 103–131). London; New York: Routledge.

Latour, B. (2005). *Reassembling the social: An introduction to actor-network-theory.* New York: Oxford University Press.

Letherby, G. (2011). Feminist methodology. In M. Williams & W. P. Vogt (eds.), *The Sage handbook of innovation in social research methods* (pp. 62–79). London; Thousand Oaks, CA: Sage Publications.

Maddocks, S. (2018). From non-consensual pornography to image-based sexual abuse: Charting the course of a problem with many names. *Australian Feminist Studies, 33*(97), 345–361.

Martens, T. (2011, December 8). No clothes, no problem? *Edmonton Journal.* Retrieved from www.pressreader.com/canada/edmonton-journal/20111208/282948152056978.

May, V. M. (2015). *Pursuing intersectionality, unsettling dominant imaginaries* (1st edn). New York: Routledge.

McGlynn, C., & Rackley, E. (2017). Image-based sexual abuse. *Oxford Journal of Legal Studies, 37*(3), 534–561.

McGlynn, C., Rackley, E., & Houghton, R. (2017). Beyond "revenge porn": The continuum of image-based sexual abuse. *Feminist Legal Studies, 25*(1), 25–46.

McGlynn, C., Rackley, E., Johnson, K., Henry, N., Flynn, A., Powell, A., ... Scott, A. J. (2019). *Shattering lives and myths: A report on image-based sexual abuse.* Retrieved from https://claremcglynn.files.wordpress.com/2019/10/shattering-lives-and-myths-revised-aug-2019.pdf.

Pew Research Center. (2014). *Online harassment.* Retrieved from www.pewinternet. org/2014/10/22/online-harassment/.

Powell, A., & Henry, N. (2017). *Sexual violence in a digital age.* London: Palgrave Macmillan.

Powell, A., & Henry, N. (2019). Technology-facilitated sexual violence victimization: Results from an online survey of Australian adults. *Journal of Interpersonal Violence, 34*(17), 3637–3665.

Powell, A., Henry, N., & Flynn, A. (2018). Image-based sexual abuse. In W. S. DeKeseredy & M. Dragiewicz (eds.), *Handbook of critical criminology* (pp. 305–315). Abingdon, Oxon; New York: Routledge.

Powell, A., Henry, N., Flynn, A., & Scott, A. J. (2019). Image-based sexual abuse: The extent, nature, and predictors of perpetration in a community sample of Australian residents. *Computers in Human Behavior, 92*, 393–402.

Powell, A., Scott, A. J., & Henry, N. (2018). Digital harassment and abuse: Experiences of sexuality and gender minority adults. *European Journal of Criminology.* Advance online publication. doi: 10.1177/1477370818788006.

Rackley, E., & McGlynn, C. (2014, July 23). The law must focus on consent when it tackles revenge porn. *The Conversation.* Retrieved from http://theconversation. com/the-law-must-focus-on-consent-when-it-tackles-revenge-porn-29501.

Ramo, D. E., Rodriguez, T. M. S., Chavez, K., Sommer, M. J., & Prochaska, J. J. (2014). Facebook recruitment of young adult smokers for a cessation trial: Methods, metrics, and lessons learned. *Internet Interventions, 1*(2), 58–64.

Robards, B. (2013). Friending participants: Managing the researcher-participant relationship on social network sites. *Young, 21*(3), 217–235.

Tyler, M. (2016, February 24). All porn is revenge porn. *Feminist Current.* Retrieved from www.feministcurrent.com/2016/02/24/all-porn-is-revenge-porn/.

Uhl, C. A., Rhyner, K. A., Terrance, C. A., & Lugo, N. (2018). An examination of nonconsensual pornography websites. *Feminism & Psychology, 28*(1), 50–68.

Chapter 2

Victim-survivor experiences of image-based sexual abuse

Introduction

Much of the legal, media and scholarly attention on image-based sexual abuse to date has focused on the non-consensual *sharing* of nude or sexual images. In reality, image-based sexual abuse encompasses a much wider range of experiences and behaviours, such as the non-consensual taking of nude or sexual images, or threats made to share such images (McGlynn, Rackley, & Houghton, 2017; Powell & Henry, 2017). It is important that prevention interventions, legislation and other regulatory responses capture the different forms of image-based sexual abuse, as well as any new behaviours emerging due to the rapidly changing nature of digital technology.

This chapter examines the nature and pervasiveness of image-based sexual abuse victimisation as reported by our survey respondents and interview participants in Australia, New Zealand and the United Kingdom. We explore victim-survivor experiences in reference to three categories: The non-consensual taking of nude or sexual images; the non-consensual sharing of nude or sexual images; and threats made to share nude or sexual images. The first section of the chapter reports on our survey and interview data, including a description of the demographic breakdown of those who reported experiencing image-based sexual abuse across the three geographical sites. The second section situates image-based sexual abuse as part of a "continuum of sexual violence" (Kelly, 1988). We further argue that "continuum thinking" across *multiple axes of harms and oppressions* can enhance understandings of the interrelationships between gender and sexuality across, for example, perpetrator performances of particular celebrated forms of aggressive masculinity, culturally specific expectations regarding gender roles and/or heteronormative expectations regarding sexuality and sexual practice (Boyle, 2019).

The pervasiveness and nature of image-based sexual abuse

As described in Chapter 1, the research reported throughout this book involved online surveys with 6,109 respondents aged 16–64 years (n=2,054: Australia; n=2,027: New Zealand; n=2,028: the United Kingdom), as well as semi-structured interviews with 75 victim-survivors who had one or more experiences of image-based sexual abuse. Strikingly, one in three survey respondents in our study reported they had experienced at least one form of image-based sexual abuse (37.7%, n=2,306). This included: One in three respondents who reported someone had taken a nude or sexual image of them without their consent (33.2%, n=2,029); one in five who had experienced a nude or sexual image of them shared without their consent (20.9%, n=1,278); and almost one in five who reported experiencing someone threatening to share a nude or sexual image of them (18.7%, n=1,142). Moreover, we found that one in seven had experienced all three forms of image-based sexual abuse (14.1%, n=862). Overall, these figures clearly demonstrate that this insidious form of abuse is commonplace, requiring urgent attention and intervention. We examine the diversity and differential rates of image-based sexual abuse victimisation in the following subsections.

Victim-survivor experiences of image-based sexual abuse

Image-based sexual abuse was reported by the survey respondents as primarily taking place in the context of an ongoing (33.5%, n=321) or previously intimate relationship (27.4%, n=262), with 60.9% (n=583) of victim-survivors experiencing the abuse in this context. However, this also means that a significant number of victim-survivors (39.1%, n=374) experienced image-based sexual abuse in other relational contexts, including where the perpetrator was a friend or acquaintance (18.6%, n=179), an unknown person or a stranger (8.3%, n=79), a family member (5.9%, n=56) or a current or previous work colleague (3.8%, n=36). We discuss the context of perpetration in more detail in Chapter 4. However, for the purposes of this chapter, these results demonstrate the diversity of contexts in which image-based sexual abuse takes place, beyond the archetype of "revenge porn".

Only a very small percentage of the victim-survivors who responded to our survey reported experiencing the non-consensual *sharing* of their nude or sexual images in isolation (4.9%, n=112). Rather, many victim-survivors reported experiencing multiple forms of image-based sexual abuse, with 11.6% (n=268) experiencing the non-consensual taking *and* sharing of their nude or sexual images; 5% (n=115) experiencing the non-consensual taking *and* threats to share their nude or sexual images; 1.6% (n=36) experiencing the non-consensual sharing *and* threats to share their nude or sexual images; and 37.4% (n=862) experiencing *all three forms of image-based sexual abuse*. These findings are similarly reflected in our qualitative study, where almost two thirds of our interview participants (64%, n=48) reported being subject to more than one form of image-based sexual abuse and, again, victim-survivors most frequently reported they had experienced all three forms of abuse. Therefore, our findings from both datasets emphasise that the different forms of image-based sexual abuse can and, more often than not, do coalesce in victim-survivors' lived experiences.

It is also important to stress that we expect many of the figures presented here to underestimate the extent of image-based sexual abuse. For example, several of the victim-survivors we interviewed mentioned that in addition to the abuse they told us about, they suspected that other forms of abuse involving the taking or sharing of intimate images had been perpetrated covertly. We also know from other qualitative research that images are being traded in secret online without either the knowledge or consent of the victim-survivor (Henry & Flynn, 2019).

Our data also reveals that victim-survivors experienced image-based sexual abuse alongside multiple forms of other violence and abuse. In the literature, this is known as "poly-victimisation" (see DeKeseredy et al., 2019; DeKeseredy, Schwartz, Nolan, Mastron, & Hall-Sanchez, 2019; Finkelhor, Ormrod, Turner, & Hamby, 2005; Hamby et al., 2018). In our qualitative study, participants reported not only multiple experiences of image-based sexual abuse by the same perpetrator or by multiple perpetrators, but also multiple experiences of sexual violence, domestic violence, stalking and sexual harassment – in both online and offline settings. For approximately one third of the victim-survivors we interviewed, the taking and sharing of nude or sexual images without consent (including threats to share) formed part of a broader, ongoing context of domestic abuse perpetrated by a current or former intimate partner. Furthermore, in our quantitative study, 59.4% (n=568) of the 957 respondents who provided information regarding their most significant experience reported multiple experiences by the same perpetrator. This included 8.3% (n=79) who reported that the same person also physically hurt them, and 28.2% (n=270) who reported that the same person kept contacting them after they asked them to stop. Our interviews also highlighted that for many victim-survivors, individual experiences of image-based sexual abuse sit alongside earlier, ostensibly disconnected, experiences of sexual harassment and violence, or sexuality- or race-based abuse or harassment. We touch on some of the diverse harms and motivations underpinning image-based sexual abuse later in the book.

Images taken without consent

Of the victim-survivors of image-based sexual abuse who responded to our survey (n=2,306), a substantial majority (88%, n=2,029) reported at least one experience of a nude or sexual image being *taken* of them without their consent. This was the most common form of image-based sexual abuse reported in our study. However, as discussed above, there was a substantial cross over of forms of image-based sexual abuse, such that many victims experienced having images being taken and shared (11.6%, n=268), images taken and threatened (5%, n=115), and images taken, threatened and shared (37.4% n=862).

Almost two-thirds (n=47) of the victim-survivors we interviewed had likewise experienced someone taking a nude or sexual image of them without their consent. In the majority of cases, victim-survivors said they were filmed without their knowledge by an intimate long-term or casual partner. For instance, many participants told us that their partners had taken photos or videos of them while they were asleep. Others mentioned photographs or videos taken of them without their knowledge or consent while they were unconscious due to alcohol or drug use. In some instances, the victim-survivor had been drugged and filmed. For others, they were conscious, but not initially aware that their partner had filmed them. Julia (Aus), for example, described a casual sexual partner filming her during intercourse without her knowledge and then posting it on Snapchat. Other participants discovered their partners had a particular fixation on secretly filming sexual encounters or intimate, private moments. As Rachel (NZ) told us:

> He was really into secretly filming us when we were having sex. So, quite a few times I would, sort of, turn around and see that he was filming, and then I would grab his phone and take it off him, delete the thing and say, 'You can't do that. That's totally not allowed'. ... There was also an incident, too, where I was in the shower and he was filming me without me knowing, and I pulled a tampon out to go and put it in the bathroom, and he filmed the whole thing, and I got mad at him for that. He said he was going to delete it, but that was one of the videos that he threatened me with, as well, in the end.

Katherine (UK) described discovering that her partner had been taking intimate images of her without her knowledge or consent across their entire relationship, in situations ranging from her getting dressed, to coming out of the shower, to performing oral sex. The extent to which he hid this from her was evident in several of the images she later discovered, where she described the image being taken from behind his hand or from behind her son: "... there's a picture of him taking it from behind my son of me coming out of the shower and getting dressed in my own bedroom".

Several participants also experienced having their intimate images captured through the aid of a secret device. Esther (NZ), for example, discussed how a friend had hidden a camera in his bedroom and had filmed her getting changed in his room. Another participant, Stephen (UK), discovered a large number of images had been taken of him by a former friend without his knowledge or consent, and in situations where he had "no idea how she was able to be in a position to take them":

> Like there's me sleeping on the bed when I'm sick. There's me in the shower. There's – the most embarrassing of them all is like I'm in the shower, but I'm bent over and it's like the most, you know, visual shot that you can possibly imagine and it's obvious it's me. I mean you can see my face. You could see everything ...

For many participants, non-consensual nude or sexual imagery was taken of them by intimate partners either in the context of an otherwise consensual sexual encounter, or in everyday private settings such as bathing or toileting. For some of our participants, they later discovered videos or photographs of them being raped or sexually assaulted while they were asleep or unconscious. Sally (NZ), for example, described finding footage of her then partner raping her as she lay unconscious:

> I was trying to look at this USB and it was like it was encrypted. You could see there was something on it, but it was like the old school TVs when they go fuzzy, black and white. So, [my friend] played around with it for a while, I'm not sure how long it took him, and then [he] came and got me and told me to come and have a look. There were about 12 videos. ... Some with [my partner's] ex-partner and other people that he'd hooked up with, and then there was about six of me. ... But it was the one where I was unconscious pretty much from within about a minute or two. It's a [long] video. [I] [w]atched this video and didn't know what to do or how to react or what I should feel. Even though it was [an] incredibly dysfunctional and crazy [relationship], I never thought that he would do that to me. ... There were other times where I would wake up from being passed out ... and I'd wake up to cameras. There'd be cameras set up either side of me.

Linda (Aus) also described finding out from several friends who had seen the footage of her being raped by her former partner:

> My partner and me had been drinking and then he gave me a bit of something else that I hadn't ever had and, basically, I was quite unconscious. He filmed a video of us. I actually wasn't aware of it at the time. I became aware of it when my friends started talking to me about this video that they'd all seen. So it turns out that he had shared that video with his guy friends over a few drinks and they were concerned and talked to me because they were like, 'You seemed completely out of it and actually unaware of this so we wanted to let you know because it's a pretty awful video'. A bit later down the track he was trying to blackmail me because he wanted to live at my house because he needed somewhere to stay so he threatened if I didn't let him that he was going to send that video to my parents.

Jennifer (UK) too described her experiences of being raped and discovering that she had been filmed:

> I was raped, and then halfway through, there was a video taken of the act. Then it was shown to others. I don't think it was posted anywhere, but it was definitely shown to others in my town where I used to live.

Although our qualitative study involved only two victim-survivors who had intimate images of them digitally altered, our survey data suggests that this form of abuse is becoming increasingly common. Our survey findings revealed that 14.1% (n=864) of all respondents disclosed that someone had either created digitally altered nude or sexual images of them without their consent, shared digitally altered images without their consent and/or threatened to share such images. The significant extent of digitally altered images represented in the experiences of our survey respondents is consistent with the increasingly accessible and sophisticated tools which permit the easy manipulation of everyday, personal and professional images, readily available online. Maya (Aus), for example, described how people she did not know had taken ordinary images of her from her social media sites, and created digitally altered, sexual images of her, by superimposing her head onto pornographic images, and then posting these online:

> People had been following me on social media and stealing or lifting ... photos [of me] – ordinary photos of me and then doctoring them or altering them into pornography and then posting them online. That was involved with a lot of very, very highly explicit sexual commentary with my details, like name, where I lived, where I studied. ... They'd Photoshop my face onto naked women. They would Photoshop me onto images where I was having sexual intercourse. They Photoshopped me into images where I was being ejaculated on, where they would literally have to Photoshop sperm onto my face to make it look like there's sperm on my face and the body of the woman.

As Maya's example demonstrates, not all interview participants said that it was intimate partners taking or creating intimate images without consent. Dee (Aus), for instance, described how she had a photograph of her genitals taken by a nurse while she was under anaesthetic in the operating theatre. Alana (Aus) described a friend and colleague of hers taking a photo of her going to the toilet which later appeared on a series of porn websites. In one case of "upskirting", Margaret (UK) recounted how a male student at the school in which she taught took images up her skirt on various occasions. Interview participants also told us that bystanders had filmed or photographed intimate acts between couples or in a group sex context, going on to share the images online, such as on YouTube, Facebook or porn sites. Olivia (NZ), for instance, told us:

> It was about six years ago, so [I was] 19, 20 [years of age] ... I actually thought these people were my friends. And you know, as far as I was concerned it was just another consensual hook-up, friends with benefits

kind of scenario, but I didn't realise that there was another friend who had somehow managed to video me. ... He kind of peeked in the door, stuck a phone or something. He filmed me performing a sexual act on the person and then put it on Facebook.

Some of our participants further described their experiences resulting from an online sexual encounter, where screenshots were taken of them naked or performing sexual acts. For those participants who knew that their images had been taken (without their consent), they were not always sure whether the person or others had deleted the images or had shared them further. Some participants only discovered much later that the images had been uploaded online or shared among a group of friends. A number of interview participants also described being pressured or coerced into having their photos or videos taken.

Images shared without consent

Our survey found that the majority (55.4%, n=1,278) of victim-survivors had experienced their nude or sexual images being shared without their consent on at least one occasion. This included victim-survivors who had initially consensually shared intimate images with others, those who had consented to others taking images of them, and those who had not consented or known at the time that they were being photographed or filmed. However, only a small number of victim-survivor survey respondents (4.9%, n=112) reported experiencing their images being non-consensually shared without also experiencing other forms of image-based sexual abuse. Many more respondents reported having had nude or sexual images taken and shared (11.6%, n=268), shared and threatened (1.6%, n=36) or taken, shared and threatened (37.4%, n=862).

The non-consensual sharing of nude or sexual images is often accompanied by personal details being provided about the person depicted in the image, such as their name, age, occupation, address, phone number or social media handle (also known as "doxing"). Survey respondents who provided further information regarding their most significant experience (n=957), told us that in two thirds (66.6%, n=637) of cases, their intimate images were non-consensually shared with accompanying information by which they could be identified. Examples of such identifying information included: the respondent's name (35.4%, n=339), face (25.1%, n=240), identifying body marks such as a tattoo (14.2% n=136), social media information (9.4%, n=90), email address (7.6%, n=73), phone number (6.2%, n=59), home town or house address (6%, n=57) and employment details (4.8%, n=46).

Respondents also reported a variety of distribution methods. Although a third (34%, n=325) of victim-survivor respondents reported they did not know the means by which their images had been shared, others reported that their images had been shared via mobile messaging (20.6%, n=197), email (16.3%, n=156), messaging apps (15.3%, n=146) or shown physically, such as via a screen (6.9%, n=66). These experiences were similarly reflected in our interviews with victim-survivors, where many also described how images of them were shown to friends or colleagues via text message or through a messenger service like WhatsApp or Messenger. One participant, Kerry (NZ), who was in high school at the time her image was shared, told us about how her image was sent around the entire school by text message:

> I was dating a guy and we'd been dating for about two months and I cringe to look back on. I guess it was the thing to do, like you share nudes with your partner or boyfriend, and we broke up. ... We didn't end on very good terms, and I didn't think that he would [share them], so I wasn't too worried, but, you know, it was almost, like, trendy, I guess, to kind of send your ex's photos around the school. ... I didn't think that he would do it though, because I didn't think that he was that kind of person. But he did ... everyone kind of got my photo during class.

Chelsea (Aus) similarly described finding out her partner had shared intimate images of her with his friend in a series of text messages:

> He was looking through his own phone and he was scrolling down something [in a series of text messages between him and his friend] and I was sitting next to him and I saw the screen shot of the video of me. ... And so, when his friend went to sleep, I went through his friend's phone and it was the video ... I don't know how many friends he'd sent it to.

Julia (Aus) described finding out that images of her engaging in sexual acts with a casual partner had been taken without her consent and that he had later shared these and other images he had surreptitiously taken, or that she had consensually sent him, with a group of around 50 men from his sporting club on Snapchat:

> A casual partner who filmed me during intercourse without me knowing at all ... and posted me in a Snapchat. ... I didn't find out until later on that he did that. ... The ones that were shared around, they were images – the two main ones were images that I took with sex toys. And the one that he had taken was a shower one. And then the most recent was close ups, videos of me performing head and just them penetrating me. Everything [was shared] pretty much.

It was common for participants to identify the "viral" spread of intimate photographs or videos of them among their social networks. Anna (UK), for instance, described the moment she found out intimate videos of her had been shared among people in her community via mobile phone:

> I had a phone call one morning and I'll never forget it. It was actually the moment my whole world just crumbled. It was a friend phoning me to say, 'there are videos going about of you everywhere'. And I said, 'What do you mean, everywhere?' She said, 'Everywhere'. Her husband works in a factory just a few miles away and she said, 'All the men have them on their phones in the factory'. That was that morning, and by the time I got home from work that afternoon – I had to leave work – my husband had been phoned from men from his work, and his brother had phoned to say the building firm that he works for, the guys had them on their phone. They were absolutely everywhere in my area and there were seven videos in total.

Olivia (NZ) likewise told us about the moment she discovered that her partner had shared images of her with his work colleagues:

> Because he was away for a couple of months and so I sent that to him a video and he showed the entire fishing boat. These are people who I had to deal with every day when they came back because I was with him in a shop that they all frequented. And I had to look at these people in the eye. They were all friends.

Another experience our participants discussed was finding out that their intimate images were part of a collection of images involving other women. Alice (NZ) discussed this in the context of her and her friend finding out that their partners were "pooling" their images within their (all male) friendship group:

> [My friend] found on her boyfriend's laptop pictures of me, her and another friend and she was also being taped in the shower. … That's how I found out about it – through her, that they were, I guess, pooling these images … which made me feel quite sick. … I would say there would be at least 20 [photos] that I had taken but there would probably be maybe at least that many more that he'd taken. Maybe 40, I don't know, I didn't keep track.

Feeling pressured or coerced to take or share images was identified by several participants. Some participants described experiences of this occurring in adulthood, while others discussed being coerced into sharing images when they were children. Zoe (Aus), for instance, met someone through an online dating site who pressured her into sending intimate images which he then shared with his friends:

> And so, chatting away and they said, 'could you send me a picture of your breasts?' And I'd been talking to this person for a while and I said 'well, no, I don't think that's particularly appropriate'. And they said, 'oh come on, everyone does it'. And so, I sent this photo of my breast to this particular person. And then they asked for more and more and more. So ... after goading, goading, goading. I sent these pictures. Explicit photos of myself. But I never sent with my face on it. Except one, which was the guy who I'd been seeing for months and months. And I was meant to be moving up there to live with him. That's when he told me that he showed three of his friends what I'd sent him.

Other participants described being pressured or coerced into sharing images as part of an intimate relationship and the images were then used as a tool to control them, with the constant fear (and sometimes explicit threat) that the images would be being shared with other people:

> It started being things of 'oh I'm away for work. Can you send me a picture?' And they gradually got more sexual. And then it started being a way for him to control me. So, for example, he would say 'can you send me a picture?' Which I would. And he would say specific things I needed to be doing or wearing. And then he would say 'I'm just with the boys'. And it was that thing of not knowing if he was showing them.
>
> (Frances, UK)

Many of our survey respondents also indicated that their images had been shared online, via social media, in chatrooms or on imageboard sites. A third (36.3%, n=347) of those victim-survivor respondents who provided more detail about their experience reported that they discovered their intimate images had been uploaded online, including on mainstream social media sites such as Facebook (13.6%, n=130), Instagram (7%, n= 67), Twitter (5.3%, n=51), Tumblr (3.1%, n=30) and imageboard sites, such as Reddit (3.4%, n=33). Some of our interview participants spoke further about how their social media accounts were hacked. For instance, Kyle's (Aus) Facebook account was hacked by an acquaintance and his profile picture changed to an intimate image:

> [I got] a call from my best friend who at the time had recently relocated back to [his hometown]. He never calls me. He doesn't do phone calls, so it was a bit weird. So, he called me up, and he said, 'What have you done with your Facebook page?' I'm just like, 'What are you talking about?' ... He's like, 'Yeah, okay, I didn't think it was you, you might want to check it out'. ...There was a nude picture of me using a sex toy on myself as the

display picture on Facebook. I couldn't get into it, which I thought was really quite odd. I just was in shock and horror. ... [I was] totally mortified.

Casey (Aus) similarly described her Facebook profile picture being changed to an intimate image after her ex-partner hacked into her account:

I can't remember if at some point I had to give him my [Facebook] login details because that was the kind of person that he was or if he just sort of got them somehow, but he logged into my page and basically posted the photo. ... I was visiting my mum in a different state and it was actually her that went on Facebook on her phone and was like, 'You better get on the computer right now', because it had been up for like an hour or something like that, because I'm not on my phone all the time.

Kristy (NZ) described having consensual images she sent to her partner being saved by a friend of his and sent around her school and friendship groups, leading to her "getting messages on Facebook from people I'd never met, telling me I had a nice body".

"Victim-survivor respondents also reported that their intimate images had been uploaded onto pornographic websites. One in five survey respondents (21.9%, n=210) reported that their images had been posted on pornographic websites, including...". One in five survey respondents (21.9%, n=210) who had their images shared reported their images had been posted on pornographic websites, including on specific "revenge porn" sites (8.2%, n=78). Esther (NZ), for example, told us, "the next time I knew about [the image] was a couple of years later, a year to two years later which is when one of my friends contacted me saying, that I was on pornhub". Julia (UK) described finding out that she had "a whole profile on xHamster with my name, details about myself. ... And then I looked at the photos and I was like the only person to have ever seen these photos was my ex". In many cases, this was part of ongoing abusive and harassing behaviour by the perpetrator. As Frances (UK) described:

He kept messaging me saying 'I'm really sorry, take me back' and all this stuff. And he was very harassing. ... And then it got pretty bad. He was stalking me and my friends and my family. And then he messaged me one day, just a link. And I was like 'what the hell is this?'. And I was curious. And I shouldn't have done it, but I clicked on it. And it took me to a porn site, and he'd uploaded the videos of me onto it.

Participants also spoke about their images being shared on multiple digital platforms with other individuals joining in on the abuse. As Rhona (UK) told us:

I was at work and my friend texted me a screenshot of a fetish Twitter account that had my profile picture, like my face and my first name on it and asked me if it was like … you know, [done] as a joke? … And then in amongst that was like intimate photos of me. And then through those there was also a link to amateur porn sites and darker corners of the internet if you like. And there were more pictures of me. And someone was … commenting on them, trying to persuade people and tell people to share them and encourage comments, encourage weird fictional stories to be written about me. … I was kind of in shock because this somebody was sort of impersonating me. I didn't really understand what was happening.

Once images are shared online, it may be very difficult, or in some cases impossible, to ensure that they are permanently removed from the internet or digital devices. We discuss the significant impacts this can have on victim-survivors in Chapter 3.

Threats to share images

Our survey data revealed that half of the respondents (49.5%, n=1,142) who had experienced image-based sexual abuse reported that someone had threatened to share a nude or sexual image of them. Threats to share nude or sexual images has been identified by Australian stakeholders and practitioners working in the domestic and family violence field as a common form of image-based sexual abuse (see e.g., Henry, Flynn, & Powell, 2018, 2019). It has also been identified as a particular problem within internet dating and as a way to further victimise members of the Lesbian, Gay, Bisexual, Transgender, Queer and Intersex (LGBTQI) community by threating to "out" a person with nude imagery, unless they meet the perpetrator's demands (Powell, Scott, & Henry, 2018). As with the other abuse categories, respondents rarely experienced threats in isolation and instead reported having experienced threats as well as their images being taken and/or shared (43.9%, n=1,013).

Regarding our interview participants, more than half had experienced threats to share nude or sexual images of them. For instance, Noni (NZ) described how she had been having an affair with a man whose wife had discovered the sexual photographs they had taken together:

[She said] 'I found your photos with my husband and I'm going to use them, I'm going to post them. I'm going to create these profiles, and I'm going to put all your photos on them and tell the world that you're a bitch'. … I think at one stage she said to me that she would use my photo to create a hooker website, sort of thing, or like a hooker profile, to show everybody that I was a bitch, and a slut, and all that sort of stuff.

Most participants, however, said that it was a partner or ex-partner who made the threats. These threats were commonly made in order to exert control, to coerce the victim into an unwanted act, such as performing a sexual act or getting them to send more images or as a way to prevent them from leaving the relationship. Rachel (NZ), for example, told us:

> I was with this guy for about eight months and towards the end of the relationship that I was having with him, I realised that he wasn't the right man for me, and there was a lot of, sort of, warning flags, as well during our relationship. ... So I tried to end the relationship which is when he went very unstable and he made threats that he was going to send photos to my friends and family, upload them and everything like that ... in the end, he started threatening me and blackmailing me saying that he was going to do poster drops of naked photos of me around my workplace. ... He was going to send videos to my work, to my parents, and my friends, and create a naked Instagram account of me, which really frightened me, and he could either come over now to my house and we will talk about this. He said, 'Come over now and we will talk about this, and if you have sex with me then I will give you the passcode to your naked Instagram account'.

Zoe (Aus) experienced this form of image-based sexual abuse at the hands of her former partner when she started a new relationship:

> He threatened me ... by saying 'I'm going to put this all online'. ... He said to me, 'you're a fucking slut'. He said 'I've shown all my mates'. ... He said he was going to put it online. ... So that's why to this day, I'm still Googling my name.

Nicole (Aus) was similarly subjected to threats by an ex-partner when she started a new relationship:

> I own a business ... it's a [sports] league. And one of the players who I'd known him before he started playing, so he and I had an intimate relationship and then he joined the league. So, in the time that we were together I had sent him intimate photos of myself and then he was playing in my league and everything and it was fine. ... And then I started dating somebody new and he was all jealous and angry about it and he consistently threatened me that he would post my photos on my business's Facebook page and so obviously that would have been super detrimental.

Casey (Aus) experienced a barrage of abuse from her ex-partner when she left the relationship, including threats to "end my career ... [because] he would send it [the intimate images] to everyone and that would be the end of whatever". Other participants described the threats happening months or even years after they had had any contact with the perpetrator. As Pania (Aus) described:

> When I was younger, I was seeing this guy and he apparently recorded me while we were intimate and, at the time, I was unaware of it. As we got older, he contacted me again to see how I was and to talk, and then he got kind of rude when I didn't like some of the questions that he had asked me – some sexual questions – and I was like, 'What are you getting at? I am happy in my life, just leave me alone', and he was like, 'I have got videos of you. ... I am going to release this video if you don't answer my questions'. ... I think he just wanted attention, and he was just so desperate that he would use anything against me. I can't even explain why he would stoop so low ... because everything – like, we didn't have an ugly relationship, or anything like that.

Xia (NZ) similarly described her ex-partner reaching out several months after they broke-up saying he wanted to catch-up. When she refused, he said "well, I've got some photos you might want".

For a small number of participants, the perpetrator was a stranger or someone they had only met online. Kyle (Aus) for example, described an experience with a potential male partner he had met through the dating app Grindr:

> I was on a ... dating app on Grindr, and I was just at home and Grindr works on proximity. There was someone close. The profile just had a picture of a torso which I found appealing. Messaged them and then we were engaged in communication. ... I didn't find them attractive. They then got upset. ... When I declined and said that I wasn't interested, they were like, 'oh why not?' and started getting very defensive about it. ... Then they started threatening me, it's like, 'oh I've got your pictures, I've got your IP address as well, I'm going to post them up and send them around to people'.

In a persistent series of abusive communications and experiences, Cassie (NZ) described being groomed by sexual predators online from the age of ten. The perpetrators made threats to send the images to her parents unless she sent them more explicit images:

> I was a young impressionable child and I was persuaded into sending them, and when I decided that, 'No, this is bad, I shouldn't be doing this', as was kind of inevitable at various different stages, I would stop. At that stage, quite often, they would threaten to share the ones I'd already sent in order to persuade me to send more. ... So, it started off with '[send an image with] just a little bit of cleavage or whatever', then

it would move to full topless and then naked, and then 'spread your legs, and play with yourself, and toys, butt stuff', all sorts of things. ... [Then it would be] 'send me more [images] or I'll send these to your parents'.

After having an intimate image taken without his consent, Jordan (NZ) described being further victimised by means of sexual extortion, in which the perpetrator threatened to share his image unless he paid them $200 (USD):

> I found one person, who's an attractive woman, and talked for an hour with no hint of sexual stuff, nothing, it was just a convo [conversation]. And then she said, 'Do you want to talk on Skype?' ... So, I went quickly and made a new email address and a new Skype account and linked my Skype account to a new email address, so it'd be completely untraceable, in theory, back to me or so I thought. So Skyped for a bit, chatted for a bit. Probably two and a half hours of chatting at this point. And then she tried to step it up to something sexual, which I wasn't entirely comfortable with. She revealed herself on camera. Exposed her breasts and stuff. ... And so, she asked me to show my penis on camera. So, I did. And that was really that, there was nothing else. At which point she probably shot off the camera as soon as I exposed myself and then sent me my full name and a list of my friends from Facebook. ...They asked for money.

While many participants reported explicit threats being made against them, some also spoke about implicit threats. Georgia (Aus), for example, told us:

> I was interested in someone I think about two years ago. I had found them through social media as well, so I had met up with him, gone on a few dates, and I was very interested in dating him properly, and I don't think he was at the time, but I exchanged photos with him both on Snapchat and on Facebook, and it turned out that we weren't compatible in the end, or he was not interested in me anyway, and I just didn't really think about it again. But now, more recently in the past few months – he has shared photos that I sent to him two years ago back to me, when one, I didn't know that he was keeping them, and two, I didn't expect him to be sending those photos back to me ... I was very interested in him and I sent those photos when I was in that mindset of wanting to be with him, and then now ... I mean, I haven't seen this person in maybe a year and a half even. ... It doesn't sound like a threat. It's more just egging me on and then sort of reminding me of the time that I did send these photos and to keep bringing them up. ... I feel threatened that he might do something more as opposed to telling me he's going to send these around. He hasn't actually told me that, but just the fact that he's bringing it up with me feels like he might.

Amy (NZ) similarly described her ex-partner contacting her a year after their relationship had ended, sending her intimate photos he had kept of her with a message: "just remember I've got this on you". Anna (UK) also experienced a "reminder" from her partner as the relationship was coming to an end:

> I can remember one night, like I say, as the relationship was falling apart, and I think he must have realised and thought, you know, this isn't going well, and we were sitting watching TV, and he got up and he stuck a memory stick in the side of the TV and all these videos just ping, ping, ping up onto the screen, and he just looked at me as if to say, 'I've got these, and just remember I have'.

While the majority of interview participants described ex-partners making threats to share nude or sexual images, there were some who said the perpetrator was a friend or other known person. Stephen (UK), for example, described how a former friend threatened to share intimate images of him:

> The pictures that she had taken of me [without consent] started coming with attachments, started coming with this is going online: 'Either you will speak to me or this gets put on Twitter. … I am going to start a Facebook page and put these up, but I am not going to use your name. I will send the link out to people, so you won't be able to search for yourself'.

Making threats to share nude or sexual images constitutes a significant harm to victim-survivors. Even in the absence of explicit threats, the knowledge that an ex-partner or other person has nude or sexual images in their possession can be troubling because there is no way of knowing when and where the images might materialise in the future.

Diversity and image-based sexual abuse victimisation

Although our interview data clearly demonstrate the complexity of image-based sexual abuse, and the different nature of victimisation experiences, we were not able to recruit evenly across demographic categories for the victim-survivor interviews. Consequently, the narrative accounts we have presented in this chapter do not speak comprehensively to marginalised peoples' experiences, nor to the range of intersectional contexts in which image-based sexual abuse victimisation can occur. In our survey, however, we were able to investigate in more detail the differentiation of experiences according to demographics. Our survey data, for instance, showed clear intersections of marginalisation with regard to experiences of image-based sexual abuse particularly in relation to sexuality, age, race, ethnicity and indigeneity. First, in relation to gender, we found similar rates of image-based sexual abuse victimisation for both women (38.1%, n=1,211) and men (37.4%, n=1,095), although we also noted the limitations of our survey method in Chapter 1 and the likely undercount of victim's *unknown victimisation*. As we explore further in Chapters 3 and 4, while the victimisation rates may be similar among women and men, the impacts and perpetration of image-based sexual abuse were experienced differently according to gender.

Second, existing research has demonstrated that those from certain minority and/or marginalised groups face increased risk of experiencing sexual violence and harassment more broadly. For example, the Australian Human Rights Commission (2017) *Change the Course* report into sexual assault and harassment in university contexts found high rates of violence against LGBTQI people, people living with a disability, Aboriginal and Torres Strait Islanders, and culturally and linguistically diverse students, compared to heterosexuals, able-bodied people, non-Indigenous and Australian-born people. These findings are consistent with other studies. For instance, Indigenous Australian women are three times more likely to experience sexual violence compared with non-Indigenous women (e.g., Mouzos & Makkai, 2004), and in general, women from non-racial or ethnic majority groups, such as New Zealand Māori and other indigenous women, as well as BAME women, face a much higher risk of exposure to violence, suffer more severe forms of abuse, and face additional and specific barriers when seeking support (e.g., Al-Yaman, Van Doeland, & Wallis, 2006; Fanslow, Robinson, Crengle, & Perese, 2010; Memmott, Stacy, Chambers, & Keys, 2001; New Zealand Ministry of Justice, 2015). Although evidence is limited, researchers have also indicated high rates of domestic and sexual violence against LGBTQI people (e.g., Leonard, Mitchell, Pitts, Patel, & Fox, 2008).

Little research currently exists on the pervasiveness of image-based sexual abuse within diverse population groups. In a 2017 representative study commissioned by the Australian Office of the eSafety Commissioner (OeSC, 2017), image-based sexual abuse victimisation was found to be highest for young women, with 24% of women aged 18–24 years reporting experiences of image-based sexual abuse, compared with 16% of men the same age. Ruvalcaba and Eaton's (2019) study of 3,044 participants found that one in twelve (8%) respondents reported having been a victim of "non-consensual pornography at some point in their lives", with women (9.2%) reporting higher rates than men (6.6%). They also found that gay men (10.2%) were more likely to report victimisation than heterosexual men (5.6%), but they found no difference between lesbian (4.23%) and heterosexual women (6.7%). In contrast, Lenhart, Ybarra and Price-Feeney's (2016) study of US adults (n=3,002) found that LGB respondents (7%) were more likely than heterosexual respondents (2%) to report having experienced the non-consensual sharing of nude or semi-nude images, and LGB respondents (15%) were significantly more likely than heterosexual respondents (2%) to have experienced threats to share nude or semi-nude images.

In our survey, experiences of image-based sexual abuse vary according to differing contexts, including sexuality, age and indigeneity.

Table 2.1 shows that there were no significant country or sex differences in the reported pervasiveness of image-based sexual abuse victimisation. Respondents in Australia (35.2%, n=724), New Zealand (39%, n=791) and

Table 2.1 Pervasiveness of image-based sexual abuse victimisation (n=6,109)

	Taken % (n)	Shared % (n)	Threatened % (n)	At least one % (n)	All three % (n)
Country					
Australia	31.1 (638)	19.4 (399)	17.2 (354)	35.2 (724)	12.9 (265)
New Zealand	35.1 (712)	21.7 (439)	19.9 (403)	39 (791)	15.5 (315)
United Kingdom	33.5 (679)	21.7 (440)	19 (385)	39 (791)	13.9 (282)
Gender					
Female	32.9 (1,047)	18 (571)	16.9 (539)	38.1 (1,211)	11.4 (362)
Male	33.5 (982)	24.1 (707)	20.6 (603)	37.4 (1,095)	17.1 (500)
Sexuality					
Heterosexual	30.9 (1,678)*	18.8 (1,022)*	16.9 (918)*	35.4 (1,923)*	12.5 (677)*
LGB+	51.7 (351)	37.7 (256)	33 (224)	56.4 (383)	27.2 (185)
Age					
16–19	37.5 (140)*	27.9 (104)*	27.9 (104)*	45.3 (169)*	19.6 (73)*
20–29	43.9 (619)	32.1 (453)	29.9 (422)	50.7 (715)	23.2 (327)
30–39	39.5 (625)	26.8 (425)	23.8 (377)	44.5 (704)	19 (301)
40–49	30.4 (345)	15.9 (180)	13 (147)	33.6 (381)	9.4 (107)
50–64	18.7 (300)	7.2 (116)	5.7 (92)	21 (337)	3.4 (54)
Race/Ethnicity					
White, European or Pākehā	31.8 (1,431)	19.5 (876)	17.1 (768)	36.5 (1,644)	12.4 (556)
Indigenous & BAME	37.1 (598)	25 (402)	23.2 (374)	41.1 (622)	19 (306)

Note: Percentages and numbers relate to respondents who have experienced each form of image-based sexual abuse victimisation (Taken, Shared, Threatened), at least one of the three forms of image-based sexual abuse, or all three forms of image-based sexual abuse. * indicates significant differences between groups within this form of image-based sexual abuse (at p < .05 with a minimum of a small effect size).

the United Kingdom (39%, n=791) were similarly likely to report having experienced one or more forms of image-based sexual abuse, as were female (38.1%, n=1,211) and male respondents (37.4%, n=1,095). However, there were significant differences according to sexuality, with LGB+ respondents significantly more likely than heterosexual respondents to report having experienced image-based sexual abuse. For example, 56.4% (n=383) of LGB+ respondents had experienced one or more forms of image-based sexual abuse, compared with 35.4% (n=1,923) of heterosexual respondents.

Our survey data also found significant differences according to age, with younger respondents more likely than older respondents to report experiencing image-based sexual abuse. For example, 47.2% (n=1,588) of respondents aged 16–39 years had experienced one or more forms of image-based sexual abuse, compared with 26.2% (n=718) of respondents aged 40–64 years.

Regarding race, ethnicity and indigeneity, there was a non-significant trend whereby respondents from non-majority ethnic backgrounds were more likely to report having experienced all three forms of image-based sexual abuse. Importantly, the pattern of victimisation for sexuality, age, race, ethnicity and indigeneity was consistent irrespective of whether respondents identified as female or male. In Australia, Indigenous respondents (65.6%, n=42) were significantly more likely than non-Indigenous respondents (34.3%, n=682) to report having experienced one or more forms of image-based sexual abuse (not shown in the table). Comparable figures were not significantly different in New Zealand or the United Kingdom, though the trend was towards higher rates for Māori (48.4%, n=109 vs. 37.8%, n=682 for non-Māori) and BAME (41.1%, n=104 vs. 38.7%, n=687 for non-BAME) respondents. Yet when it came to those who had experienced all three forms of image-based sexual abuse, a clearer trend according to indigeneity emerged. In Australia, 35.9% (n=23) of respondents identifying as Indigenous had experienced all three forms of image-based sexual abuse, compared with 12.2% (n=242) of non-Indigenous respondents. The equivalent percentages were 28.4% (n=64) for respondents identifying as Māori and 13.9% (n=251) for non-Māori respondents in New Zealand, and 23.7% (n=60) for respondents identifying as BAME and 12.5% (n=222) for non-BAME respondents in the United Kingdom (not shown in the table).

Overwhelmingly then, our survey data suggests that individuals are differentially exposed to image-based sexual abuse and the risk of victimisation is distributed unequally across demographic patterns and vectors of marginalisation, including age, sexuality, indigeneity, race and ethnicity. In accounting for both the pervasiveness and the diversity of image-based sexual abuse victimisation reported here, it is clear that a nuanced conceptualisation of image-based sexual abuse is needed. As we suggest throughout the book, an account of image-based sexual abuse needs to engage not only with the dominant conceptual paradigms of sexual violence as predominantly reflective of systems of gender inequality, but also with the multiple structural inequalities that produce multiple relations of power and abuse. We argue in the final section of this chapter that "continuum thinking" (Boyle, 2019) is a useful way to think about image-based sexual abuse in order to recognise men's differential experience within the context of relative power and privilege, and at the same time to acknowledge the differential experiences and risks of image-based sexual abuse victimisation across different societal sectors.

Conceptualising image-based sexual abuse

Liz Kelly (1988) proposed that women's lived experiences of sexual violence should not be confined within existing legal parameters that define sexual offences and harm. Her research, which involved in-depth interviews with 60 victim-survivors of sexual violence, showed that many women experienced a spectrum of unwanted sexual violations across their lifetimes, some of which do not constitute either a criminal offence or unlawful conduct under the law. Kelly (1988) conceptualised these different, but interlinked experiences, as a "continuum of sexual violence". Continuum here is understood in two main ways: First, as a "continuous series of elements or events that pass into one another and which cannot be easily distinguished"; and second, these experiences have a "basic common character" underpinning and linking what might otherwise be seen as disparate phenomena (Kelly, 1988: 76). These common elements include "abuse, intimidation, coercion, intrusion, threat and force" (see further McGlynn et al., 2017: 27). Kelly argued that many women experience multiple forms of victimisation in their lifetime across the continuum of sexual violence.

Understanding victim-survivor experiences in this way allows connections to be made between all forms of sexual harassment and abuse, including everyday "intimate intrusions" (Stanko, 1985), such as street, workplace or online forms of sexual harassment (e.g., Fileborn, 2016; Vera-Gray, 2017), as well as rape, sexual assault and other forms of sexual violence. This conceptualisation also allows for a better understanding of the cumulative effects of sexual abuse in women's lives. For example, when women report feeling fearful of sexual violence, it is in a context of never knowing when the catcall or stares on the street, the unwanted touch or the persistent sexual requests, may escalate into a rape or sexual assault (Powell, Flynn, & Henry, 2019). It also means that the impacts and harms experienced in any one incident of sexual violence can connect with, or reinforce and amplify, the impacts of a lifetime of these experiences.

McGlynn and colleagues (2017) have argued that Kelly's continuum concept has value in two particular ways when analysing image-based sexual abuse. First, that the multiplicity of experiences of image-based sexual abuse mean that understanding these different behaviours as a "continuum of image-based sexual abuse" enables better understanding of the fluidity and complexity of these behaviours. Second, many victim-survivors of image-based sexual abuse experience these behaviours in ways connected to other forms of sexual violence, meaning that understanding the phenomenon of image-based sexual abuse as part of a "continuum of sexual violence" helps to better understand it and how it impacts and constrains engagement in the digital public sphere (McGlynn et al., 2017; see also see Henry & Powell, 2015a, 2015b; Powell & Henry, 2017). In her analysis of "continuum thinking", Boyle (2019: 29) describes image-based sexual abuse as "conceptually and experientially similar to more well-documented patterns of abuse", as well as distinct from those other experiences on the sexual violence continuum. This was evident in the voices of many of our interview participants who described their experiences as occurring within the context of ongoing abuse (e.g., domestic violence), or as similar or distinct to their other (connected or unconnected) experiences of sexual violence.

As well as situating image-based sexual abuse within a context that explores the connections and structural underpinnings of multiple forms of violence against women, it is also important to acknowledge the intersections of gender with other societal inequalities and oppressions in society, including racism, xenophobia, ableism, homophobia and ageism (Crenshaw, 1991; Price, 2012; Sokoloff & Dupont, 2005; Sokoloff & Pratt, 2005). In relation to street harassment, for instance, Vera-Gray (2017: 128) notes that:

> Although all women and girls are in some way subject to gender discrimination, all women and girls are not discriminated against in the same way. Hierarchies of worth situate women and girls in relation to each other, as well as in relation to men and boys.

Connecting different experiences of sexual abuse, harassment and violence to gender, alongside other markers of identity and inequality, "allow[s] us to see multiple connections in different contexts and support the broader argument … about the value of (re)conceptualising Kelly's continuum in the plural", but it also "demonstrates that not everything is related in the same way and distinctions are important" (Boyle, 2019: 29–32).

It is also important to acknowledge similarities and differences in terms of the impacts and harms of victimisation (further discussed in Chapter 3). In our survey, of the 2,306 respondents who had experienced one or more forms of image-based sexual abuse victimisation, 41.5% (n=957) provided further information regarding their most significant experience. When asked how their most significant victimisation experience made them feel, 61.1% (n=585) of respondents indicated that they did not think it was okay, flattering and/or funny (i.e., they did not report any neutral or positive feelings). There was a clear gendered pattern, with female respondents (71.7%, n=369) being significantly more likely than male respondents (48.9%, n=216) to indicate that they did not think their experience was okay, flattering and/ or funny. Moreover, across the 75 interviews we conducted with victim-survivors of image-based sexual abuse, while no participants described their experiences as "flattering" or "funny", a few participants reflected they had felt ambivalent or confused about what had happened to them, for example feeling unsure how to perceive or interpret, or react and respond to their experiences. As Chelsea (Aus) observed:

> I didn't know how to react to it, so I didn't want to cause a scene because no one likes to be the girl who causes a scene about a joke. I didn't really want to break up with my boyfriend so I didn't know whether I should keep quiet about it and just pretend like it didn't happen or whether I should confront him, so I was just trying to work out what to do about it and how I felt about it.

Additionally, some participants told us that their perceptions had changed over time, indicating, for example, that they wished they had felt more confident to identify their experience as significant, or had sought help or reported it – whether to a teacher, a parent, a friend or even the police. For example, Sofia (UK), whose boyfriend had showed a consensually taken intimate image of her on his phone to one of his friends, told us she had "brushed off" what had happened:

> I really liked [my boyfriend] at the time…[his actions] were definitely immature, but he wasn't trying to hurt anyone…So because he didn't send [the intimate picture], I was okay with it – I told myself that it didn't matter, it wasn't a big deal.

However, Sofia later reflected that she had played down her boyfriend's actions, partly because she had been "blinded" by her feelings for him, but also because she blamed herself and was "in denial" about what had happened:

> I did blame myself a little bit for being stupid enough to let myself be in the position where he would take a picture and not saying no … and I know girls kind of tend to be in denial … But yeah if something like that were to happen now, now that I'm more informed … even if he was just being careless, I would have definitely told him that it wasn't right and … I wouldn't have just brushed it off.

As Sofia's comment reflects, powerful gendered messages minimising the impact and nature of image-based sexual abuse are common, and they can be normalised and internalised by victim-survivors. Similarly, Katie (NZ) described not wanting "any more attention" or for others to know what had happened, especially her parents. This, she told us, prevented her from saying or doing anything about the experience and resulted in her downplaying her experiences as a minor form of abuse. By way of contrast, many participants we interviewed described their experiences as having profound "life shattering" effects, which we discuss in detail in the next chapter.

The differing responses to image-based sexual abuse experiences demonstrates the utility of conceptualising image-based sexual abuse as part of a continuum of sexual violence. While one person might describe their experience as "relatively minor", for others, it is deeply impactful, signalling a significant "rupture" to their lives (see Chapter 3). Even in relation to those who describe the behaviour as less significant at one point in time, some come later to experience greater harm, such as victim-survivors who are unable to secure employment because sexualised images of them are available online. Moreover, the collective effects of other experiences of sexual intrusions and violations over a person's lifetime can accumulate to make the experience of a sexual intrusion more harmful.

Another way in which continuum thinking can be applied to image-based sexual abuse is in considering the ways in which differing behaviours by men as perpetrators can shade into one another (Kelly, 1988: 75). As Boyle (2019: 29) observes:

> The continuum of men's violences allows us to think of violence as being gender based not because of who it targets but, rather, because of how that violence is understood in relation to perpetrators' gender performances. This can allow us to make gendered sense of behaviours which don't seem to fit comfortably on the continuums we have explored so far.

Boyle (2019) argues that highly visible "aberrant" and "abusive" masculine behaviours are overlooked, accepted or even celebrated because they are seen as "typical" masculine behaviour. She contends that the concept of "hegemonic masculinity" is thus useful to demonstrate the ways in which celebrated male behaviours (not always abusive behaviours) are "enacted in culture and institutions as well as in gender performance and inter-personal relationships – which allow men's dominance over women to continue" (Boyle, 2019: 29) (see Chapter 5 for further discussion).

Conclusion

This chapter has shed light on the diverse and complex nature of image-based sexual abuse. Among our survey and interview cohorts, participants were most likely to report having experienced multiple forms of image-based sexual abuse, whether by the same perpetrator, by different perpetrators, or by multiple perpetrators. It was also not uncommon for participants to disclose other experiences of sexual violence, domestic violence, stalking and sexual harassment in online and offline settings, either as part of the image-based sexual abuse victimisation, or as separate from it.

We have also sought to explore the nature of image-based sexual abuse, arguing that the variety and complexity of experiences are best understood as being on a "continuum of image-based sexual abuse". This approach enables an understanding of the breadth of different ways in which image-based sexual abuse is both experienced and perpetrated.

Overall, our survey data suggests that certain groups are more likely to experience image-based sexual abuse victimisation, across all forms of abuse. In particular, we found that LGB+ respondents, people aged 16–39 years, individuals with minority racial and ethnic identities and Indigenous/Māori respondents were more likely to experience image-based sexual abuse. Our interviews provided further insight into both the diversity and shared experiences of victim-survivors, further highlighting the complexity of image-based sexual abuse, as well as locating image-based sexual abuse within a broader discursive sociocultural system whereby coercive sexuality and gender inequality, particularly in intimate relationships, is the norm. In the next chapter, we further explore these insights more deeply through an analysis of the relational contexts, harms and impacts of image-based sexual abuse.

References

Al-Yaman, F., Van Doeland, M., & Wallis, M. (2006). *Family violence among Aboriginal and Torres Strait Islander peoples* (cat. No. IHW 17). Canberra, ACT: Australian Institute of Health and Welfare.

Australian Human Rights Commission (AHRC). (2017). *Change the course: National report on sexual assault and sexual harassment at Australian universities 2017.* Sydney, NSW: AHRC. Retrieved from www.humanrights.gov.au/our-work/sex-discrimination/publications/change-course-national-report-sexual-assault-and-sexual.

Boyle, K. (2019). What's in a name? Theorising the inter-relationships of gender and violence. *Feminist Theory, 20*(1), 19–36.

Crenshaw, K. (1991). Mapping the margins: Intersectionality, identity politics, and violence against women of color. *Stanford Law Review, 43*(6), 1241–1299.

DeKeseredy, W. S., Schwartz, M. D., Harris, B., Woodlock, D., Nolan, J., & Hall-Sanchez, A. (2019). Technology-facilitated stalking and unwanted sexual messages/images in a college campus community: The role of negative peer support. *Sage Open, January–March*, 1–12.

DeKeseredy, W. S., Schwartz, M. D., Nolan, J., Mastron, N., & Hall-Sanchez, A. (2019). Polyvicitmization and the continuum of sexual abuse at a college campus: Does negative peer support increase the likelihood of multiple victimizations? *The British Journal of Criminology, 59*(2), 276–295.

Fanslow, J., Robinson, E., Crengle, S., & Perese, L. (2010). Juxtaposing beliefs and reality: Prevalence rates of intimate partner violence and attitudes to violence and gender roles reported by New Zealand women. *Violence Against Women, 16*(7), 812–831.

Fileborn, B. (2016). *Reclaiming the night-time economy: Unwanted sexual attention in pubs and clubs*. New York: Springer.

Finkelhor, D., Ormrod, R. K., Turner, H. A., & Hamby, S. L. (2005). Measuring poly-victimization using the Juvenile Victimization Questionnaire. *Child Abuse & Neglect, 29*(11), 1297–1312.

Hamby, S., Taylor, E., Jones, L., Mitchell, K. J., Turner, H. A., & Newlin, C. (2018). From poly-victimization to poly-strengths: Understanding the web of violence can transform research on youth violence and illuminate the path to prevention and resilience. *Journal of Interpersonal Violence, 33*(5), 719–739.

Henry, N., & Flynn, A. (2019). Image-based sexual abuse: Online distribution channels and illicit communities of support. *Violence Against Women, 25*(16), 1932–1955.

Henry, N., Flynn, A., & Powell, A. (2018). Policing image-based sexual abuse: Stakeholder perspectives. *Police Practice and Research: An International Journal, 19*(6), 565–581.

Henry, N., Flynn, A., & Powell, A. (2019). *Responding to "revenge pornography": Prevalence, nature and impacts*. Report to the Criminology Research Advisory Council. Canberra, ACT: Australian Institute of Criminology. Retrieved from http://crg.aic.gov.au/reports/1819/08-1516-FinalReport.pdf.

Henry, N., & Powell, A. (2015a). Beyond the "sext": Technology-facilitated sexual violence and harassment against adult women. *Australian & New Zealand Journal of Criminology, 48*(1), 104–118.

Henry, N., & Powell, A. (2015b). Embodied harms: Gender, shame, and technology-facilitated sexual violence. *Violence Against Women, 21*(6), 758–779.

Kelly, L. (1988). *Surviving sexual violence*. Cambridge, UK: Polity Press.

Lenhart, A., Ybarra, M., & Price-Feeney, M. (2016). *Nonconsensual image sharing: One in 25 Americans has been a victim of "revenge porn"*. New York: Data & Society Research Institute. Retrieved from https://datasociety.net/pubs/oh/Nonconsensual_Image_Sharing_2016.pdf.

Leonard, W., Mitchell, A., Pitts, M., Patel, S., & Fox, C. (2008). *Coming forward: The underreporting of heterosexist violence and same-sex partner abuse in Victoria* (Monograph Series No. 69). Melbourne, VIC: Australian Research Centre in Sex, Health & Society, La Trobe University.

McGlynn, C., Rackley, E., & Houghton, R. (2017). Beyond "revenge porn": The continuum of image-based sexual abuse. *Feminist Legal Studies, 25*(1), 25–46.

Memmott, P., Stacy, R., Chambers, C., & Keys, C. (2001). *Violence in Indigenous communities*. Canberra, ACT: Commonwealth Attorney-General's Department.

Mouzos, J., & Makkai, T. (2004). *Women's experiences of male violence: Findings from the Australian component of the International Violence against Women Survey*. Research and Public Policy Series No. 56. Canberra, ACT: Australian Institute of Criminology.

NZ Ministry of Justice. (2015). *2014 New Zealand crime and safety survey: Main findings*. Wellington, NZ: Ministry of Justice. Retrieved from www.justice.govt.nz/assets/Documents/Publications/NZCASS-201602-Main-Findings-Report-Updated.pdf.

Office of the eSafety Commissioner (OeSC). (2017). *Image-based abuse national survey: Summary report*. Melbourne, VIC: OeSC. Retrieved from www.esafety. gov.au/sites/default/files/2019-07/Image-based-abuse-national-survey-summary-report-2017.pdf.

Powell, A., Flynn, A., & Henry, N. (2019). Sexual violence in digital society: Human, technical and social factors. In T. J. Holt & R. Leukfeldt (eds.), *The human factor of cybercrime* (pp. 134–155). Abingdon, Oxon; New York: Routledge.

Powell, A., & Henry, N. (2017). *Sexual violence in a digital age*. London: Palgrave Macmillan.

Powell, A., Scott, A. J., & Henry, N. (2018). Digital harassment and abuse: Experiences of sexuality and gender minority adults. *European Journal of Criminology*. Advance online publication. Doi: 10.1177/1477370818788006.

Price, J. M. (2012). *Structural violence: Hidden brutality in the lives of women*. New York: State University of New York Press.

Ruvalcaba, Y., & Eaton, A. A. (2019). Nonconsensual pornography among US adults: A sexual scripts framework on victimization, perpetration, and health correlates for women and men. *Psychology of Violence*. Advance online publication. https://doi.org/10.1037/vio0000233.

Sokoloff, N. J., & Dupont, I. (2005). Domestic violence at the intersections of race, class, and gender: Challenges and contributions to understanding violence against marginalized women in diverse communities. *Violence Against Women, 11*(1), 38–64.

Sokoloff, N. J., & Pratt, C. (eds.). (2005). *Domestic violence at the margins: Readings on race, class, gender and culture*. Piscataway, NJ: Rutgers University Press.

Stanko, E. A. (1985). *Intimate intrusions: Women's experience of male violence*. London; Boston, MA; Melbourne, VIC; Henley: Routledge & Kegan Paul.

Vera-Gray, F. (2017). Outlook: Girlhood, agency and embodied space for action. In B. Formark, H. Mulari, & M. Voipio (eds.), *Nordic girlhoods: New perspectives and outlooks* (pp. 127–136). Cham: Palgrave Macmillan.

Chapter 3

The harms of image-based sexual abuse (with Erika Rackley & Nicola Gavey)

Introduction

While few would dispute that image-based sexual abuse can cause considerable harm, we know surprisingly little about the nature of the harms, particularly those which are less visible, consequential or which do not fit the paradigmatic "revenge" narrative so commonly told in media and other public discourses. On the one hand, qualitative studies, which have focused on the harms of image-based sexual abuse, have tended to be with small samples and/or have concentrated on one specific form of such abuse, such as the non-consensual sharing of nude or sexual images (e.g., Bates, 2017). Quantitative studies, on the other hand, have tended to be with samples from a single country and/or have concentrated on victim-survivors' most recent experiences, rather than their most significant experiences. Accordingly, this chapter seeks to address gaps in our understanding with a focus on the nature and impacts of the harms of image-based sexual abuse.

In this chapter, we report on the findings of our 2019 survey with 6,109 respondents from Australia, New Zealand and the United Kingdom regarding their self-reported experiences of image-based sexual abuse. In particular, we focus on the *impacts* of image-based sexual abuse with a subsample of respondents who provided further information regarding their most significant experience. We also examine the harms and impacts experienced by the 75 victim-survivors we interviewed, exploring the following five key themes: Social rupture; constancy; existential threat; isolation; and constrained liberty.

The first section of the chapter examines the feelings, concerns and harms reported by a diverse group of survey respondents. The second section explores the impacts of image-based sexual abuse, examining the shortcomings of medicalised models. Using a phenomenological approach, we argue that a nuanced, holistic approach to understanding the harms of image-based sexual abuse should move beyond a medicalised, trauma-focused framework. We argue that the varying and differential ways in which people experience image-based sexual abuse must be taken into account, especially in the context of minoritised individuals and communities. Such an approach will support the varied responses necessary to challenge and prevent image-based sexual abuse, as well as the differing needs and mechanisms for providing redress (see Chapters 7 and 8).

Feelings, concerns and harms: survey findings

Our survey revealed that a large number of respondents (37.7%, n=2,306) had experienced at least one form of image-based sexual abuse. Respondents who had experienced image-based sexual abuse were asked about their most significant experience and to indicate their level of agreement ("not at all", "not really", "neutral", "somewhat", "very much") with various consequential feelings and concerns. In this context, we asked respondents a range of questions that related to: Whether they experienced negative responses concerning the abusive actions (i.e., whether they felt annoyed, embarrassed, humiliated, ashamed, depressed, angry, or were fearful for their safety); and whether they experienced neutral or even positive responses (i.e., whether they felt okay, flattered or found it funny). We also asked respondents if they experienced any reputational concerns (i.e., whether they were concerned about their reputation, relationships with others, employment, other people having seen the images and/or thinking badly of them), or safety concerns (i.e., whether they were concerned about the person physically, verbally or emotionally hurting them and/or others using the images to harass or hurt them). These questions were asked concerning their most significant experience of image-based sexual abuse.

Of the 957 respondents that provided further information regarding their most significant experience, 38.9% (n=372) reported some positive feelings (i.e., "somewhat" or "very much" agreement), whereas 61.1% (n=585) did not have any positive feelings (i.e., "not at all", "not really", "neutral" agreement). When examining those respondents who reported neutral or negative feelings (n=585),[1] Table 3.1 shows that there were significant differences across all reported feelings and concerns according to respondent sex, with female respondents significantly more likely than males to report experiencing negative feelings (92.1%, n=340 vs. 75.9%, n=164), as well as reputational concerns (82.7%, n=305 vs. 72.1%, n=155), and safety concerns (74%, n=273 vs. 59.1%, n=127). Although there were no significant differences in respondents' feelings or concerns based on sexuality or age, there were differences regarding negative feelings for respondents from racial or ethnic minority communities. White, European or Pākehā respondents (88.9%, n=376) were more likely than those from minority racial or ethnic communities (79%, n=128) to report negative feelings. There were no significant country differences in respondents' reported feelings and concerns.

Table 3.1 Feelings and concerns regarding the most significant victimisation experience (n=585)

	Negative feelings % (n)	Reputational concerns % (n)	Safety concerns % (n)
Country			
Australia	88.8 (167)	79.3 (149)	71.8 (135)
New Zealand	82.2 (162)	76.5 (150)	63.8 (125)
United Kingdom	87.5 (175)	80.5 (161)	70 (140)
Gender			
Female	92.1 (340)*	82.7 (305)*	74 (273)*
Male	75.9 (164)	72.1 (155)	59.1 (127)
Sexuality			
Heterosexual	86.2 (388)	77.6 (349)	66.7 (300)
LGB+	85.9 (116)	82.8 (111)	74.6 (100)
Age			
16–19	85.7 (42)	77.6 (38)	73.5 (36)
20–29	87.6 (190)	82.5 (179)	71.4 (155)
30–39	87.3 (145)	78.3 (130)	69.9 (116)
40–49	81.6 (71)	73.6 (64)	62.1 (54)
50–64	84.8 (56)	75.4 (49)	60 (39)
Race/Ethnicity			
White, European or Pākehā	88.9 (376)*	80.9 (342)	69 (292)
Indigenous & BAME	79 (128)	73.3 (118)	67.1 (108)

Note: Percentages and numbers relate to respondents who have experienced negative feelings, and reputational and safety concerns (i.e., "somewhat" or "very much" agreement). Response percentages exceed 100% as the questions allowed respondents to select multiple answers. * indicates significant differences between groups within this category of feelings and harms (at $p < .05$ with a minimum of a small effect size).

The pattern of findings for sexuality and age was consistent irrespective of whether respondents were female or male. Regarding respondent race and ethnicity, although White, European or Pākehā females (94.9%, n=261) were more likely than females from racial or minority ethnic communities (84%, n=79) to report negative feelings, there was no significant difference for males based on race or ethnicity (77.7%, n=115 vs. 72.1%, n=49) (not shown in the table). These findings suggest both a difference in victims' negative feelings as a result of image-based sexual abuse according to gender, and an intersectional impact for women from racial or ethnic minority communities.

In addition to providing information regarding various consequential feelings and concerns, respondents who provided further information regarding their most significant experience of image-based sexual abuse victimisation were asked to indicate their level of agreement ("not at all", "not really", "neutral", "somewhat", "very much") as to whether they experienced various consequential harms. We asked respondents about the impacts of the abuse on their health (i.e., whether it negatively affected their mental and physical health), on their relationships (i.e., whether it negatively affected their intimate/sexual partners and friends/family relationships, their work or study performance, and their professional reputation) and on any experiences of harassment (i.e., whether they were teased, harassed or stalked by others in relation to the abuse).

More than half of those respondents (55.1%, n=322) reported that their most significant experience of image-based sexual abuse harmed their health. Similarly, more than half (55.7%, n=325) reported harms to their relationships, and over a third (39.7%, n=232) reported experiencing harassment. Table 3.2 shows that there were significant differences according to respondent sex, with females significantly more likely than males to report harms to their health (61%, n=225 vs. 45.1%, n=97) and/or adverse relational impacts (59.6%, n=220 vs. 48.8%, n=105). A larger proportion of males reported having experienced harassment (43.3%, n=93) related to image-based sexual abuse, compared to females (37.7%, n=139). This difference was not statistically significant. Additionally, LGB+ respondents tended to be more likely than heterosexual respondents to report some harms as a consequence of their most significant victimisation experience. For example, LGB+ respondents (64.9%, n=87) were significantly more likely than heterosexual respondents (52.9%, n=238) to report experiencing adverse relational impacts.

There were no clear patterns of findings for the harms experienced across the different age groups, except in the context of harassment, where younger respondents were more likely than older respondents to report these harms. For example, 57.1% (n=28) of respondents aged 16–19 years reported experiencing subsequent harassment related to image-based sexual abuse compared with 18.5% (n=12) of respondents aged 50–64 years. In relation to respondents from racial or ethnic minority communities, they were also significantly more likely to report experiencing harassment (50.3%, n=81) compared with White, European or Pākehā respondents (35.7%, n=151). Though our survey did not ask respondents about the nature of the harassment (for instance, whether it was sexuality- or race-based), it is notable that these minority groups were more likely to experience subsequent harassment, suggestive of an interaction between sexism, heterosexism and racism and image-based sexual abuse.

The pattern of findings for age was consistent irrespective of whether respondents were female or male. There was, however, a clear interaction between respondent gender and sexuality. Female LGB+ respondents (74.4%, n=61) were more likely than female heterosexual respondents (55.4%, n=159) to report relational harms (although there was no significant sexuality

Table 3.2 Harms as a consequence of the most significant victimisation experience (n=585)

	Health harms % (n)	Relational harms % (n)	Harassment % (n)
Country			
Australia	58 (109)	56.9 (107)	42.6 (80)
New Zealand	50 (98)	57.7 (113)	37.2 (73)
United Kingdom	57.5 (115)	52.5 (105)	39.5 (79)
Gender			
Female	61 (225)*	59.6 (220)*	37.7 (139)
Male	45.1 (97)	48.8 (105)	43.3 (93)
Sexuality			
Heterosexual	52.9 (238)	52.9 (238)*	37.8 (170)
LGB+	62.7 (84)	64.9 (87)	46.3 (62)
Age			
16–19	51 (25)	57.1 (28)	57.1 (28)*
20–29	56.7 (123)	59.9 (130)	42.9 (93)
30–39	59 (98)	51.8 (86)	41 (68)
40–49	50.6 (44)	54 (47)	35.6 (31)
50–64	49.2 (32)	52.3 (34)	18.5 (12)
Race/Ethnicity			
White, European or Pākehā	56.7 (240)	54.1 (229)	35.7 (151)*
Indigenous & BAME	50.9 (82)	59.6 (96)	50.3 (81)

Note: Percentages and numbers relate to respondents who have experienced negative health harms, reputational harms and harassment (i.e., "somewhat" or "very much" agreement). * indicates significant differences between groups within this category of harms (at p < .05 with a minimum of a small effect size).

difference for males, 50%, n=26 vs. 48.5%, n=79) (not shown in the table). Furthermore, although there was no overall significant difference for sexuality (as discussed above), female LGB+ respondents (50%, n=41) were more likely than female heterosexual respondents (34.1%, n=98) to report experiencing harassment. Again, there was no significant difference for males (40.4%, n=21 vs. 44.2%, n=72). The pattern of findings for harassment was consistent irrespective of whether respondents were White, European or Pākehā, or from minority racial or ethnic communities. However, there was again a clear pattern of race or ethnicity interacting with gender, with females from racial or ethnic minority groups (69.1%, n=65) being were more likely than White, European or Pākehā females (56.4%, n=155) to report relational harms, whereas there was no corresponding difference for males (46.3%, n=31 vs. 50%, n=74) (not shown in the table).

Overall, our survey results indicate that the impacts and harms of image-based sexual abuse can be significant for many, but that the nature and extent of these harms can vary across different demographic groups. Women report more significant negative feelings, reputational and safety concerns, health and relational impacts than men, with LGB+ women being particularly affected. In general, LGB+ respondents were more likely to experience harassment, as were respondents from minority ethnic and racial groups, and young people. These findings possibly point to, at least in part, a connection between image-based sexual abuse and hate crime, where LGB+ and minority ethnic individuals' increased reports of harassment might be related to racialised, homophobic and/or xenophobic harassment. However, further investigation is needed to adequately understand the nuance and context of these findings in future research. Similarly, there may be a multiplicity of factors as to why White, European or Pākehā women reported higher levels of negative feelings than women from minority racial or ethnic communities, including the possibility of women from minority ethnic communities articulating harms differently, or internalising and minimising higher levels of adverse impacts.

In future research it will be useful to investigate further the experiences of those who described the abuse as "funny" or said that they were "okay" with it or were "flattered". On the one hand, it is possible that, even though their experiences still sit on a continuum of image-based sexual abuse, several respondents genuinely felt amused or flattered, and consequently do not characterise what happened as "abusive". On the other hand, it may be that societal norms on gender and sexuality serve to shape the way in which people react. For instance, in the context of masculine bonding and status building, men may feel they are expected to find it amusing when someone takes or shares nude or sexual images of them without their consent. Similarly, some women may express feeling "flattered" by images being taken or shared of them without their consent in a context where their physical appearance is lauded and subject to judgement.

The wrongs of image-based sexual abuse

While our survey found that the majority of those who experienced image-based sexual abuse reported negative feelings and adverse impacts, there were some who reported no such consequences. Nonetheless, we argue that all acts of image-based sexual abuse are wrongs because they constitute breaches of an individual's "fundamental rights to dignity and privacy, as well as their freedom of sexual expression and autonomy" (McGlynn & Rackley, 2017: 546; see also Citron & Franks, 2014; McNeilly, 2019).

It may be helpful therefore to distinguish between the wrong (in this case, the non-consensual taking or sharing of nude or sexual images) and the harm caused (that is, the *consequences* of the wrong). This is not to suggest that both elements are – or should be – required for it to be a criminal wrong. Indeed, such an approach would not only fail to recognise the inherent wrong of the act, but it also risks expecting particular responses from victim-survivors (see Flynn & Henry, 2019; Gavey & Farley, in press). Rather, it is to suggest that our understanding of, and in turn our responses to, image-based sexual abuse may be improved once we distinguish the wrongful act from the harm it causes. Put another way, there is a need to recognise that *all* forms of image-based sexual abuse involve some form of *prima facie* wrong, even though the nature and impacts of that wrong may be experienced differently across different populations. Therefore, while some may report being "okay" with the behaviours, the acts still amount to a fundamental wrong.

Beyond the wrong per se, there are often serious, harmful consequences for those who have experienced image-based sexual abuse. In our survey, as described above, many respondents reported adverse impacts on their health and well-being, on their relationships with others, as well as experiencing harassment and abuse. Our interviews with victim-survivors shed further light on the nature and extent of some of these consequential harms, which can vary according to the form the abuse takes, and also depend, as our survey also found, on the context and positionality of the victim-survivor. In the section below, we examine the "consequential" harms of image-based sexual abuse, critiquing the use of medicalised trauma models. We propose a phenomenological approach that provides a more holistic and nuanced understanding of the harms victim-survivors can experience.

The consequential harms of image-based sexual abuse

We have come to understand more about the nature and extent of the harms and impacts of image-based sexual abuse via victim-survivor testimonies (Evans, 2016), academic analyses of the significance of these testimonies (Bloom, 2014; Cecil, 2014; Citron & Franks, 2014; Kamal & Newman, 2016), qualitative studies (Bates, 2017) and quantitative research (Powell & Henry, 2019; Powell, Henry, & Flynn, 2018; Powell, Henry, Flynn, & Scott, 2019; Ruvalcaba & Eaton, 2019). While this research has been important in developing our understanding of the harms of image-based sexual abuse, it has primarily conceptualised harms through a medicalised trauma-based framework, drawing upon biomedical discourses of trauma – describing, for example, discrete forms of psychological (and physical) injury or distress (see e.g., Bates, 2017; Kamal & Newman, 2016; Ruvalcaba & Eaton, 2019). For instance, Bates' (2017) study of 18 US and Canadian survivors, whose sexual images were shared without their consent, reported serious mental health effects, including post-traumatic stress disorder (PTSD), suicidality, anxiety, depression, as well as negative psychological impacts such as lack of trust, loss of control and potentially harmful coping mechanisms, such as high alcohol use.

Foregrounding the harms of image-based sexual abuse through a trauma lens can help to legitimise victim-survivors' experiences as "real", conveying the extent of their violation and validating the harm and suffering that many experience (Wasco, 2003). For some, it might provide a framework that helps to make sense of their experiences. More instrumentally, medicalised trauma models lend themselves to quantifiable, clinical measurements of harm – for instance, providing "authoritative evidence" of the severe and widespread effects of sexual violence in society (Morrison, Hardison, Mathew, & O'Neil, 2004: 4). These models thus serve a practical function, informing developments in policy and practice and helping to justify the allocation of resources for prevention and support to victim-survivors (DiTullio & Sullivan, 2019; Gilfus, 1999; Root, 1992; Wasco, 2003).

However, we have argued elsewhere (McGlynn et al., in press), that a medicalised trauma model risks categorising and defining the harms in narrow ways that do not adequately capture the wide array of complex and interconnected harms associated with image-based sexual abuse. As such, the nature of harm experienced by victim-survivors risks being missed, minimised and misunderstood within a trauma model. In addition, a medicalised trauma model can inadvertently collude with the gendered status quo to decontextualise and depoliticise the harms of sexual violence (even though this is anathema to earlier feminist landmark trauma formulations – see e.g., Burgess & Holmstrom, 1974; Herman, 1992; see also Vera-Gray, 2019 for an excellent summary). While it is well-established that sexual violence occurs in particular intersectional, gendered and sociopolitical contexts, all of which may co-produce, shape and extend the harms experienced, a reductive focus on the discrete mental health effects or psychological distress an individual victim-survivor suffers tends to lock our attention on that individual. This can orientate our focus towards a "pathologised subject", wherein harms are framed as medical "symptoms" or signs of individual distress and dysfunction which are disconnected from broader contexts of misogyny, racism and other forms of oppression in which sexual violence is experienced (see e.g., Burstow, 2003; Gavey, 2005, 2007; Gilfus, 1999; McKenzie-Mohr & Lafrance, 2011; Vera-Gray & Fileborn, 2018; Wasco, 2003).

In focusing on individual mental health effects and "trauma", we risk diverting attention away from social injustice as a source of harm, obscuring the potential of harm prevention strategies which might be secured through social change (Vera-Gray & Fileborn, 2018: 81). Accordingly, we have sought to develop a feminist phenomenological approach to better understand the nature and extent of the harms of image-based sexual abuse (McGlynn et al., in press). Feminist phenomenological works, for instance, have conceptualised suffering as an embodied, conscious and subjective happening, experienced and situated in a particular time and place (Butler, 1989; de Beauvoir, 2012; Scarry, 1985; Young, 1990).[2] Within this framework, the harms of sexual violence can be conceptualised holistically, centring everyday experience within an analysis of how this is inflected by our situatedness: "opening up a theoretical space to talk about the realities of sexual violence as a constraining context for women without denying their 'space for action'" (Vera-Gray & Fileborn, 2018: 92).

Furthermore, a phenomenological perspective can take account of the fact that victim-survivors may talk in terms of commonly understood ideas of trauma, while not confining or limiting those harms and experiences to medicalised understandings. Some victim-survivors in the present study, for example, described symptoms and diagnoses of PTSD and many experienced mental health and psychological trauma-related harms which must be appropriately recognised and treated.

Our argument, therefore, is that a feminist phenomenological perspective better captures the totality, extent and diversity of the harms experienced. It can help us to recognise that image-based sexual abuse and the consequential harms remain relatively fluid concepts, embedded within contingent "networks of values, attitudes and relations which are, inter alia, gendered" (Conaghan, 2019: 180).

A feminist phenomenological approach then provides a holistic way to understand the consequential harms of image-based sexual abuse. In our interviews, victim-survivors expressed their experiences of harms in ways beyond medicalised, trauma-based approaches, emphasising the overlapping and interconnected nature of their experiences. We develop this holistic, nuanced approach through reference to five inter-related themes described by victim-survivors in our study: Social rupture; constancy; existential threat; isolation; and constrained liberty. Each theme is discussed below.

Social rupture: "devastating, like it broke me" (Faith (NZ))

A significant number of our interview participants described their experience of image-based sexual abuse as one of utter devastation. Participants described feeling "completely, completely broken" and characterised their experiences as "life-ruining", "hell on earth" and "a nightmare ... which destroyed everything". Their narratives conveyed a sense in which the abuse was experienced as a marked and overwhelming breach – or rupture – that radically disrupted their lives, altering their sense of self, their identity and their relationships with their bodies and others. For these participants, their victimisation was experienced as a point of "fracture" and discontinuity which generated far-reaching change, causing them to delineate their lives and sense of self as "before" and "after" the abuse. In Maya's (Aus) words, image-based sexual abuse "impacts your sense of self on every level". This was echoed by Louise (UK) who said: "it completely changes you". Jennifer

(UK) similarly reflected: "it obviously does define my life now … it has completely changed my life in horrific ways". While Anna (UK) told us: "I'm nowhere near the person I once was. That's gone and it's rebuilding a new part of me now".

While differences in life experience, social identity and age meant that the ramifications of the image-based sexual abuse varied between participants, collectively there was a common experience of the abuse as an extreme, unsettling and intrusive violation. These participants identified the consequential impacts as all-encompassing and pervasive, as radically altering their everyday life experiences, relationships and activities, causing harms which permeated their personal, professional and digital social worlds: "It impacts you emotionally, physiologically, professionally, in dating and relationships, in bloody every single factor of your life" (Maya, Aus).

Additionally, many participants reflected on how their experience of image-based sexual abuse was embodied – experienced in and through their bodies, altering their sense of bodily integrity, and their corporeal, social and sexual subjectivity. Jennifer (UK), for example, described how the image-based sexual abuse touched her "very core" – the harms she described were experienced "really deep within your body … it really penetrates you". Frances (UK) recounted how her awareness of, and relationship with, her body has changed since the abuse in that she now feels very "conscious" of her body and uncomfortable if anyone gets "too close". Anna (UK) further commented:

> I've changed my hair colour. I intentionally put on weight, because I was quite thin and I always had quite an athletic sort of figure, and it sounds so ridiculous because I intentionally made myself put on [substantial weight] so people wouldn't [recognise me].

We invoke the notion of "social rupture" here as a means of encapsulating and better understanding the experiences of a significant number, though not all, of our participants, who spoke of the totality of harm experienced, conveying at that time a sense of complete devastation. In so doing, we are building on works which examine the biographical disruption embodied in narratives or testimonies of traumatic experiences – the radical undoing of the self – in order to convey the way in which such experiences can profoundly disturb situated understandings of the self, the world and others (Brison, 2003; Brockmeier, 2008; Bury, 1982; Caruth, 1996; Du Toit, 2009; Langer, 1991). This approach allows us to move beyond decontextualised, discretely conceived forms of psychological injury or distress, as conceived in some medicalised trauma-based frameworks, to better represent and understand how the impacts of image-based sexual abuse can unfold across the *entirety* of participants' lifeworlds, as they relate to and interact with others.

Previous phenomenological works also discuss the processual experience and consequence of sexual violence in terms of disjointedness, intrusion and fracture (e.g., Brison, 2003; Du Toit, 2009). Within these works, this sense of discontinuity has been used to convey the *nature* of traumatic experience. In contrast, we intend to foreground the intrusion experienced by victim-survivors as a harm in its own right – conceived as an *ontological violation* which can inflict harm across all the facets of an individual's lifeworld. In this way, social rupture provides a conceptual framework which reveals the holistic, situated and relational nature of harms – relocating the locus of "harm" from the individual and/or their symptoms (as in medicalised trauma models), to the entirety of the social fabric of the victim-survivor's life, to the wholeness of their being-in-the-world.

The idea of social rupture permits us to understand the harms generated by image-based sexual abuse as *contextual*, where meaning and consequences are inflected by and contingent upon a range of interlocking factors, such as victim-survivors' particular social locations, intersectional identities and experiences in relation to broader systemic and structural inequalities and oppressions, such as misogyny, racism, ableism and homophobia (see also Vera-Gray & Fileborn, 2018). It enables us to see the socially constructed nature of these harms and the ways in which they are heightened in particular social and political contexts, such as where dominant sexual scripts legitimise forms of victim-blaming, minimisation and harassment.

Many of our women participants spoke not only of the violation of having their images shared without consent, but also how they felt "degraded", "mortified", "ashamed", "disgusted" and "stupid", reflecting gendered social expectations and sexual scripts. They spoke about how they were blamed for the abuse and were subjected to sexualised insults. Several women participants said that the "worst" harm (hypothetical or realised) was their families finding out about the abuse: "The worst thing ... is the shame of your parents being disappointed. ... I don't want my family ... to even know that I'm a sexual being" (Georgia, Aus). Others, who had experienced image-based sexual abuse in the context of a previous or ongoing intimate relationship, spoke of their former or current partner's "controlling", "manipulative", "obsessive" or "belittling" behaviours:

> It started being ... 'oh, I'm away for work – can you send me a picture?' And then it started being a way for him to control me ... [it] ends up ... where we were being intimate and he wanted ... to film it – which I wasn't happy with. But the threat of being hit ... was greater. So I just said okay.
>
> (Frances (UK))

In addition, some victim-survivors we interviewed spoke about the intersectional nature of the harms, and the additional risks and barriers these might generate. Tia (NZ), for example, reflected that not only was her experience of abuse deeply violating, but it also potentially jeopardised her safety by putting her at increased risk of so-called "honour-based" violence. Also, Maya (Aus) described how the harassment and victim-blaming she experienced was inflected with racism and misogyny after someone created digitally altered images of her and then circulated them online,:

> I got a lot of hate and a lot of it was because I'm brown skinned, I'm a woman of colour, I'm not conventionally attractive in that I'm not skinny and I'm not white. The hate was not only sexist and sexualised but it was also racialised as well. I had racialised hate and misogynistic hate, and the commentary was, 'You're ugly and gross, why would this happen to you?', or 'You should be flattered', or 'You're asking for it, you're a slut, you're a whore, what do you expect?'

Another common theme identified by participants living with a disability and/or a long-term health condition was that the experience of image-based sexual abuse, and the social rupture it caused, significantly destabilised or worsened their health. This, in turn, caused further harm, which negatively affected many aspects of their lives, including their work or education, relationships with others and well-being.

Constancy: "a level of permanence which affects everything" (Margaret, UK)

Most of our participants spoke of the relentless, constant nature of the harms experienced; of their "ongoingness" and "endlessness". For some, this was reflected in the continuing nature of the abuse itself, of living each day in "utter fear" that the images would be discovered. The material was "out there", beyond their control, constantly available to be shared online, viewed and rediscovered, with each viewing or distribution another itera-tion of the abuse:

> It is permanent ... and so people know it, you can't not know it. ... Maybe you could have something happen to you that was traumatic, but you don't have to necessarily feel like you're defined by it for the rest of your life. But with this, there's such a level of permanence which af-fects everything ... especially if it's impossible now to take photos down, especially if it's impossible to stop the dissemination of the images. ... There will never be a day in my entire lifetime that all of the images of me could ever be deleted.
>
> (Maya, Aus)

Anna (UK) also commented on the seeming infinitude of the acts of image-based sexual abuse:

> There is no end to it, there is no stop, there is no finale. ... It's like, I'm quite aware that if I was to go on the internet or the porn websites now, I would ... find the videos of me. ... It's a crime that doesn't just happen and then that's done. It's something that is continual, and this could continue for I don't know how long. It could go on for bloody ever.

Some spoke of constantly "feeling on the edge". As Stephen (UK) described: "[It's become] a hidden obsession to always check my phone ... And that's kind of become the way that I've coped with it, constantly checking my phone, to the detriment of like my work".

Reminiscent of Brison's (2003: 45) description of embodied traumatic memories of sexual violence, particularly the effects of the lingering, sensory, physiological and emotional intrusions or "flashbacks" in everyday life, other participants spoke of the ubiquity of the images in their lives: "you have the image in your head, and it revisits and it revisits and revisits. ... It haunts you ..." (Alana, Aus).

Existential threat: "I live with it all the time, just waiting" (Anna, UK)

Merging into this sense of constancy, and due to the very real possibility of the abuse continuing or re-emerging, is the unnerving sense of fear, worry and uncertainty experienced by some victim-survivors of image-based sexual abuse. Heather (UK) described this as follows: "It was more constant apprehension, every time I was getting an email or a message, it was, 'is this somebody telling me it's finally been shared?'" For Louise (UK), being subject to threats to disclose sexual images was overwhelming: "I was embarrassed and I was ashamed ... and I felt stupid. Even now I'm still not sure whether or not she will send them ... I took an overdose".

As with some other forms of violence and abuse, the ongoing threat, fear and constraint it can engender, crossed time and space, and persisted almost regardless of how victim-survivors responded. As Stephen (UK) further explained:

> [It's] having this continuing threat that the images could be re-shared, or re-emerge online, that new people could see these intimate images. ... And I think it's the unknowing; that not knowing aspect that you have to deal with every day.

Victim-survivors described feeling they needed to be perpetually vigilant, ready to take action should the threat materialise in either their "online" or "offline" interactions. Many described how they continuously check the internet, particularly pornography websites or social media, in case their images have been posted or re-posted. Others described hyper-analysing all of their social interactions, trying to establish and manage who might know about or have seen their images, and consequently harbour negative opinions of them, often generating additional harms in their professional and personal lives.

These experiences demonstrate how the constancy of image-based sexual abuse can create a particularly pernicious violation – a sense of ongoing, existential threat which can cast a shadow over victim-survivors' lives. This was particularly the case for participants situated in precarious contexts underpinned by unequal power relations, where they were denied the instrumental means to protect themselves from harm, and thereby exercise control or containment of the abuse and its subsequent fallout (see also Johnson, 2017). This closely parallels the harms experienced by victim-survivors of other forms of sustained abuse, such as domestic abuse experienced as a pattern of coercive control which occurs "along a broad spatial and temporal continuum" (Stark, 2009: 1517). Furthermore, this existential threat was also felt by those whose experiences were outside of the context of an intimate partnership. The seemingly interminable and indomitable nature of the internet renders the potential threat limitless – extending across social relationships to encounters with faceless strangers.

Isolation: "it made me very reclusive in general" (Danielle, UK)

Image-based sexual abuse can engender a profound sense of isolation from family and friends, from the online world and from society as a whole. Often this is due to a profound breach of trust, not only in relation to the abuser, but from family, friends and the world around them (see also Bates, 2017; Short, Brown, Pitchford, & Barnes, 2017). Due to the constancy of image-based sexual abuse, and its continuing impacts, these isolating and destabilising effects can themselves be ongoing and intense. Thus, many victim-survivors told us that following the abuse, they withdrew from their social lives and relationships: "I cut myself off from all of my friends. I cut myself off from my family ... and just stayed at home in my room ... because I couldn't face the world" (Faith, NZ).

The isolation was often compounded by the negative reactions of others, both anticipated and realised, compelling victim-survivors to "go into hiding" (Lucy, UK) or "hide in shame" (Linda, Aus). Heather (UK) explained, "I had nobody to turn to because everyone had turned against me, so I was totally isolated". Other participants similarly described feeling "judged", "alone" and "unsupported", which only exacerbated their suffering. Maya (Aus), for example, told us:

> It was so isolating ... especially getting hate [online and] from 'friends' who don't want to associate with you ... because you're associated with something [they perceive to be] explicit and gross. Oftentimes I feel like the people you think would get it don't. ... It is so harmful and isolating.

This meant that many of our participants felt they could no longer "trust anyone" or "anything", and that they had to be "suspicious of everyone", with their loss of "faith" permeating their lives. Margaret (UK) explained: "My trust ... has been shattered on so many levels". This aligns with DiTullio and Sullivan's (2019) assertion that image-based sexual abuse can impact on an individual's relationships, from a relational and systemic perspective, engendering an "intense shift" towards a position of lack of trust which can have a marked effect on individuals' lives.

Many women participants emphasised the gendered impact of this isolation and lack of trust. Rachel (NZ) described this as follows: "Especially men, I just had a big distrust in them and I thought they are all out there to, sort of, do horrible things to you if you don't give them what they want". This was mentioned by Alison (Aus): "I would say that [the abuse] has definitely affected my trust in men specifically". Colleen (Aus) similarly explained:

> With strangers ... I just never trust people the way I used to and I'm always more closed off with males. Not towards females, it's just always with males, and I know that that's awful but it's just the way it is.

Many victim-survivors also told us that their continual living in fear, and the constancy of the harms they experienced, negatively affected their experiences and trust of digital space, exacerbating any sense of isolation. They came to see the internet as a dangerous place which they could not "trust", they no longer felt "safe" online, and instead viewed it as a site of potential re-traumatisation. Jennifer (UK) told us how she felt "terrified" at the thought of going back on social media for fear of "opening something back up". Julia (UK) also described:

> In a lot of ways it sort of isolates you even more in this day and age. ... I'm not on anything other than Facebook ... because I'm just petrified. It's just a scary, scary thought and I don't know who's watching.

This was expressed by Lucy (UK): "I don't really have an online presence anymore because I'm just so terrified of ... people contacting me because they've seen these pictures".

Consequently, some victim-survivors completely shut down their online profiles, with many others severely restricting their online information and interactions. When some returned to social media, it was an entirely different experience and practice compared to before the abuse, involving less interaction, reduced use and fewer communications. Thus, the abuse markedly affected people's online interactions. It was no longer a positive social activity, but a "necessary evil" in today's world. This echoes research from the European Women's Lobby (EWL, 2017: 17) which found that online abuse engenders "isolation" as one of its real-world effects. They note that "all the objects that empower them [women] on a personal and professional level become off-limits". In more stark terms, these lived realities resonate with Scarry's (1985: 40) description of how ordinary objects, in the context of torture, lose their everyday meaning and are themselves turned into instruments of torture.

Constrained liberty: "that feeling of vulnerability... distrust ...
and being unsafe actually affects you potentially forever"
(Clara, UK)

Many women participants talked about feeling consciously "unsafe", reflecting the omnipresent threat of sexual violence that women experience in their everyday lives. They reported experiencing a sense of jeopardy, distrust and wariness of men which permeated their experiences in public spaces, as well as their broader experience of the world in which they are situated. Some participants described how they subsequently felt they had to be constantly "aware" of their surroundings and take steps to protect themselves from men, as well as safeguard other women and girls in their lives. Clara (UK), for example, told us that she would deliberately cover up her and her daughters' bodies with extra clothing when in public spaces, to deter (further) sexualised abuse or harassment:

> I don't feel like I can feel comfortable walking down the street, without having sort of extra layers on, just in case. The chances are probably quite small but ... I feel like I sort of have to protect myself and my daughters.

Connecting this sense of jeopardy in public spaces, with a more systemic (lack of) safety when living within a wider culture of sexism and misogyny, Alana (Aus) explained:

> Like my whole sense of safety in the world [has been] profoundly damaged. ... If I go online or I go to a shopping centre or a public place and I'm just bombarded with sexualised images of women and children ... [it] just brings up all that trauma and just the proliferation of it, the extent of it. ... The enormity of it is such a burden.

These reflections speak to Brison's (2003: 56) suggestion that, for some, the lived experience of rape "shatters fundamental assumptions about the world and one's safety in it". This can generate perceptions that the world is a hostile place, imbued with the "imminent potentiality" of further harm (Cahill, 2008: 810; Du Toit, 2009). In this way, we can see how the threat and lack of trust women experienced extends beyond individual men to encompass what Gavey (2012: 722) refers to as the "cultural conditions of possibility"; namely the current socio-symbolic context of gender inequality (see also Cahill, 2008; Vera-Gray & Fileborn, 2018).

These experiences of unease and jeopardy, which were engendered or compounded by the image-based sexual abuse, connects with the extensive literature which recognises that women's experiences of spaces are inflected by the threat and fear of sexualised harassment, abuse and violence from men (e.g., Brison, 2003; Pain, 1993; Stanko, 1987; Valentine, 1989; Vera-Gray, 2017a). As with the notion of existential threat, victim-survivors told us how the sense of living in a hostile world, pervaded by misogyny and underpinned by the possibility of sexual violence, constrained their liberty and what has been termed their "space for action" (Jeffner, 2000; Kelly, 2003; Lundgren, 1998). This idea focuses on how individual perpetrators, together with broader social expectations, opportunities and experiences, can curtail victim-survivor choices and therefore their "space" for taking action and exercising agency. It aligns with the idea of how experiencing some forms of abuse, in the context in which we live, can constrain one's "horizons of possibility" (Vera-Gray, 2017b) by serving to limit what seems viable in a world where a pervasive sense of existential threat may also exist. Crucially, this notion does not erase agency, but recognises that agency is exercised in context.

It is important to note that image-based sexual abuse is a situated experience, varying according to each individual's position with intersecting axes of power and privilege. Thus, experiences of reduced "space for action" will vary according to each individual, being particularly felt in situations of precarity, where multiple inequalities intersect. Nevertheless, our interview participants commonly told us that the abuse "narrowed down [their] world", making it "small and claustrophobic". Victim-survivors felt like they had to "limit" themselves and their lives, to be "closed" and "put walls up" to "keep [themselves] safe". Some victim-survivors reflected that this in itself constituted a harm which negatively inhibits their everyday lives, adversely altering their sense of belonging and freedom in the world, and subsequently their participation in public life and experiences of citizenship.

These reflections evoke Stark's (2007: 13) assertion that to understand harm comprehensively, we must not only look at what is "done" to victim-survivors, but also what they are stopped from doing. In other words, image-based sexual abuse comprises a "liberty crime" (Stark, 2007), with enduring impacts which restrict a victim-survivor's "right to everyday life" (Beebeejaun, 2017). All of these interconnected forms of harm are threats to victim-survivors' liberty, diminishing their capacity for freedom, social connection and dignity.

Conclusion

This chapter has focussed on examining the significance of the harms that many victim-survivors experience as a consequence of image-based sexual abuse. Our survey revealed that of the respondents who reported negative consequences from their experience, those particularly affected were women, respondents identifying as LGB+ and those from minority racial and ethnic communities. Our interviews shed further light on how women in particular experienced these negative consequences, with our findings emphasising the holistic and interconnected nature of the harms.

In this context, it is important to re-emphasise the experiential, contingent and intersectional nature of the harms described, with each experience located in a particular time, place and context. We must also recognise that the consequences of image-based sexual abuse are often shaped by gendered cultural values, attitudes and practices that, while difficult to shift, are in fact amenable to change.

Notes

1   To focus on the harms of image-based sexual abuse, respondents who reported positive feelings concerning their most significant victimisation experience have been excluded from the subsequent analyses in this chapter. Of the 585 respondents who reported neutral or negative feelings, 86.2% (n=504) reported experiencing negative feelings in relation to their most significant experience of image-based sexual abuse victimisation. Additionally, 78.8% (n=460) reported experiencing reputational concerns, and 68.5% (n=400) reported safety concerns.

2   Indigenous approaches also explain the meaning, causes and effects of sexual violence in ways that are profoundly contextual and holistic. Māori scholars, for instance, explain how Māori experience and view discrete acts of sexual violence within a wider historical and sociocultural context (e.g., Cavino, 2016; Pihama et al., 2016; Wilson, Mikahere-Hall, Jackson, Cootes, & Sherwood, 2019). This includes recognising the ongoing relevance of colonisation and coloniality in both contributing to its causes, as well as compounding its harms. Furthermore, as Pihama et al. (2016: 48) explain, for Māori, the harms of sexual violence are felt,

> not only as a form of physical violence but also as a cultural and spiritual transgression that impacts both the individual and the collective wellbeing of their entire whakapapa line [genealogy] and whanau [extended family]. What that means is that acts of sexual violence are considered to be acts of both individual and collective violence.

References

Bates, S. (2017). Revenge porn and mental health: A qualitative analysis of the mental health effects of revenge porn on female survivors. *Feminist Criminology, 12*(1), 22–42.

Beebeejaun, Y. (2017). Gender, urban space, and the right to everyday life. *Journal of Urban Affairs, 39*(3), 323–334.

Bloom, S. (2014). No vengeance for "revenge porn" victims: Unraveling why this latest female-centric, intimate-partner offense is still legal, and why we should criminalize it. *Fordham Urban Law Journal, 42*(1), 233–289.

Brison, S. J. (2003). Beauvoir and feminism: Interview and reflections. In C. Card (ed.), *The Cambridge companion to Simone de Beauvoir* (pp. 189–207). Cambridge, UK: Cambridge University Press.

Brockmeier, J. (2008). Language, experience, and the "traumatic gap": How to talk about 9/11? In L.-C. Hyden & J. Brockmeier (eds.), *Broken narratives: Health, illness and culture* (pp. 16–35). Abingdon, Oxon; New York: Routledge.

Burgess, A. W., & Holmstrom, L. L. (1974). Rape trauma syndrome. *American Journal of Psychiatry, 131*(9), 981–986.

Burstow, B. (2003). Toward a radical understanding of trauma and trauma work. *Violence Against Women, 9*(11), 1293–1317.

Bury, M. (1982). Chronic illness as biographical disruption. *Sociology of Health and Illness, 4*(2), 167–182.

Butler, J. (1989). Foucault and the paradox of bodily inscriptions. *The Journal of Philosophy, 86*(11), 601–607.

Cahill, A. J. (2008). A phenomenology of fear: The threat of rape and feminine bodily comportment. In A. Bailey & C. J. Cuomo (eds.), *The feminist philosophy reader* (pp. 810–825). Boston, MA: McGraw Hill.

Caruth, C. (1996). *Unclaimed experience: Trauma, narrative, and history*. Baltimore, MD; London: Johns Hopkins University Press.

Cavino, H. M. (2016). Intergenerational sexual violence and Whānau in Aotearoa/ New Zealand: Pedagogies of contextualisation and transformation. *Sexual Abuse in Australia and New Zealand, 7*(1), 4–17.

Cecil, A. L. (2014). Taking back the internet: Imposing civil liability on interactive computer services in an attempt to provide an adequate remedy to victims of nonconsensual pornography. *Washington and Lee Law Review, 71*(4), article 9. https://scholarlycommons.law.wlu.edu/cgi/viewcontent.cgi?referer=&httpsredir= 1&article=4431&context=wlulr.

Citron, D. K., & Franks, M. A. (2014). Criminalizing revenge porn. *Wake Forest Law Review, 49*(2), 345–391.

Conaghan, J. (2019). The essence of rape. *Oxford Journal of Legal Studies, 39*(1), 151–182.

de Beauvoir, S. (2012). *The second sex* (C. Borde & S. Malovany-Chevallier, trans.). New York: Vintage. (Original work published 1949).

DiTullio, M., & Sullivan, M. (2019). A feminist-informed narrative approach: Treating clients who have experienced image-based sexual abuse. *Journal of Feminist Family Therapy, 31*(2–3), 100–113.

Du Toit, L. (2009). *A philosophical investigation of rape: The making and unmaking of the feminine self*. New York: Routledge.

European Women's Lobby (EWL). (2017). *#HerNetHerRights: Mapping the state of online violence against women and girls in Europe*. Strasbourg: European Women's Lobby.

Evans, L. (2016, April 5). My experience with revenge porn. *Huffington Post*. Retrieved from www.huffingtonpost.co.uk/lauren-evans2/revenge-porn_b_9610018. html.

Flynn, A., & Henry, N. (2019). Image-based sexual abuse: An Australian reflection. *Women and Criminal Justice.* Advance online publication. https://doi.org/10.1080 /08974554.2019.1646190.

Gavey, N. (2005). *Just sex? The cultural scaffolding of rape.* London; New York: Routledge.

Gavey, N. (2007). Rape, trauma and meaning. In C. M. Elliott (ed.), *Global empowerment of women: Responses to globalization and politicized religions* (pp. 233–246). London; New York: Routledge.

Gavey, N. (2012). Beyond "empowerment"? Sexuality in a sexist world. *Sex Roles, 66*(11–12), 285–301.

Gavey, N., & Farley, J. (in press). Reframing sexual violence as "sexual harm" in New Zealand policy: A critique. In G. Torres & K. Yllo (eds.), *Conceptualizing sexual violence in marriage: Research and policy.* New York: Routledge.

Gavey, N., & Schmidt, J. (2011). "Trauma of rape" discourse: A double-edged template for everyday understandings of the impact of rape? *Violence Against Women, 17*(4), 433–456.

Gilfus, M. E. (1999). The price of the ticket: A survivor-centered appraisal of trauma theory. *Violence Against Women, 5*(11), 1238–1257.

Herman, J. L. (1992). *Trauma and recovery: The aftermath of violence – from domestic abuse to political terror.* New York: Basic Books.

Jeffner, S. (2000). *Different space for action: The everyday meaning of young people's perception of rape.* Paper presented at the ESS Faculty Seminar, University of North London.

Johnson, K. (2017). *Domestic violence, liminality and precarity in the British Borderlands: Polish women's experiences of abuse and service engagement in Edinburgh.* Unpublished PhD thesis, Durham University, Durham, UK.

Kamal, M., & Newman, W. J. (2016). Revenge pornography: Mental health implications and related legislation. *Journal of the American Academy of Psychiatry and the Law, 44*(3), 359–367.

Kelly, L. (2003). The wrong debate: Reflections on why force is not the key issue with respect to trafficking in women for sexual exploitation. *Feminist Review, 73*(1), 139–144.

Langer, L. L. (1991). *Holocaust testimonies: The ruins of memory.* New Haven, CT: Yale University Press.

Lundgren, E. (1998). The hand that strikes and comforts: Gender construction and the tension between body and soul. In R. E. Dobash & R. P. Dobash (eds.), *Rethinking violence against women* (pp. 169–196). Thousand Oaks, CA: Sage Publications.

McGlynn, C., & Rackley, E. (2017). Image-based sexual abuse. *Oxford Journal of Legal Studies, 37*(3), 534–561.

McGlynn, C., Johnson, K., Rackley, E., Henry, N., Gavey, N., Flynn, A., & Powell, A. (in press). "It's torture for the soul": The harms of image-based sexual abuse. *Social and Legal Studies.*

McKenzie-Mohr, S., & Lafrance, M. (2011). Telling stories without the words: "Tightrope talk" in women's accounts of coming to live well after rape or depression. *Feminism and Psychology, 21*(1), 49–73.

McNeilly, C. (2019, May 17). Teacher victim of upskirting pupil breaks silence to tell of her trauma. *Belfast Telegraph.* Retrieved from www.belfasttelegraph.co.uk/ news/northern-ireland/teacher-victim-of-upskirting-pupil-breaks-silence-to-tell-of-her-trauma-38119262.html.

Morrison, S., Hardison, J., Mathew, A., & O'Neil, J. (2004). *An evidence-based review of sexual assault preventive intervention programs.* Washington, DC: National Institute of Justice. United States Department of Justice. Retrieved from www.ncjrs.gov/pdffiles1/nij/grants/207262.pdf.

Pain, R. (1993). Women's fear of sexual violence: Explaining the spatial paradox. In H. Jones (ed.), *Crime and the environment: The Scottish experience* (pp. 55–68). Aldershot: Avebury.

Pihama, L., Te Nana, R., Cameron, N., Smith, C., Reid, J., & Southey, K. (2016). Māori cultural definitions of sexual violence. *Sexual Abuse in Australia and New Zealand, 7*(1), 43–51.

Powell, A., & Henry, N. (2019). Technology-facilitated sexual violence victimization: Results from an online survey of Australian adults. *Journal of Interpersonal Violence, 34*(17), 3637–3665.

Powell, A., Henry, N., & Flynn, A. (2018). Image-based sexual abuse. In W. S. DeKeseredy & M. Dragiewicz (eds.), *Handbook of critical criminology* (pp. 305–315). Abingdon, Oxon; New York: Routledge.

Powell, A., Henry, N., Flynn, A., & Scott, A. J. (2019). Image-based sexual abuse: The extent, nature, and predictors of perpetration in a community sample of Australian residents. *Computers in Human Behavior, 92*, 393–402.

Root, M. (1992). Reconstructing the impact of trauma on personality. In L. S. Brown & M. Ballouds (eds.), *Personality and psychopathology: Feminist reappraisals* (pp. 229–265). New York; London: Guilford.

Ruvalcaba, Y., & Eaton, A. A. (2019). Nonconsensual pornography among US adults: A sexual scripts framework on victimization, perpetration, and health correlates for women and men. *Psychology of Violence.* Advance online publication. https://doi.org/10.1037/vio0000233.

Scarry, E. (1985). *The body in pain.* New York: Oxford University Press.

Short, E., Brown, A., Pitchford, M., & Barnes, J. (2017). Revenge porn: Findings from the Harassment and Revenge Porn (HARP) Survey – preliminary results. *Annual Review of Cybertherapy and Telemedicine, 15*, 161–166.

Stanko, E. A. (1987). Typical violence, normal precaution: Men, women and interpersonal violence in England, Wales, Scotland and the USA. In J. Hanmer & M. Maynard (eds.), *Women, violence and social control* (pp. 122–134). London: Macmillan.

Stark, E. (2007). *Coercive control: How men entrap women in personal life.* New York: Oxford University Press.

Stark, E. (2009). Rethinking coercive control. *Violence Against Women, 15*(12), 1509–1525.

Valentine, G. (1989). The geography of women's fear. *Area, 21*(4), 385–390.

Vera-Gray, F. (2017a). *Men's intrusions, women's embodiment: A critical analysis of street harassment.* Oxon and New York: Routledge.

Vera-Gray, F. (2017b). Outlook: Girlhood, agency and embodied space for action. In B. Formark, H. Mulari, & M. Voipio (eds.), *Nordic girlhoods: New perspectives and outlooks* (pp. 127–136). Cham: Palgrave Macmillan.

Vera-Gray, F. (2019). The whole place self: Reflecting on the original working practices of rape crisis. *Journal of Gender-Based Violence.* Advance online publication. https://doi.org/10.1332/239868019X15682997635986.

Vera-Gray, F., & Fileborn, B. (2018). Recognition and the harms of "cheer up". *The Philosophical Journal of Conflict and Violence, 2*(1), 78–95.

Wasco, S. M. (2003). Conceptualizing the harm done by rape: Applications of trauma theory to experiences of sexual assault. *Trauma, Violence, & Abuse, 4*(4), 309–322.

Wilson, D., Mikahere-Hall, A., Jackson, D., Cootes, K., & Sherwood, J. (2019). *Aroha* and *Manaakitanga* – That's what it is about: Indigenous women, "love," and interpersonal violence. *Journal of Interpersonal Violence*. Advance online publication. doi: 10.1177/0886260519872298.

Young, I. M. (1990). *Throwing like a girl and other essays in feminist philosophy and social theory*. Bloomington, IN: Indiana University Press.

Chapter 4

Image-based sexual abuse perpetration

Power and control

Introduction

Digital communication technologies have radically transformed intimate relationships over the past two decades. These technologies enable users to engage in relationships in creative, efficient and exploratory ways, through various means such as email, text, instant messaging, apps, webcams, video chat, dating sites and social media (Hobbs, Owen, & Gerber, 2017). At the same time, these communications devices are being harnessed as tools or weapons by motivated perpetrators to enact power and control over both known and unknown victims. Indeed, domestic and family violence service providers report the increasing use of digital technologies in the tactics and strategies of perpetrators (Douglas, Harris, & Dragiewicz, 2019; Henry & Powell, 2015; Southworth, Finn, Dawson, Fraser, & Tucker, 2007; Woodlock, 2017). Such behaviours include harassing text messages, GPS tracking, impersonation, computer hacking, restricting access to technology, using technology to access, monitor and control, as well as image-based sexual abuse. Researchers note that digital technologies form part of a "constellation of tactics" that perpetrators of domestic abuse employ alongside other more widely recognised forms of physical and psychological abuse that take place in face-to-face encounters (Douglas et al., 2019; Reed, Tolman, & Ward, 2016).

While image-based sexual abuse is part of the repertoire of abusive intimate partners in the context of domestic violence or other forms of intimate partner abuse, not all cases of image-based sexual abuse conform to this pattern. As our research has demonstrated, perpetrators of image-based sexual abuse may also be friends, family members, colleagues or acquaintances. Perpetrators might also be unknown to the victim-survivor, for instance, a stranger-rapist who films his assault, or a computer hacker who accesses victim-survivors' personal files and threatens to share their images unless they receive monetary payment or more nude or sexual images. Moreover, although the term "revenge porn" implies that the primary motive for the non-consensual sharing of nude or sexual images is vengeance, the diverse examples we have discussed thus far in the book strongly demonstrate that there is no one dominant motivation common to all forms of image-based sexual abuse perpetration.

This chapter focuses on the diverse contexts of image-based sexual abuse perpetration, particularly the divergent, multifaceted and often overlapping motivations for engaging in the abuse. The first section reports on the key findings from our survey of 6,109 respondents from Australia, New Zealand and the United Kingdom regarding their self-reported engagement in image-based sexual abuse behaviours. The second section discusses findings from a combination of existing qualitative studies on image-based sexual abuse perpetration and the reflections of victim-survivors on perpetrator motivations from the 75 interviews that we conducted. Drawing together these primary and secondary data sources, we argue that many aspects of image-based sexual abuse have been normalised – to the extent that the non-consensual sharing of intimate images can be argued to constitute a form of "social currency" for a particular social identity online. Additionally, we suggest that, like other forms of sexual violence, a key motivation for the perpetration of image-based sexual abuse is power and control. As such, we argue that image-based sexual abuse should be conceptualised as a form of social control, which operates as both a cause and a consequence of gendered and other intersectional inequalities. It is crucial that we understand the complexity of image-based sexual abuse perpetration across these contexts in order to devise more effective responses and interventions.

Image-based sexual abuse perpetration: quantitative research

Research on image-based sexual abuse perpetrators currently remains limited. A number of studies investigating issues such as sexting, technology use or technology-facilitated abuse have asked survey respondents about limited aspects of image-based sexual abuse behaviours. Findings across these studies suggest that the sharing or distribution of nude or sexual images is relatively common (e.g., Crofts, Lee, McGovern, & Milivojevic, 2015; Garcia et al., 2016; Morelli, Bianchi, Baiocco, Pezzuti, & Chirumbolo, 2016; Patrick, Heywood, Pitts, & Mitchell, 2015; Strohmaier, Murphy, & DeMatteo, 2014; Thompson & Morrison, 2013). However, only a few studies have taken a more comprehensive approach in focusing specifically on image-based sexual abuse perpetration (Powell, Henry, Flynn, & Scott, 2019; Ruvalcaba & Eaton, 2019). In the discussion below, we develop this knowledge further, presenting the findings from our survey in relation to perpetration of all three forms of image-based sexual abuse. Through conducting a quantitative survey, we were able to explore self-reported perpetration demographics across Australia, New Zealand and the United Kingdom, as well as the motivations that people report for taking, sharing, or threatening to share, nude or sexual images without consent.

Self-reported image-based sexual abuse perpetration: survey findings

Our survey revealed that more than one in six, or 17.5% (n=1,070), of all re-spondents (n=6,109) reported engaging in at least one form of image-based sexual abuse perpetration across their lifetime against a person over the age of 16 years. This included 15.8% (n=967) who said they had engaged in the non-consensual *taking* of a nude or sexual image, 10.6% (n=648) who said they had *shared* a nude or sexual image without consent, and 8.8% (n=536) who reported having *threatened* to share a nude or sexual image of another person. Coinciding with our finding that most victim-survivors experience multiple forms of image-based sexual abuse (see Chapter 2), 7.8% (n=479) – which is almost half (44.8%, n=479) of all respondents who self-reported perpetration – disclosed they had engaged in *all three* forms of image-based sexual abuse.

Table 4.1 Pervasiveness of image-based sexual abuse perpetration

	Taken % (n)	Shared % (n)	Threatened % (n)	At least one % (n)	All three % (n)
Country					
Australia	14.8 (304)	9.1 (186)	7.6 (156)	16.2 (332)	6.6 (135)
New Zealand	18.1 (366)	12.8 (260)	10.5 (213)	19.9 (403)	9.9 (200)
United Kingdom	14.6 (297)	10 (202)	8.2 (167)	16.5 (335)	7.1 (144)
Gender					
Female	11.4 (363)*	7.2 (230)*	5.8 (184)*	13.1 (417)*	5.1 (163)*
Male	20.6 (604)	14.3 (418)	12 (352)	22.3 (653)	10.8 (316)
Sexuality					
Heterosexual	14.6 (794)	9.3 (507)*	7.8 (426)	16.1 (876)*	6.9 (374)*
LGB+	25.5 (173)	20.8 (141)	16.2 (110)	28.6 (194)	15.5 (105)
Age					
16–19	20.4 (76)*	17.2 (64)*	14.5 (54)*	22.3 (83)*	13.7 (51)*
20–29	23 (325)	16.5 (233)	14.2 (201)	25.7 (362)	12.5 (176)
30–39	19.3 (306)	14.4 (228)	11.7 (186)	21.2 (335)	11.1 (176)
40–49	11.9 (135)	7.1 (81)	6.3 (71)	13.1 (149)	5.4 (61)
50–64	7.8 (125)	2.6 (42)	1.5 (24)	8.8 (141)	0.9 (15)
Race/Ethnicity					
White, European or Pākehā	14.4 (646)	9 (406)	7.2 (326)	16 (721)	6.4 (289)
Indigenous & BAME	19.9 (321)	15 (242)	13 (210)	21.7 (349)	11.8 (190)

Note: Percentages and numbers relate to respondents who have engaged in each form of image-based sexual abuse perpetration (Taken, Shared, Threatened), at least one of the three forms of image-based sexual abuse, or all three forms of image-based sexual abuse. * indicates significant differences between groups within this form of image-based sexual abuse (at p < .05 with a minimum of a small effect size).

Again, and similar to our victimisation data presented in Chapter 2, there were no significant country differences in the reported pervasiveness of image-based sexual abuse perpetration (see Table 4.1). Respondents in Australia (16.2%, n=332), New Zealand (19.9%, n=403) and the United Kingdom (16.5%, n=335) were similarly likely to report having engaged in one or more forms of image-based sexual abuse perpetration. However, there were significant differences according to gender, with male respondents significantly more likely than female respondents to report having engaged in all forms of image-based sexual abuse. For example, one in five men (22.3%, n=653) self-reported engaging in one or more forms of image-based sexual abuse perpetration, compared with one in eight women (13.1%, n=417). Men were almost twice as likely to report having engaged with each behaviour, as shown in Table 4.1.

There were significant differences according to sexuality. For example, 28.6% of respondents identifying as LGB+ had engaged in one or more forms of image-based sexual abuse perpetration, compared with 16.1% (n=876) of heterosexual respondents. There were also important patterns in perpetration when examining both sexuality and gender, with sexual minority men (34.3%, n=122) more likely than sexual minority women (22.3%, n=72), heterosexual men (20.6%, n=531) and heterosexual women (12.1%, n=345) to self-disclose engaging in at least one form of image-based sexual abuse behaviour (not shown in table). There are likely a range of factors associated with these patterns. For instance, there is a higher uptake of digital technologies among sexual minority men for consensual sexual self-expression and dating, perhaps because online spaces are potentially safer than many public, non-online spaces (see Waldman, 2019).

There were significant differences for age across all forms of image-based sexual abuse perpetration. Respondents aged 16–39 years (23.2%, n=780) were more likely than respondents aged 40–64 years (10.6%, n=290) to report engaging in one or more forms of image-based sexual abuse (not shown in the table). Again, there were important patterns in perpetration when examining both age and gender, as young men aged 20–29 years were the most likely to self-disclose engaging in at least one form of image-based sexual abuse overall (33.5%, n=189), closely followed by men aged 30–39 years (29.9%, n=211) and young men aged 16–19 years (28.8%, n=51) (not shown in the table). Young women aged 20–29 years were fourth most likely to self-disclose engaging in any image-based sexual abuse (20.4%, n=173). These findings clearly demonstrate the importance of working with young men in order to respond to and prevent image-based sexual abuse.

Image-based sexual abuse perpetration was statistically similar, when all countries were analysed together, in relation to respondents from minority racial and ethnic communities (21.7%, n=349) compared with those identifying as White, European or Pākehā (16%, n=721). However, there were consistent and significant differences when the three countries were analysed separately (not shown in the table). In Australia, respondents who identified as Indigenous (39.1%, n=25) were more likely than non-Indigenous respondents (15.4%, n=307) to report engaging in image-based sexual abuse. This pattern was mirrored in New Zealand with respondents who identified as Māori (32%, n=72) being more likely to report engaging in these behaviours compared with non-Māori respondents (18.4%, n=331), and to a lesser extent in the United Kingdom, where respondents who identified as BAME (26.9%, n=68) were more likely than non-BAME respondents (15%, n=267) to report perpetration. Once again, there were differences according to gender. For example, men from racial or ethnic minorities (26.9%, n=211) were among those most likely to self-disclose engaging in at least one form of image-based sexual abuse perpetration, compared with White, European or Pākehā men (20.6%, n=442), women from racial or minority ethnic communities (16.7%, n=138), or White, European or Pākehā women (11.8%, n=279). Notably, these patterns also reflect the higher impacts of victimisation within these groups, suggesting that any correlation between image-based sexual abuse and racial or ethnic identity is complex. Some Australian research does suggest that the uptake of mobile technologies in some Indigenous communities is very high, with greater sharing of devices within family and peer communities (Carlson, 2019), which may in turn place individuals at greater risk of both victimisation and opportunity for perpetration. Nonetheless, there is currently very little in-depth research into the particular nature and contexts of image-based sexual abuse within indigenous or racial and ethnic minority communities.

These results present a complex picture of those who self-report having engaged in some or all forms of image-based sexual abuse. While gender and age provide particular indications of likely perpetration, further investigation is needed to consider the circumstances giving higher rates of self-reported perpetration, and indeed the impacts on victims, for those identifying as LGB+ and those from minority ethnic, racial and indigenous communities.

Motivations for image-based sexual abuse perpetration

In our survey, we also asked respondents who reported having taken, shared and/or threatened to share nude or sexual images to indicate their motivations for each of the three behaviours. Motivations included for fun, to flirt or be "sexy", impressing friends, maintaining relationships, attention-seeking, revenge or "getting back" at the person, embarrassment, control, financial gain or to obtain further images. Respondents were able to select multiple motivations (as such the data discussed below do not add up to 100% for all items) and many did so, suggesting that a mixture of motivations are common from the perspective of perpetrators.

One common motivation reported by respondents was for "fun" or to be "sexy" (61.2%, n=592 for taking; 58%, n=376 for sharing; 55.8%, n=299 for threatening).

Table 4.2 Motivations for image-based sexual abuse perpetration: funny/sexy

	Taken % (n)	Shared % (n)	Threatened % (n)
Country			
Australia	58.6 (178)	55.9 (104)	47.4 (74)*
New Zealand	61.7 (226)	55 (143)	58.2 (124)
United Kingdom	63.3 (188)	63.9 (129)	60.5 (101)
Gender			
Female	62.3 (226)	59.6 (137)	58.7 (108)
Male	60.6 (366)	57.2 (239)	54.3 (191)
Sexuality			
Heterosexual	63.7 (506)*	61.9 (314)*	58.7 (250)*
LGB+	49.7 (86)	44 (62)	44.5 (49)
Age			
16–19	61.8 (47)	60.9 (39)	61.1 (33)*
20–29	60.3 (196)	54.5 (127)	56.7 (114)
30–39	62.1 (190)	61.8 (141)	53.2 (99)
40–49	65.2 (88)	60.5 (49)	64.8 (46)
50–64	56.8 (71)	47.6 (20)	29.2 (7)
Race/Ethnicity			
White, European or Pākehā	61.1 (395)	58.4 (237)	57.1 (186)
Indigenous & BAME	61.4 (197)	57.4 (139)	53.8 (113)

Note: Percentages and numbers relate to respondents who were motivated to engage in each form of image-based sexual abuse perpetration (Taken, Shared, Threatened) because they thought it was funny/sexy. * indicates significant differences between groups within this form of image-based sexual abuse (at p < .05 with a minimum of a small effect size).

Table 4.2 shows that with the exception of threatening to share nude or sexual images, there were no significant country or gender differences in motivations to engage in image-based sexual abuse perpetration because of the belief that it was fun or sexy. The one significant difference is where respondents in the United Kingdom (60.5%, n=101) and New Zealand (58.2%, n=124) were more likely to report this motivation than respondents in Australia (47.4%, n=74). With regard to sexuality, heterosexual respondents were significantly more likely than LGB+ respondents to report being motivated because of the belief that it was funny or sexy to: Take nude or sexual images without consent (63.7%, n=506 vs. 49.7%, n=86); share images without consent (61.9%, n=314 vs. 44%, n=62); or threaten to share images (58.7%, n=250 vs. 44.5%, n=49). Finally, there were no significant differences relating to the racial or ethnic background of respondents in Australia, New Zealand and the United Kingdom who reported that they had engaged in the behaviour because they thought it was funny or sexy. Likewise, there were no significant differences within these countries for indigenous/BAME as compared with non-indigenous/BAME respondents in each country.

Other motivations included wanting to "impress friends" and/or "trade the images" (37.8%, n=366 for taking; 54.9%, n=356 for sharing; 54.9%, n=294 for threatening); and wanting to "control the person in the image" (45%, n=435 for taking; 57.1%, n=370 for sharing; 63.2%, n=339 for threatening). Perhaps unsurprisingly, wanting to "control the person" was among the highest of perpetrator motivations for threatening to share images.

Table 4.3 Motivations for image-based sexual abuse perpetration: impress friends/trade the images

	Taken % (n)	Shared % (n)	Threatened % (n)
Country			
Australia	35.5 (108)	55.9 (104)	51.3 (80)
New Zealand	37.7 (138)	50.8 (132)	55.4 (118)
United Kingdom	40.4 (120)	59.4 (120)	57.5 (96)
Gender			
Female	36.4 (132)	57.4 (132)	56.5 (104)
Male	38.7 (234)	53.6 (224)	54 (190)
Sexuality			
Heterosexual	37.9 (301)	57.6 (292)*	57 (243)
LGB+	37.6 (65)	45.4 (64)	46.4 (51)
Age			
16–19	51.3 (39)*	56.3 (36)*	59.3 (32)
20–29	43.1 (140)	55.8 (130)	55.7 (112)
30–39	42.2 (129)	56.1 (128)	55.4 (103)
40–49	33.3 (45)	61.7 (50)	56.3 (40)
50–64	10.4 (13)	28.6 (12)	29.2 (7)
Race/Ethnicity			
White, European or Pākehā	33.7 (218)*	53.4 (217)	54.3 (177)
Indigenous & BAME	46.1 (148)	57.4 (139)	55.7 (117)

Note: Percentages and numbers relate to respondents who were motivated to engage in each form of image-based sexual abuse perpetration (Taken, Shared, Threatened) because they wanted to impress friends / trade the images. * indicates significant differences between groups within this form of image-based sexual abuse (at p < .05 with a minimum of a small effect size).

Tables 4.3 and 4.4 show that there were no significant country or gender differences in motivations to engage in image-based sexual abuse perpetration because of the desire to impress friends, trade the images or control the person. With regard to sexuality, heterosexual respondents were more likely than LGB+ respondents to be motivated to non-consensually share nude or sexual images because of the desire to impress friends or trade the images (57.6%, n=292 vs. 45.4%, n=64) as well as control the person (60.6%, n=307 vs. 44.7%, n=63). There were consistent age differences relating to these motivations, with respondents aged 50–64 years being significantly less likely to take (10.4%, n=13) or share (28.6%, n=12) nude or sexual images because of the desire to impress friends or trade images. Those aged 50–64 years were also significantly less likely than other age groups to be motivated by control when taking (14.4%, n=18), sharing (19%, n=8), or threatening to share (33.3%, n=8) nude or sexual images. Finally, the only differences in relation to race and ethnicity were in relation to the non-consensual taking of nude or sexual images, with those from minority racial and ethnic communities being more likely than White, European or Pākehā respondents to be motivated by the desire to impress friends or trade the images (46.1%, n=148 vs 33.7%, n=218) or control the person (52.6%, n=169 vs. 41.2%, n=266).

Although there were few differences in motivations according to racial and/or ethnic minority demographics across the three countries as a whole, there were some significant differences when the three countries were analysed separately (not shown in the table). For example, there were significant differences for "impress friends/trade the images" in New Zealand (Māori 53.7%, n=36 vs. non-Māori 34.1%, n=102) and the United Kingdom (BAME 54.1%, n=33 vs. non-BAME 36.9%, n=87) as a motivation for the *taking* of nude or sexual images without consent. Meanwhile in Australia, there were significant differences for "impress friends/trade the images" as a motivation for the *sharing* of images (Indigenous 88.9%, n=16 vs. non-Indigenous 52.4%, n=88). Also, in Australia, there were significant differences for "control the person" as a motivation for the taking of images (Indigenous 64%, n=16 vs. non-Indigenous 40.9%, n=114).

Finally, respondents reported being motivated to "embarrass" and/ or "get back at the person" depicted in the image (38%, n=367 for taking; 51.7%, n=335 for sharing; 61.4%, n=329 for threatening), as shown in Table 4.5 below.

Again, Table 4.5 shows that there were no significant country or gender differences in motivations to engage in image-based sexual abuse perpetration because of the desire to embarrass or get back at the person. With regard to sexuality, heterosexual respondents (55%, n=279) were more likely to be motivated to non-consensually share nude or sexual images because of the desire to embarrass or get back at the person than respondents identifying as LGB+ (39.7%, n=56). Again, there were consistent age differences relating to this motivation, with respondents aged 50–64 years being

Table 4.4 Motivations for image-based sexual abuse perpetration: control the person

	Taken % (n)	Shared % (n)	Threatened % (n)
Country			
Australia	42.8 (130)	57 (106)	59 (92)
New Zealand	42.3 (155)	53.5 (139)	63.8 (136)
United Kingdom	50.5 (150)	61.9 (125)	66.5 (111)
Gender			
Female	44.4 (161)	57.4 (132)	64.1 (118)
Male	45.4 (274)	56.9 (238)	62.8 (221)
Sexuality			
Heterosexual	45.7 (363)	60.6 (307)*	66 (281)*
LGB+	41.6 (72)	44.7 (63)	52.7 (58)
Age			
16–19	53.9 (41)*	62.5 (40)*	68.5 (37)*
20–29	51.1 (166)	60.1 (140)	63.7 (128)
30–39	49.3 (151)	58.3 (133)	64 (119)
40–49	43.7 (59)	60.5 (49)	66.2 (47)
50–64	14.4 (18)	19 (8)	33.3 (8)
Race/Ethnicity			
White, European or Pākehā	41.2 (266)*	55.7 (226)	62.9 (205)
Indigenous & BAME	52.6 (169)	59.5 (144)	63.8 (134)

Note: Percentages and numbers relate to respondents who were motivated to engage in each form of image-based sexual abuse perpetration (Taken, Shared, Threatened) because they wanted to control the person. * indicates significant differences between groups within this form of image-based sexual abuse (at p < .05 with a minimum of a small effect size).

significantly less likely to take (10.4%, n=13), share (21.4%, n=9) or threaten to share (33.3%, n=8) nude or sexual images because of the desire to embarrass or get back at the person. Consistent with the previous two motivations, respondents identifying as being from minority ethnic and racial communities (44.9%, n=144) were more likely than White, European or Pākehā respondents (34.5%, n=223) to non-consensually take nude or sexual images because of the desire to embarrass or get back at the person. In addition to these overall across-country differences, there were again differences according to minority ethnic and racial communities when the three countries were analysed separately (not shown in the table). For instance, there were significant differences for embarrass/get back at the person in New Zealand (Māori 53.7%, n=36 vs. non-Māori 34.4%, n=103) as a motivation for

Table 4.5 Motivations for image-based sexual abuse perpetration: embarrass/
get back at the person

	Taken % (n)	Shared % (n)	Threatened % (n)
Country			
Australia	34.9 (106)	48.9 (91)	60.3 (94)
New Zealand	38 (139)	49.2 (128)	61 (130)
United Kingdom	41.1 (122)	57.4 (116)	62.9 (105)
Gender			
Female	38 (138)	57.8 (133)	65.2 (120)
Male	37.9 (229)	48.3 (202)	59.4 (209)
Sexuality			
Heterosexual	38.4 (305)	55 (279)*	63.4 (270)
LGB+	35.8 (62)	39.7 (56)	53.6 (59)
Age			
16–19	43.4 (33)*	57.8 (37)*	70.4 (38)*
20–29	43.1 (140)	55.8 (130)	61.2 (123)
30–39	43.5 (133)	49.6 (113)	61.3 (114)
40–49	35.6 (48)	56.8 (46)	64.8 (46)
50–64	10.4 (13)	21.4 (9)	33.3 (8)
Race/Ethnicity			
White, European or Pākehā	34.5 (223)*	50.7 (206)	61 (199)
Indigenous & BAME	44.9 (144)	53.3 (129)	61.9 (130)

Note: Percentages and numbers relate to respondents who were motivated to engage
in each form of image-based sexual abuse perpetration (Taken, Shared, Threatened)
because they wanted to embarrass / get back at the person. * indicates significant differences between groups within this form of image-based sexual abuse (at p < .05 with
a minimum of a small effect size).

the *taking* of images. Similarly, in Australia embarrass/get back at the per-
son was more commonly reported as a motivation for the *sharing* of images
(Indigenous 83.3%, n=15 vs. non-Indigenous 45.2%, n=76) and also in New
Zealand (Māori 61.5%, n=32 vs. non-Māori 46.2%, n=96).

Overall, what these findings suggest is that there are a range of diverse
motivations for engaging in image-based sexual abuse that extend well beyond those of the stereotypical "vengeful" or "jilted" ex-partner. In some
cases, perpetrators reported motivations which appeared to be less about
personally targeting a specific victim and more about their own capacity to
either make money or gain status. Significantly, many respondents did not
appear to recognise the harms caused to victims. Even when respondents
described their motivations as to "control", "embarrass" or "get back at the

person", they also labelled them as "funny" or "sexy". Crucially, these findings are at odds with what many victim-survivors describe as the serious and lasting impacts of image-based sexual abuse, as was described by our interview participants in Chapter 3.

Image-based sexual abuse perpetration: qualitative research

Qualitative studies have also begun to investigate the contours of image-based sexual abuse perpetration, which, in addition to the quantitative findings as described above, provide further insight into this problem. In one recent study, Hall and Hearn (2017) examined the online comments that accompanied the postings of non-consensual nude or sexual images on a popular "revenge porn" website. They found that most of the images were of women and were shared by male users. They also found that the text accompanying many of the images occurred in a context of homosocial bonding in which men presented themselves as "real men" within an online community of mostly male peers. Similar conclusions were made in Langlois and Slane's (2017) study, in which they analysed 193 images and 183 comments contained on one "revenge porn" site, finding that not only is image-based sexual abuse a form of heteronormative misogyny, but also a profitable business enterprise. In another study, Uhl, Rhyner, Terrance and Lugo (2018) undertook a content analysis of 134 non-consensual photographs contained on seven different websites. They similarly found that 92% of victims depicted in the images were women. They also investigated the motivations for the sharing of non-consensual sexual images through examining the text accompanying the image, noting that perpetrators' reasons for sharing nude or sexual images without consent included because the woman was their ex-partner, "hot" or "sexy", a "slut" or unfaithful.

These studies exclusively examined revenge-oriented sites (also known as "revenge porn" sites). In a digital ethnography of 77 different websites, Henry and Flynn (2019) examined a much broader array of sites (including porn sites, social media, "revenge" sites, community forums, imageboards and blogging sites) that host nude or sexual non-consensual imagery, to provide a more comprehensive investigation into the phenomenon of image-based sexual abuse beyond the "revenge porn" frame. Consistent with the aforementioned studies, Henry and Flynn (2019) found that image-based sexual abuse online was a highly gendered practice, with the majority of exchanges of images (of predominantly women) occurring among male users. They observed that image-based sexual abuse material was shared and distributed via public sites, such as social media or revenge-oriented websites, or "public shaming sites", corresponding more closely with the paradigmatic "revenge porn" scenario. In addition, they found that image-based sexual abuse material was being shared in greater volumes on private contexts, such as imageboards, pornography sites, community forums and other less visible online communities – what they call "private sharing sites". In the latter context, perpetrators did not appear to be motivated specifically by revenge, but rather by peer bonding and esteem-building. This bonding took place among an online network of peers who collectively used the sexual objectification and humiliation of known or unknown women as a conduit for sexual gratification and social status building. Due to their private nature, these illicit forms of image-sharing may go unnoticed or undetected by victims, unless someone in their peer network alerts them to it or they inadvertently stumble across their images online (Henry & Flynn, 2019). Their study, therefore, underscores the extent to which it is difficult to comprehensively quantify both victimisation and perpetration, because of the private and illicit nature of many of these sites and victims being unaware that their images are being shared.

While these studies provide clear indications as to the motivations of perpetrators, very little qualitative research has thus far been undertaken directly with perpetrators of image-based sexual abuse. One Australian study undertook semi-structured interviews with 16 adult perpetrators who had engaged in image-based sexual abuse behaviours, as well as interviews with 12 stakeholders, such as defence lawyers, police, forensic psychologists and men's behaviour change program facilitators (OeSC, 2019). The study found that many of the perpetrators' behaviours were underpinned by motivations that related to obtaining, exerting or attempting to reclaim, power and control. Relatedly, some of the more instrumental motivations highlighted in the study included a perpetrator's desire to: Punish or embarrass victims; to boost social status by boasting about sexual prowess and accomplishment; or to obtain sexual gratification. The study also found that few perpetrators were aware that their behaviour was against the law, instead viewing the behaviour as normalised among their peers. Accordingly, participants in this study downplayed and minimised their behaviour (e.g., "I only shared it with a few friends") as well as blamed the victim (e.g., "they shouldn't have sent the image to me in the first place"). Finally, the study found that overall perpetrators demonstrated little remorse. Any regret that they felt was largely to do with being detected, prosecuted or punished, with little thought given to the impacts of their behaviours on the victim-survivors (OeSC, 2019).

In light of these qualitative research findings, it is possible that our survey respondents who reported perpetrating image-based sexual abuse because they thought it was "funny" or "sexy" were similarly minimising their behaviours, justifying their actions as normal and acceptable. Further, the OeSC (2019) qualitative study identifies motivations that are similar to the ones identified in our survey (discussed above). Together, what these data suggest is that those engaging in image-based sexual abuse perpetration behaviours may not fully understand, or even give any thought to, the po-tentially harmful impacts upon victims. Additionally, such minimising of the harms may also be symptomatic of self-reported data in which perpetra-tors of abuse avoid taking full responsibility for their actions, and likewise avoid viewing their own behaviour as ultimately "wrong". This is a "tech-nique of neutralization" (Sykes & Matza, 1957) which has been identified in other studies on perpetrators of sexual violence more broadly (e.g., Boyle & Walker, 2016).

Image-based sexual abuse perpetration: interview findings

To complement the findings from our survey, in our interviews with 75 victim-survivors of image-based sexual abuse, we asked them to reflect on and contextualise what they believed to be the motivations of the perpe-trators who had taken, shared, or threatened to share, their nude or sexual images without their consent. A few participants commented that they did not know the reasons why the perpetrator acted as they did, with some even saying they were "at a loss" to understand why. The remainder reported a wide variety of motivations for image-based sexual abuse behaviours, in-cluding control, attention-seeking, jealousy, obsession, misogyny, sexual gratification, a "prank", distress, humiliation, entitlement and social cap-ital. Therefore, consistent with the findings from our cross-national survey, our interviews revealed a complex picture of image-based sexual abuse perpetration.

Through analysing victim-survivors' qualitative accounts, it became clear that there was rarely a single motivation for image based-sexual abuse. Rather, participants identified multiple, overlapping motivations. This is evident in the following comment from Heather (UK), who reflected on why she thought a boy she had been seeing had shared her intimate images across her school:

> I think, to be honest, I think he just wanted to humiliate me. I think he just had something over me and I guess we stopped being intimate and he just thought he was going to humiliate me and maybe try and get himself a bit of a reputation for being a ladies' man... I think he just clicked on to what other people were doing as well, it was quite common in our area, people sharing photos and videos around like that, and I think he was just cottoning on to what everyone was doing.

Participants similarly reflected that perpetrator motivations for committing or continuing the abuse may shift and change over time. This was indicated by Zoe (UK), who spoke about her partner threatening to share her intimate images while they were together as a form of control, and then sharing her images once they had broken up to "pay her back":

> So he tried to use [my intimate images] as a bargaining tool to stop me from ending it, but I still did [end it]. And then [when he did share them] it was a revenge thing; him not wanting me to be happy and that's what he said to me, he said 'if you get into another relationship, I'll send them around.' ...It was a control thing whilst I was in the relationship and then it was a revenge thing afterwards.

Across these diverse motivations, *power and control* emerged as a dominant theme – particularly in the sense of image-based sexual abuse taking place in an asymmetrical power dynamic, where the perpetrator's sense of entitlement to coercively conduct their abusive behaviours superseded the sexual autonomy and privacy rights of the victim-survivor. This parallels extensive research on other forms of sexual violence which identifies power and control as being a central motivation of perpetrators (see e.g., Griffin, 1986; Kelly, 1988).

Many of the interview participants who identified control as being a primary motive had experienced image-based sexual abuse in the context of either an ongoing or previous intimate relationship. Approximately a third of the participants we interviewed (30.7%, n=23) had experienced image-based sexual abuse within a broader context of ongoing domestic abuse perpetrated by an intimate partner. This clearly emphasises the strong relationship between image-based sexual abuse, domestic abuse and coercive control (Stark, 2007). As Liz (UK) reflected:

> He just was not a nice guy ... he was very controlling and manipulative. So, when we were going out ... he would jokingly say ... 'If we ever fall out, I can show people these photographs' ... And in hindsight now I realise that that is very controlling behaviour.

Liz situated her partner's threats to share intimate images of her within a broader pattern of his coercive and controlling behaviour. Nicole (Aus) likewise felt that her abusive partner was motivated by power and control when he took intimate images of her without her consent. Nicole explained that her partner used the threats as a control tactic, so he could "try and get what he wanted":

> I think he just wanted me to be like controlled by him, or me to be scared and just do whatever he said because I was scared that he could, I don't know, inflict these consequences on me ... I guess it's a power thing ... He was just generally like a really awful person. He was really abusive to me in the time that we were together anyway, so I guess I

couldn't really expect more. I just didn't know that he'd go to that level. Like, I thought he was just a dickhead, I didn't realise that he'd actually like kind of commit those kinds of offences against me.

In a number of victim-survivor accounts which involved ongoing domestic abuse, participants reflected they had been conscious their partner might use their intimate imagery as a means through which to further enact their abuse. Accordingly, some told us how they had sought to protect themselves by refusing to take and/or send private sexual images, only to find that the perpetrator had taken images without their knowledge. This is evident in Katherine's (UK) words, where she describes how she discovered her abusive intimate partner had been secretly recording images of her:

> It wasn't just isolated; this had been going on for ages. He controlled me, who my friends were … he's controlled my reproductive, contraception. So I've had to get secret tablets, coils … And he's sexually assaulted me on numerous occasions … [But I was] totally unaware [these photos were being taken]. I would have got him to delete them straightaway if I'd known about these images … the thought of him taking images makes me feel quite sick, because I at least thought I was safe in that, the fact that he could never threaten me with anything in terms of images because we don't have any.

There were, however, several cases where the image-based sexual abuse took place in the context of an intimate or former relationship, but the victim-survivor did not characterise the perpetrator's actions as being part of a broader context of domestic abuse. Yet, even if there was no sustained pattern of domestic abuse present, many of these participants still perceived that the image-based sexual abuse was significantly motivated by power and control. For example, Xia (NZ) told us she felt her partner always expected to be "in charge" in their relationship, and perceived that his taking non-consensual intimate images of her was geared towards asserting his power and control over her:

> I think, more than anything, it was in the relationship he was always the leader. We went where he wanted to go. We did things he wanted to do. Even when we went away together, we went to the destination he picked. It was almost like 'I have to be the one to control it'. And I think with the images, it was a bit the same. It was like 'I've finally got control of you. I couldn't quite keep a lid on it and keep a grip on you, but now I've got these [images] and I can keep a tighter grip'.

Even outside the context of intimate partnerships, participants still identified power and control as being a motivation for the image-based sexual abuse perpetration. Tara (Aus), for example, experienced image-based sexual abuse when she was a teenager when she hooked up with someone at a party, which some boys filmed without her knowledge and then uploaded and circulated the video online. Reflecting on the motivations of the perpetrators, Tara said:

> Sixteen/17-year-old boys are dickheads. I think [they did it] because they thought it was funny and they don't think about things from other people's perspectives, and probably don't think about the long-term consequences of things either ... But I think it's also like a power thing – to take advantage when someone's vulnerable ... it was definitely meant to either make me feel vulnerable or embarrassed.

Additionally, we noted the relevance of power and control in participants' reflections where they identified the image-based sexual abuse had been motivated in some sense by "revenge", where the abuse was perpetrated in a bid to assert or regain power and control in response to a perceived "transgression", such as ending an intimate relationship. This was evident in Rachel's (Aus) reflections about her ex-partner's motivations:

> He is just a sociopath. He has got a lot of emotional issues from things that had happened in his past. Abandonment issues, as well, too. He is never to blame for anything. The reason his life isn't going well is because of everyone else but him. And so he thought that he never did anything wrong and I was a bitch, [a] piece of shit who had led him on and broken his heart and ruined his life ... He said, 'I want you to feel as horrible as I feel. ... What you did to me, I want to do back to you. I want to make you feel the way that I am feeling right now. I want to ruin your life'.

Harriet (NZ) similarly told us about how her ex-partner had wanted to hurt her when he hacked into her Facebook page and replaced her profile pictures with nude images of her because he believed she was cheating on him:

> He thought that I was seeing my ex while I was with him, but that wasn't actually the case, and he was seeing [someone else] ... so it was the other way around. So he did it to hurt me because I had hurt him.

Even though Sarah (UK), whose ex-partner digitally altered images of her to make them pornographic and then posted them online, did not believe that the perpetrator ever intended for her to see the images, she still felt he wanted to punish her for rejecting him. Sarah commented that she was his first girlfriend and he had become "obsessed" with her. When they first started going out, he initially put her on a "pedestal" and then when she broke up with him, he became "very, very angry" and it then went "to the other extreme" and she became the "spawn of Satan":

> I do think it was revenge and he felt that I needed punishing for, as far as he was concerned, 'cheating' on him and 'lying' about our relationship to our mutual friends. So I do think [revenge was] involved, but also definitely sexual gratification because he was very angry that as a teenager I had not slept with him and he very much wanted me to. Hence him [sexually] assaulting me and not being great with boundaries and consent when we were together and stuff ... I don't know, 'revenge porn' takes into account how my ex viewed it, that it was his revenge and it was porn ... but it doesn't really have anything to do with me.

As Sarah's experience indicates, revenge, jealousy and resentment are closely interrelated with misogyny, sexual entitlement and "lad culture". Some victim-survivors felt male perpetrators were more motivated by how they were perceived by others, as opposed to harming the victim-survivor. For example, Vicky (UK) told us:

> It's this whole thing of 'how many girls have you slept with?' 'I've slept with this many', it's all this 'lad point', laddish lifestyle. And I feel like my boyfriend at the time he was very 'oh my girlfriend's fit' and he was just being very immature and wanted to show me off to his mates, just for the sake of being 'look at this fit girl that I'm sleeping with'.

Similarly, Mary (UK) described how she thought that "for him, it was just about getting more notches on his bedpost, 'Oh yeah, she's good fun, she's up for this'". Many other participants echoed this, with Linda (Aus), for instance, talking about how her partner wanted to show off to his friends: "It was never really revenge. Showing his friends, he just wanted to be able to brag and be like, 'Look this ... is who I'm getting to sleep with' to his mates". Related to a sense of entitlement and misogyny is the perception by some victim-survivors that the perpetrator simply did not really care. According to Mary (UK):

> It was quite hurtful and embarrassing, and I just think for me the biggest thing is that it meant nothing to him, but it meant everything to me because I felt there were so many implications of that being exposed. So for him it was a laugh or a good time, but for me it was this could ruin my job, this could make me the black sheep of the family, and I have a son.

Similarly, as Linda (Aus) reflected:

> He just kind of laughed it off ... it was just one of those things to show the boys. We were having a few drinks. He didn't think too much of it. I don't think he understood why I was so upset.

Sometimes characterised as being driven by desire to have "fun", the victim-survivors we spoke to understood "having a laugh" as being about the perpetrator's feeling of entitlement as well as lack of interest in the impacts on the victim. The perpetrators, if they thought about their actions at all, often minimised any wrongdoing or harm. This parallels the findings of the research discussed above, namely the aforementioned Australian study that undertook interviews with perpetrators (OeSC, 2019), finding that participants failed to reflect on the seriousness of their actions and had little to no insight or remorse for the pain and trauma experienced by victim-survivors.

Like Sarah (UK), a small number of participants reflected that the perpetrator seemed likely to be motivated, at least partially, by sexual gratification. Maya (Aus) discussed how images of her were digitally altered into pornographic videos and widely shared on various internet sites. Although she never knew who the perpetrators were, she concluded that sexual gratification must have been what motivated them to create and share images of her without her consent:

> They wanted gratification sexually ... [On this website] they have these tributes where they'd ejaculate on images and post it as if it somehow – I don't know the psyche behind that, but they would post it and it's almost like maybe a conquest for them or something why they would feel compelled to ejaculate on an image and then take a photo of their sperm and penis on the image of me and then post that onto porn sites. That is a weird psyche.

Financial gain was also mentioned as another motivation. Jordan (NZ), for instance, was the victim of a sexual extortion scam (also known as "sextortion"), in which scammers demanded money from him after they had screen-captured images of him during an online conversation with a woman. He told us:

> I don't think [it's] revenge porn really, because there's no revenge. I didn't do anything wrong to that person. And so it wasn't a revenge thing. It was just a simple money thing. They wanted money. They clearly found what they thought was a good gig and scam.

Overall, our research with victim-survivors revealed a complex picture of multiple, often overlapping motivations, with power, control and misogyny being particularly dominant. Participants reflected that perpetrators were "insecure", "not nice", "controlling", "abusive", "sadistic", "belittling", "insecure" and "manipulative" – and commonly their aim was to "have something over" them. These attributes are consistent with the motivations discussed in Pina, Holland and James's study (2017), which found an association between higher levels of ambivalent sexism Machiavellianism, narcissism and psychopathy, with a greater self-reported proclivity to engage in non-consensual sexual image sharing. Though the low numbers of male participants in this study precluded a gender analysis, the findings reflect those of broader sexual violence research in which characteristics, such as sexism and narcissism, are frequently found to be associated both with perpetration, and to be higher among male participants.

While a focus on individual perpetrators contributes to our understanding of image-based sexual abuse, it is important that future work also considers the role that digital platforms play in facilitating the perpetration of image-based sexual abuse. Digital platforms are arguably complicit in image-based sexual abuse perpetration when they fail to respond to the non-consensual sharing of nude or sexual images. They uphold the discourses for supporting and legitimising those acts, as well as facilitating forums for individuals to engage in the discussion of those illicit acts, providing further support to those normalising discourses. As we discuss in more detail in Chapter 5, there are also cultural and structural forces at play that are part of the underlying drivers of image-based sexual abuse. These include economic profit and excessive individualism, as well hypersexuality, "compulsory heterosexuality" and hegemonic masculinity. These individual, sociocultural, structural and organisational factors must be considered in not only creating a better understanding of image-based sexual abuse, but also providing better responses to it.

Conclusion

The term "revenge porn" has been widely denounced by victim-survivors, scholars and activists alike for failing to account for the spectrum of behaviours and motivations involving the abuse and misuse of intimate imagery. Our study adds to these voices, emphasising the need for a far more nuanced approach to understanding why image-based sexual abuse is perpetrated in the first place and by whom. In particular, we must recognise that there are many complex motivations for engaging in image-based sexual abuse, often overlapping and intersecting, with power and control commonly playing a central role. With men far more likely than women to be perpetrators of this form of abuse, misogyny and entitlement dominated victim-survivors' perspectives on why the abuse was perpetrated. This is also evident in studies examining the nature of image-based sexual abuse on online platforms, which clearly shows that this is a heavily gendered phenomenon with the vast majority of images being shared and traded online being of women (Hall & Hearn, 2017; Henry & Flynn, 2019; Uhl et al., 2018).

In light of our findings on the extent of self-reported perpetration and the diverse range of motivations, we argue that many aspects of image-based sexual abuse have been normalised. Indeed, the non-consensual sharing of intimate images can be argued to constitute a form of social currency in some social contexts. Further, we suggest that image-based sexual abuse should be conceptualised as a form of social control which operates as both a cause and a consequence of gendered violence. Understanding the complexity of image-based sexual abuse perpetration is crucial for designing appropriate responses to image-based sexual abuse, such as effective criminal and civil laws, as well as educational resources and programs. We need to better understand the broader social context and communities that facilitate, support, encourage, condone and excuse these behaviours.

We urge further work that investigates the role that other human and non-human actors (e.g., machines, organisations and systems) play in facilitating the perpetration of image-based sexual abuse, including the digital platforms (e.g., search engines, social media), as well as the broader overarching systems of "surveillance capitalism" (Zuboff, 2019), social inequality and patriarchy. In the next chapter, we build further on these insights to construct a theoretical framework for conceptualising the causes and drivers of image-based sexual abuse perpetration, which recognises the complex interplay of individual, socio-cultural and structural factors.

References

Boyle, K. M., & Walker, L. S. (2016). The neutralization and denial of sexual violence in college party subcultures. *Deviant Behavior, 37*(12), 1392–1410.

Carlson, B. (2019). Love and hate at the cultural interface: Indigenous Australians and dating apps. *Journal of Sociology.* Advance online publication. doi: 10.1177/1440783319833181.

Crofts, T., Lee, M., McGovern, A., & Milivojevic, S. (2015). *Sexting and young people.* Basingstoke: Palgrave Macmillan.

Douglas, H., Harris, B., & Dragiewicz, M. (2019). Technology-facilitated domestic and family violence: Women's experiences. *British Journal of Criminology, 59*(3), 551–570.

Garcia, J. R., Gesselman, A. N., Siliman, S. A., Perry B. L., Coe K., & Fisher, H. E. (2016). Sexting among singles in the USA: Prevalence of sending, receiving, and sharing sexual messages and images. *Sexual Health, 13*(5), 428–435.

Griffin, S. (1986). *Rape: The politics of consciousness* (3rd rev. & updated edn). San Francisco, CA: Harper & Row.

Hall, M., & Hearn, J. (2017). *Revenge pornography: Gender, sexuality and motivations.* Abingdon, Oxon; New York: Routledge.

Henry, N., & Flynn, A. (2019). Image-based sexual abuse: Online distribution channels and illicit communities of support. *Violence Against Women, 25*(16), 1932–1955.

Henry, N., & Powell, A. (2015). Beyond the "sext": Technology-facilitated sexual violence and harassment against adult women. *Australian & New Zealand Journal of Criminology, 48*(1), 104–118.

Hobbs, M., Owen, S., & Gerber, L. (2017). Liquid love? Dating apps, sex, relationships and the digital transformation of intimacy. *Journal of Sociology, 53*(2), 271–284.

Kelly, L. (1988). *Surviving sexual violence.* Cambridge, UK: Polity Press.

Langlois, G., & Slane, A. (2017). Economies of reputation: The case of revenge porn. *Communications and Critical /Cultural Studies, 14*(2), 120–138.

Morelli, M., Bianchi, D., Baiocco, R., Pezzuti, L., & Chirumbolo, A. (2016). Sexting, psychological distress and dating violence among adolescents and young adults. *Psicothema, 28*(2), 137–142.

Office of the eSafety Commissioner (OeSC). (2019). *Understanding the attitudes and motivations of adults who engage in image-based abuse: Summary report.* Melbourne, VIC: Social Research Centre. Retrieved from www.esafety.gov.au/sites/default/files/2019-10/Research_Report_IBA_Perp_Motivations.pdf.

Patrick, K., Heywood, W., Pitts, M., & Mitchell, A. (2015). Demographic and behavioural correlates of six sexting behaviours among Australian secondary school students. *Sexual Health, 12*(6), 480–487.

Pina, A., Holland, J., & James, M. (2017). The malevolent side of revenge porn proclivity: Dark personality traits and sexist ideology. *International Journal of Technoethics, 8*(1), 30–43.

Powell, A., Henry, N., Flynn, A., & Scott, A. J. (2019). Image-based sexual abuse: The extent, nature, and predictors of perpetration in a community sample of Australian residents. *Computers in Human Behavior, 92,* 393–402.

Reed, L. A., Tolman, R. M., & Ward, L. M. (2016). Snooping and sexting: Digital media as a context for dating aggression and abuse among college students. *Violence Against Women, 22*(13), 1556–1576.

Ruvalcaba, Y., & Eaton, A. A. (2019). Nonconsensual pornography among US adults: A sexual scripts framework on victimization, perpetration, and health correlates for women and men. *Psychology of Violence.* Advance online publication. https://doi.org/10.1037/vio0000233.

Southworth, C., Finn, J., Dawson, S., Fraser, C., & Tucker, S. (2007). Intimate partner violence, technology, and stalking. *Violence Against Women, 13*(8), 842–856.

Stark, E. (2007). *Coercive control: How men entrap women in personal life.* New York: Oxford University Press.

Strohmaier, H., Murphy, M., & DeMatteo, D. (2014). Youth sexting: Prevalence rates, driving motivations, and the deterrent effect of legal consequences. *Sexuality Research and Social Policy, 11*(3), 245–255.

Sykes, G. M., & Matza, D. (1957). Techniques of neutralization: A theory of delinquency. *American Sociological Review, 22*(6), 664–670.

Thompson, M. P., & Morrison, D. J. (2013). Prospective predictors of technology-based sexual coercion by college males. *Psychology of Violence, 3*(3), 233–246.

Uhl, C. A., Rhyner, K. A., Terrance, C. A., & Lugo, N. (2018). An examination of nonconsensual pornography websites. *Feminism & Psychology, 28*(1), 50–68.

Waldman, A. E. (2019). Law, privacy, and online dating: "Revenge porn" in gay online communities. *Law & Social Inquiry, 44*(4), 987–1018.

Woodlock, D. (2017). The abuse of technology in domestic violence and stalking. *Violence Against Women, 23*(5), 584–602.

Zuboff, S. (2019). *The age of surveillance capitalism: The fight for a human future at the new frontier of power.* London: Profile Books.

Chapter 5

Visual criminality

A theory of image-based sexual abuse

Introduction

Contemporary digital culture can be characterised by a fixation on visuality – on both the technological artefact that captures or broadcasts the visual, and the material subject/object which can be "seen" and monitored. This is evidenced through contemporary trends such as reality television, "selfies", live-streaming, webcams and amateur pornography – what Calvert (2000) calls "the voyeurism value". Understanding this cultural appetite for "authentic" visual representations of reality is important for sharpening and deepening our understandings of image-based sexual abuse. While not a new phenomenon, the non-consensual taking or sharing of nude or sexual images is far more common today, not only because of massive advances of digital communications technologies (e.g., smart phones, social media, artificial intelligence), but also due to changes in culture, including the increasingly visual, interactive and voyeuristic nature of digital communications (Andrejevic, 2004).

This chapter examines the micro and macro context that underpins the prevalence, nature and perpetration of image-based sexual abuse. The chapter brings together criminological, sociological, philosophical and social learning theories to investigate the relationship between, on the one hand, the "cultural scaffolding" of sexual violence (Gavey, 2019), in which image-based sexual abuse takes place, and on the other hand, the phenomenological, relational and "first-person" context. Our aim is to build, through "theory-knitting", a feminist ecological framework for understanding the complexity and diversity of image-based sexual abuse by bringing together key elements of the micro-macro puzzle (Bourdieu & Wacquant, 2007: 3).

We argue that image-based sexual abuse needs to be understood within a contemporary context of digital media that is characterised by a cultural obsession with visuality and realism, a fixation on feminised bodies, and a social system predicated on a gender hierarchy which pervades social interactions and conceptions of self. We first explore the usefulness of criminological approaches to understanding image-based sexual abuse. Second, we examine image-based sexual abuse through the lens of Bandura's (1986) social learning theory in conjunction with Bourdieu's theory on *habitus* and *field* (Bourdieu & Wacquant, 2007) as a way to understand the cognitive self-regulatory mechanisms that are deactivated within individuals to produce image-based sexual abuse behaviours – within a system of meaning and symbolic power. Finally, we examine trends in pornography, voyeurism and digital cultures to further understand image-based sexual abuse perpetration.

An etiology of image-based sexual abuse

As we have argued in Chapter 2, image-based sexual abuse exists on a continuum of sexual violence (see Kelly, 1988). As such, it is important to explore existing theories on sexual and other forms of gendered violence in order to better understand this phenomenon. It is best to start by acknowledging the long-standing debate about the etiology or causes of sexualised violence emerging from three basic schools of thought. First, *psychological theories* tend to focus on psychopathological explanations such as childhood abuse and neglect, exposure to pornography, poor social learning, low self-esteem, acceptance of interpersonal violence, low education, drug and alcohol use, or attachment and personality disorders as risk factors underlying gendered violence (see e.g., Malamuth, Sockloskie, Koss, & Tanaka, 1991; Marshall & Barbaree, 1990). Second, *evolutionary psychology perspectives* focus on inherited biological dispositions, such as natural selection, adaptation and sex selection, with some theorists controversially claiming that sexual aggression is an outcome of evolved reproductive traits inherited from ancestral contexts to ensure genetic survival (e.g., Thornhill & Palmer, 2000; for a critique, see Ward & Siegert, 2002). And third, *feminist sociological theories* tend to treat sexual aggression as a manifestation of social control and gender inequality within a sociocultural context of patriarchy and masculine privilege (e.g., Baron & Straus, 1987; Brownmiller, 1975; Clark & Lewis, 1977).

While all three single-factor theories are in fact more diverse and heterogenous than briefly outlined here, broadly speaking they each have their own limitations for theorising the causes of sexual violence. Evolutionary theories view sexual aggression as a natural phenomenon and tend to discount the role that power and culture play in men's violence against women. Psychological theories often gloss over the broader structural and cultural factors in perpetuating sexual violence, such as problematic beliefs, attitudes and norms around gender and sexuality, with the focus instead being on psychopathology or "proximal causes" such as mental health issues or drug and alcohol addiction. And third, sociological feminist theories tend to ignore individual-level factors and cognitive processes. As Jewkes (2012) argues in relation to understanding rape perpetration, it is useful to merge these different theoretical approaches to examine individual thought processes and social learning alongside the social and structural context of patriarchy and gender hierarchy. In the discussion below, we explore the applicability of various criminological, sociological, psychoanalytic and social learning theories on violence, with the aim of crafting a feminist ecological approach to theorising the etiology of image-based sexual abuse. Our approach is inspired by Bourdieu's dialectic on interrelations and intersubjectivity (Bourdieu & Wacquant, 2007).[1]

Criminological theories

Criminological theory is useful for understanding the nature of crime, including its causes and impacts, as well as the social responses to crime (White, Haines, & Asquith, 2017). In this section, we focus on three strands of criminological theory for developing a richer understanding of image-based sexual abuse perpetration: Routine activities theory; strain theory; and feminist criminology.

Routine activities theory

Routine activities theory focuses on three factors said to affect both the extent of the crime and the location. These include: The presence and proximity of likely offenders who are motivated to commit the crime; the absence of capable guardians to intervene; and the availability of "suitable targets" (Cohen & Felson, 1979). Routine activities theory has been increasingly used by cybercrime scholars to show how risky online behaviours puts individuals at risk of cybercrime and technology-facilitated victimisation (e.g., Grabosky, 2001; Holt & Bossler, 2008; Yar, 2005). Studies have focused on issues such as cyberstalking (e.g., Reyns, Henson, & Fisher, 2011), cyberbullying (e.g., Navarro & Jasinski, 2012), online harassment (e.g., Bossler, Holt, & May, 2012; Marcum, Higgins, & Ricketts, 2014), digital dating abuse (e.g., Van Ouytsel, Ponnet, & Walrave, 2018) and sexting (e.g., Reyns, Burek, Henson, & Fisher, 2013; Wolfe, Marcum, Higgins, & Ricketts, 2016).[2]

   Most studies applying routine activities theory to understanding technology-facilitated abuse have not adequately addressed the role of gender or applied a critical feminist lens to understanding either victimisation or perpetration. One exception is the study by Bossler et al. (2012), which found that although women are more likely to be victims of online harassment compared to men, being female was not a factor in and of itself for predicting victimisation. Instead, they found that although women were less likely to engage in online deviance, women were more likely to engage in social networking with greater identification of their gender through disclosure of personal details, and to have more friends who engaged in harassment behaviours (see also Navarro & Jasinski, 2012). Like other routine activities theories, however, the focus of this study was on the victim rather than the perpetrator, or the causes of offending.

In responding to the gender-blindness apparent within routine activities theory, Schwartz and Pitts (1995) developed a "feminist routines activity theory" in relation to sexual assault on college campuses. They observed in their study that lifestyle factors, such as alcohol and drug use, increases the risk of sexual victimisation. They also noted that the motivations of offenders have been neglected in traditional routine activities research and called on feminist theorisation to contextualise offenders' motivations within a patriarchal and "rape supportive" culture and system.

While there has not yet been empirical testing of routine activities theory in relation to image-based sexual abuse, a feminist routine activities approach can provide some insight into prevalence, as well as victimisation and perpetration experiences. All three key factors can be said to converge on the internet sites where non-consensual intimate imagery is shared. First, the online platforms bring together motivated offenders who have proximity to their victims through their existing relationships (e.g., as partners or former partners) and through their online contact with other users, victims and the victims' online networks. Second, available female targets are present in the images uploaded – images that are often taken by and/or shared with intimate partners or other known persons. And third, "capable guardians" willing to intervene are not only absent, but are themselves often perpetrators (partners, family members, friends and acquaintances). Moreover, users are actively supported by their online male peers, as well as the digital platforms, to post images, comment and abuse the women depicted in the images (Henry & Flynn, 2019).

Using a routine activity approach can help to guide practical solutions to image-based sexual abuse, including greater awareness, action, transparency and accountability of digital platforms who have the power to act as the "capable guardians" (see Chapter 8). However, exhorting the "risks" associated with online behaviour for victims is inherently problematic, given the practical implications that may arise from such an approach. For instance, this can unfairly place the burden on victims to engage in a range of online safety behaviours, such as desisting from taking or sharing intimate "selfies", deactivating social media accounts, or removing themselves altogether from online interactions. It also runs the risk of unfairly placing the blame onto victims. Moreover, while routine activity theory may be useful for understanding risk factors for victimisation, it does not adequately explain the underlying individual or sociocultural causes or "drivers" of abuse and harassment.

Strain theory

In contrast to routine activities theory, strain theory provides a more sociological approach to understanding the individual, situational and structural causes of criminal offending. Strain theorists posit that social and economic strains or pressures, including the unequal and uneven distribution of opportunities within a given society, have a powerful influence on individuals, making crime a means through which individuals can achieve socially defined goals of monetary success or middle-class status (e.g., Broidy & Agnew, 1997; Durkheim, 1893/1984; Merton, 1938). From within the strain theory tradition, subcultural theory positions crime as interpersonal, located at the level of group interaction whereby subcultures emerge from class-based status frustration, usually in poor urban environments (e.g., Cohen, 1955; Sutherland & Cressey, 1974). Through association with gangs and male delinquency, individuals within subcultures are insulated from the unachievable demands and expectations placed on them by conventional society, seeking alternative ways to achieve these means through crime and deviance. Crime is thus seen as "an attempt to make a mark on the world, to be noticed, to get identity feedback" (Braithwaite, 1979: 68).

While strain theories provide some insight into criminal behaviours, they have, by and large, failed to recognise the important role of gender, or the intersections of gender with other markers of difference, such as race, sexuality, age and ability (for a discussion, see Belknap & Holsinger, 2006; Broidy & Agnew, 1997; Burgess-Proctor, 2006). Strain theorists also focus almost exclusively on crime within lower socio-economic contexts and fail to explain crime across class and advantage or disadvantage.

Despite its limitations, strain theory is nonetheless a useful conceptual tool for understanding image-based sexual abuse because it helps to explain the interrelationships between the individual and the society, the will to power, the dynamics of subcultures, and the communications among like-minded peers. For instance, the production and distribution of nonconsensual intimate imagery within deviant online subcultures may be explained in reference to "anomie", characterised by abrupt social change, a lack of social guidance around ethics and norms, and the association of deviant peers seeking alternative means to achieve validation and recognition. On many of the sites observed by Henry and Flynn (2019) in their digital ethnography, users developed their own norms, languages and practices to create subcultures of online deviancy. On some sites, users adopt specific, customised language to describe certain actions, such as "dumps" (for uploading images), "wins" (for images of women being shared), or practices that facilitated the sharing of images, such as the use of file-sharing and chat sites (called VOLAs) that allow users to create rooms and engage in conversation and share images, or through file sharing databases and Google Drive accounts. On one site, chatrooms were temporary, meaning they were closed by the moderators after users had had a brief window of opportunity to download files containing non-consensual sexual images of women. On this site, identifying information was provided about the women depicted in the images, such as their name and links to their social media accounts (Henry & Flynn, 2019).

While not usually considered part of criminological "strain theory", feminist scholars have usefully drawn on German philosopher Friedrich Nietzsche's concept of *ressentiment* (1969: 127) to provide further explanation for individual actions and sentiments within social systems of support (e.g., Brown, 1995; Nussbaum, 2010; Powell & Henry, 2017). According to Nietzsche, *ressentiment* is a feeling of bitterness or "vengefulness" which prompts the individual to seek out a cause of his or her suffering – a "guilty agent … upon which he can, on some pretext or other, vent his affects, actually or in effigy" (Nietzsche, 1969: 127). Nietzsche (1969: 127) likened this to the "desire to deaden pain" rather than confront it with consciousness and reflexivity. Feminist postmodernist scholar Wendy Brown (1995: 69) uses his concept as a way of understanding the late modern subject, who she claims, "quite literally seethes with *ressentiment*". She argues that the liberal subject is both "starkly accountable and yet dramatically impotent" owing to the domination of capital and bureaucracies, the "unparalleled individual powerlessness over the fate and direction of one's own life", and the increased fragmentation or disintegration of community (Brown, 1995: 68).

In relation to misogynist objectification online, Nussbaum (2010: 76) also draws on the concept of *ressentiment*. She describes it as "a reactive emotion inspired by the feeling of weakness", which is deeply connected to "shame punishment". According to Nussbaum, much of the gender-based hate speech online serves to satisfy the needs of the objectifier, who reduces and debases his or her (sexed) object of hate to bodily parts and physical appearance (see also Powell & Henry, 2017). Indeed, many contemporary feminist scholars, although not specifically interpreting harassing and harmful online behaviours through the lens of strain or subcultures, or indeed *ressentiment*, have provided multiple examples of hate, bitterness and hostility through acts such as trolling, hate speech, doxing and other online forms of abuse (e.g., Gorman, 2019; Jane, 2014). Although these behaviours are arguably distinct from the non-consensual taking, sharing, or threats to share, nude or sexual images, there is much overlap because the people who engage in these behaviours are sometimes embittered, expressing misogynist, racist, homo- and transphobic attitudes and beliefs, as reported by the victim-survivors we interviewed (see Chapter 4).

Moreover, as Gavey (2019: 250) argues, men "heavily invest in the myth of masculinity" within a gender hierarchy which is shaped by broader societal discourses that position men as not only "dominant, superior, and entitled to taken-for-granted prominence and authority", but also invulnerable. Gavey (2019) contends that men who subscribe to the myth of masculinity not only perform their gender and heterosexuality according to a proscribed (unwritten) script, but also resist and defend against any threat to their privileged status and position. Perceived "threats" might include: Women who have rejected them; women who do not conform to proscribed conventions of femininity, such as lesbian, bisexual, or queer women; or women who are "outspoken" or ambitious.

Feminist criminology

Feminist criminology is a useful conceptual framework from which to understand crime victimisation, female offending and male perpetration in the context of unequal social structures of (patriarchal) power. It is important to note, however, that like other theoretical traditions, feminist criminology is not a unified theoretical approach, but rather "a diverse collection of theoretical perspectives and methods" (Renzetti, 2013: 99).

One feminist approach to understanding the causes of gendered violence is through an *ecological model*, which examines the complex interplay of individual, social and structural factors, including attitudes, beliefs, norms and values about gender and sexuality (e.g., Heise, 1998; Jewkes, 2012; Pinchevsky & Wright, 2012). Recognising the central role that gender inequality plays in gendered violence, an ecological model helps to explain the divergences in perpetrator background and experiences; for instance, why some individuals without adverse childhood experiences or mental health or drug and alcohol issues, are capable of perpetrating sexual or domestic violence.

An ecological model is useful for explaining "reciprocal causation"; that is, the social, economic and political context which shapes individual behaviours, which in turn shape the social context. An ecological model is furthermore instrumental to devising interventions and responses to the problem of men's violence against not only women, but also children and other men. For instance, addressing the multitude of individual-level risk factors, such as low self-esteem, lower socio-economic opportunities, adverse childhood experiences, and adherence to problematic beliefs and values about gender and sexuality, is equally as important as is addressing broader societal beliefs, attitudes, norms and values about gender and sexuality, including moving towards formal and substantive gender equality at the societal level.

A focus on masculinity within feminist scholarship in particular has been fruitful for further developing understandings of the underlying drivers of online harassment and violence. While many scholars argue that perpetrators of gendered violence (including both sexual and domestic violence) constitute a diverse group of (mostly) men from different racial, ethnic, age and socio-economic backgrounds, some scholars note that economic and social marginalisation, in conjunction with adherence, resistance or adaptation to hegemonic masculine norms, can help to explain subcultural forms of misogynist violence and abuse as a form of "compensatory masculinity" (e.g., Carrington & Scott, 2008; DeKeseredy & Schwartz, 2010). DeKeseredy and Schwartz's (2010: 160) feminist criminological theory examines how gender power relations intersects with other systems of inequality to shape criminal offending and victimisation experiences. Their theory embraces some of the key ideas of left realism, which contend that "people lacking legitimate means of solving the problem of relative deprivation may come into contact with other frustrated disenfranchised people and form subcultures, which in turn encourage criminal behaviors". According to DeKeseredy and Schwartz (2010), individuals who turn to patriarchal crime "behind closed doors" are marginalised men who fail to live up to the standards of hegemonic masculinity. Similarly, as Carrington, McIntosh and Scott (2010: 402) explain in relation to male-to-male violence in remote geographical locations: "Where men's place, status or territory is threatened ... violence can become a way of re-enforcing boundaries, exercising power, asserting male honour and re-establishing social status with other groups of men" (see also Gavey, 2019).

Drawing on traditional criminological theories of socio-economic strain and the importance of subcultures, DeKeseredy and Schwartz's (1993) "male peer support theory" is an important ecological model which seeks to explain the bonds of attachment of some men to their patriarchal and abusive male peers behind closed doors. The model takes into account broader social forces such as patriarchy, as well as community-level factors, such as membership in social groups (e.g., college fraternities and gangs), socio-economic status, and disinhibiting factors, such as alcohol use and lack of guardianship (DeKeseredy & Schwartz, 1993). Within these deviant peer groups of men, beliefs, values, attitudes and norms are cultivated, validated and reinforced – within the context of a patriarchal society. Gavey (2019) calls this the "cultural scaffolding" of coercive sexuality. She argues that normative heterosexuality is constructed through narratives, scripts and discourses which provide the conditions possible for coercive sexuality, where the effects are to minimise, excuse and condone men's sexual aggression. This was demonstrated in a recent study that involved 16 interviews with image-based abuse perpetrators in Australia (OeSC, 2019). The study found that for many perpetrators, image-based sexual abuse is untroubling and normative within a context of male bonding and homosociality, through peer-to-peer competition and identification.

As we demonstrated in the previous chapter, some forms of image-based sexual abuse represent a mechanism for the achievement or consolidation of social power among a subculture of male peer support and online sexual deviancy. In Henry and Flynn's (2019) digital ethnography, they identified online community forums as a particular example of this, where members come together to form part of an active community. The purpose of these community forums is discussion among a group of users, sometimes in sub-forums using threads based on particular topics of interest. Some forums specialise in the non-consensual sharing and trading of non-consensual nude or sexual photos or videos of their current partners. For instance, on one forum, specific challenges were set for users – such as taking a nude or sexual image of their wife or girlfriend in a public place and then uploading the image onto the forum without the woman's consent or knowledge. Another forum was labelled "degrade and abuse" which involved users posting images of clothed or nude women and asking others to respond with answers to what they would do to her. An even more highly interactive forum was one that encouraged users to "post their girls" for other men to download and then re-upload as a "cum tribute", where a man ejaculates on a printed image or on the screen of their phone or computer (Henry & Flynn, 2019).

A new trend in image-based sexual abuse is the rise of so-called "deepfake pornography", using sophisticated techniques in artificial intelligence (or "machine learning") which enable users to create realistic fake or "synthetic" pornographic videos (see Chesney & Citron, 2019). The creation of fake pornography is not a new issue with digitally altered images having been made available in the past (e.g., through "photoshopping" or other techniques, such as speeding, slowing, cutting and other methods – see Paris & Donovan, 2019). Yet in November 2017, a Reddit user, who called himself "deepfakes", created a video-editing desktop application, which allows users to train algorithms (through machine learning) to replace the face of one person with another's – to make it look like a person is appearing in a video when they were not. Although the Reddit forum was removed in February 2018, the Reddit user donated the "deep learning" faceswap source code to the open-source community. This means that since 2017, not only have the techniques for creating fake imagery become more sophisticated, but there appears to be soaring demand for deepfake pornography, as evidenced by the number of deepfake websites, communities, forums, tools, and services (see Ajder, Patrini, Cavalli, & Cullen, 2019).

Deepfake pornography, as well as other online practices of image-based sexual abuse, are, we contend, constitutive of a gender order – "a historically constructed pattern of power relations between men and women and definitions of femininity and masculinity" (Connell, 1987: 98–99). Connell and Messerschmidt's (2005) concept of "hegemonic masculinity" characterises this gender order as one of subordinated masculinities and femininities which serves to legitimate and stabilise patriarchy, male dominance (by the hegemonic few) and heteronormativity. According to Connell and Messerschmidt (2005: 832), "[h]egemonic masculinity [embodies] the … most honoured way of being a man, it require[s] all other men to position themselves in relation to it, and it ideologically legitimate[s] the global subordination of women to men".

Masculinities scholar Michael Flood (2008: 341) also notes that ritualised acts of sexual humiliation against women is used for men's collective amusement in the service of proving one's position in a male social hierarchy. He contends that this is achieved through the "markers of manhood", such as occupation, wealth, physicality and sexual prowess. The performance of hypermasculinity is typically achieved through the conduit of bodies and sexualities. Prior to the age of the internet, social media and camera-enabled smart phones, while some markers of manhood were no doubt easily verified (e.g., occupation, wealth and physicality), sexual prowess was much harder to prove. However, in the digital era, a nude or sexual photograph or video is incontrovertible "proof" of intimacy and conquest. While the exchange and trade of non-consensual nude or sexual imagery may be competitive in nature, it is also actively encouraged, supported and normalised within peer contexts. DeKeseredy and Schwartz (2016: 3), for instance, argue that "[d]isseminating image-based sexual abuse is a means of 'doing masculinity' in a culturally specific way ... [t]hese men provide attachments to other abusive men, and resources that involve specific verbal and emotional support".

Image-based sexual abuse may thus be seen as a conduit through which to perform one's gender. Goffman (1977) and Garfinkel (1967) argued that all persons manage and practice their gender on a metaphoric stage that follows a socially proscribed script. West and Zimmerman (1987) developed these ideas further to argue that gender is a "routine accomplishment" embedded in everyday interactions and functioning to reinforce the "naturalness" of the sexed or gendered binary. This mutually interactional and self-regulatory disciplinary practice, they argue, ensures that gender is being done "correctly".

In relation to image-based sexual abuse, gender is performed within a script premised on heteronormativity, masculine privilege and misogyny. Images then are a form of *social currency* or *social capital* (Bourdieu & Wacquant, 2007) that individuals draw upon to seek approval, sexual gratification, social control, retribution or validation from others, as indicated by many victim-survivors in the 75 interviews we conducted (see Chapter 4). This means then that the non-consensual taking or sharing of nude or sexual images is an *identity-consolidation practice* – where the subject uses an object (for instance, a nude or sexual representation of another person without their consent) as a means through which to "do gender".

This might be further explained using psychoanalytic theory which, like Goffman (1977) and Garfinkel's (1967) ethnomethodological approach, does not presuppose consciousness or cognitive intent. In Kristeva's (1982) theory on *abjection,* she argues that the abject is the "radically excluded" – that which "disturbs identity, system, order" and violates the "borders, positions, rules" (Kristeva, 1982: 2–4). The abject is a "primal repression" that precedes the subject's relationship to objects and other subjects. Abjection symbolises a breakdown of meaning caused by a loss of distinction between the "self" and the "other", and the reestablishment of the boundary between self and other. For Kristeva (1982: 12–13), abjection is a way in which "primitive societies have marked out a precise area of their culture in order to remove it from the threatening world of animals or animalism, which were imagined as representatives of sex and murder". It is that which we reject within ourselves – the maternal object which created us but which we became separated from "in order to be" (Kristeva, 1982: 10). In a similar vein, Layton's theory on *projection* is useful to explain men's sexual violence against women as "relational scenarios marked by the effects of projection of repudiated parts of self onto the other, by domination and submission and by the eroticization of positions of power and weakness" (cited in Gavey, 2019: 250).

Other theorists have described abjection in reference to the marginalisation of particular groups within the community, such as women, sex workers, transgender and intersex people, people with disabilities, single mothers and menstruating or menopausal women. The abject then is the bodily desires and fluids which transgress and threaten cleanliness, order and respectability, and as such, represent the part of ourselves that we reject, projected onto a "blameworthy" other. But there is also fascination in the abject – as demonstrated by Ringrose and Walkerdine's (2008: 227) exploration of reality makeover television, the contemporary production of neoliberal femininity, and the ways in which the "feminine" has become a new site of "limitless possibility and endless consumption".

Returning to Nietzsche's (1969) concept of *ressentiment*, disenfranchised men who subscribe to the "myth of masculinity" (Gavey, 2019), whose efforts to exert power over women have failed, including women of colour, women with disabilities, and LGBTQI women, seek out means through which to consolidate that identity and status. A pertinent example of this is the rise of "deepfake" pornography depicting well-known female celebrities, actors and musicians – women that most men will never be able to touch or possess.

Before moving on to the final theory on social learning, it is important to note that not all acts of image-based sexual abuse can be placed within the context of strain, subcultures, anomie, "toxic masculinity" or abjection/projection. Yet, for many instances of image-based sexual abuse, these theories are useful for explaining the underlying factors or drivers of image-based sexual abuse – many of which will be unconscious to the individual. While feminist, criminological, sociological or philosophical approaches are important for aiding our understanding of the complexity of image-based sexual abuse perpetration, macro-sociological theories on sexual aggression fail to account for the ways in which individuals come to engage in such behaviours in the first place. Thus, in the next section, we integrate social learning theory with Bourdieu's sociological theory on structure and agency to further develop an ecological model of image-based sexual abuse.

Social learning theory and the structure/agency puzzle

Alongside criminological theory, social learning theory is a useful conceptual tool to understand image-based sexual abuse behaviours. Bandura's

(1971: 1) social learning theory seeks to explain "why people behave as they do". This includes the ways in which individuals are socialised through observation and mimicry, and how cognitive self-regulatory mechanisms are deactivated through external situational stimuli and internal thought processes to produce behaviour (Bandura, 1986). This model embraces an interactional model of causation that examines both dispositional and environmental factors, or "reciprocal causation". This posits human functioning as "a model of triadic reciprocity in which behavior, cognitive and other personal factors, and environmental events all operate as interacting determinants of each other" (Bandura, 1986: 18). As part of this theory, Bandura identifies eight cognitive distortions that explain how individuals come to engage in antisocial or criminal behaviour: Diffusion of responsibility; displacement of responsibility; distortion of consequences; moral justification; euphemistic labelling; advantageous comparison; dehumanisation; and attribution of blame.

Below we interpret Bandura's model predominantly in *sociological terms* to suggest that these cognitive processes are not necessarily conscious or unconscious. Indeed, this is made clear by Bandura (1971: 1) who stated that the principal causes of behaviour are "often operating below the level of consciousness".

We also draw on elements of Bourdieu's philosophy of structure/agency, which

> ... refuses to establish sharp demarcations between the external and the internal, the conscious and the unconscious, the bodily and the discursive. It seeks to capture the intentionality without intention, the knowledge without cognitive intent, the prereflective, infraconscious mastery that agents acquire of their social world by way of durable immersion within it.
>
> (Bourdieu & Wacquant, 2007: 19)

Bourdieu's theory on *field* and *habitus,* in particular, is useful for understanding why people behave the way that they do, and what internal/external processes are at play (without necessarily distinguishing between the internal and the external). According to Bourdieu, a *field* is a hierarchical, historical and heterogenous system where individuals and their social positions are located "anchored to certain forms of power (or capital)", including the larger, overarching field of power relations on the basis of gender, class and race. This is a space for conflict and competition over social, economic and cultural capital (Bourdieu & Wacquant, 2007: 17). *Habitus* refers to the physical embodiment of "a set of historical relations ... in the form of mental and corporeal schemata of perception, appreciation, and action" (Bourdieu & Wacquant, 2007: 16) – the space of the "social agent" or the "cognitive structures inscribed in bodies and in minds" (Bourdieu & Wacquant, 2007: 171).

We provide a Bordieuan interpretation of Bandura's cognitive distortions, resisting the sharp or dualistic distinctions between structure/agency and the micro/macro, and instead interpreting social (or antisocial) behaviour as stemming from networks of power relations, performances and interactions where certain value is assigned to economic, social and cultural capital in particular *fields* (Bourdieu & Wacquant, 2007: 15).

Diffusion of responsibility

First, Bandura (1986) described the diffusion of responsibility as a key cognitive distortion prior to behaviour enactment, which is accomplished through the internal state of deindividuation, characterised by reduced self-awareness and self-evaluation, and a consequent diminished concern for the well-being of others. Deindividuation is understood in part as an immersion in group behaviours, where responsibility becomes diffused or displaced. This was famously illustrated by the Zimbardo (1970) Stanford Prison Experiment, which simulated a prison environment in which subjects were assigned either the role of prisoner or prison guard. Zimbardo found that through uniforms, identification numbers and group dynamics, identity loss and anonymity were facilitated, leading to the conclusion that group norms can exert a powerful influence over human behaviour, particularly when there is a common enemy. The diffusion of responsibility is also facilitated by an absence of eye contact and anonymity (Lapidot-Lefler & Barak, 2012). In online contexts, this is what Suler (2004) refers to as the "disinhibition effect", noting that people are not only more likely to share highly personal information about themselves and others online, but also more likely to engage in toxic behaviours. He argues that this is facilitated by anonymity, invisibility asynchronicity (interactions not always happening in real time), "solipsistic introjection" (e.g., imagining it's all in one's head), "dissociative imagination" (e.g., imagining it's all a game) and the minimisation of authority.

Compliance to group norms also contributes to diffusion of responsibility, often out of fear of rejection from the group or punishment. According to Walzer (1992: 315–316):

> To disobey [the group] is to breach that elemental accord, to claim a moral separateness (or a moral superiority) involves the risk that may well be greater than that of punishment; the risk of a profound and morally disturbing isolation.

As discussed above, economic, social and cultural capital, particularly around masculinity and sex in the *field* (the broader system of meaning), mean that boys and men are typically judged by their male peers on the basis of group norms within a particular *field*, and self-esteem thus is derived from these sources (O'Sullivan, 1993). This shapes and feeds the *habitus* (the internalisation and embodiment of the discourses in the *field*), and in turn, feeds back into and shapes the *field*. Again, it is important to note, as Bourdieu does, that these social practices are not necessarily either conscious or intentional (Bourdieu & Wacquant, 2007). Indeed, as political philosopher Hannah Arendt (1963/1994) so cogently explored in her book about the criminal trial of Adolf Eichmann (German-Austrian SS-Obersturmbannführer who orchestrated the Nazi concentration camps), the "banality of evil" is the incapacity for independent critical, conscious thought, and the resulting *failure to think from the perspective of the "other"*. In relation to image-based sexual abuse, this is perhaps aptly demonstrated by the comments of Kevin Bolleart, the website operator of an infamous "revenge porn" website. In an exclusive television interview while in prison after being convicted of identity theft and extortion, Bolleart said he did not realise that so many people would be harmed by his actions: "I thought it was more of, like, a joke, than damaging people's lives to that extent" (Dye, 2015).

Moral justification and euphemistic labelling

Second, Bandura (1986: 376) defined moral justification as "cognitive restructuring" – a process in which "reprehensible conduct is made personally and socially acceptable by portraying it in the service of moral ends". Bandura used military training as an example of how killing is transformed into heroic, honourable behaviour, arguing that the task of converting socialised individuals into trained combatants is achieved not through personality transformation, but through restructuring the moral value of killing. Likewise, with online abuse, again while the intentions and processes might not necessarily be conscious to individual agents, when asked to explain, perpetrators typically justify it using moral reasoning, framing it as either expressions of humour, fun or free speech. This is also an example of Bandura's (1986: 378) euphemistic labelling cognitive distortion which "provides a convenient device for masking reprehensible activities or even conferring a respectable status upon them" – for instance, terms such as "revenge porn", "nudes" or "deepfakes" are examples of euphemistic labelling that fail to capture the harms. Sometimes, moral justification is also rooted in *ressentiment* and revenge, such as embittered partners or ex-partners justifying the non-consensual sharing of intimate images for perceived wrongs done to them.

Displacement of responsibility

The displacement of responsibility refers to responsibility being displaced onto others, but also the influence (or absence) of authority figures (Bandura, 1986). In online spaces, the absence of capable guardianship to intervene in harassment and abuse when it occurs (Yar, 2005), has long been recognised as a factor that disinhibits abusive online behaviours. According to Suler (2004), people are reluctant to say what they really think in front of an authority figure for fear of disapproval, censure or punishment, but online they are more willing to express their own opinions due to the anonymity and invisibility that being online can provide. Moreover, it is not only the absence of capable guardianship that facilitates image-based sexual abuse behaviours, but many digital platforms, as semi-authority figures, implicitly or explicitly encourage the sharing and trading in non-consensual sharing of intimate imagery, or at least condone or permit these image-sharing practices through the functionality and architectural design of their sites.

Distortion of consequences

A fourth cognitive distortion identified by Bandura (1986) concerns the distortion of consequences, or the minimisation or disregard of anticipated negative consequences. This is particularly relevant in relation to image-based sexual abuse where detection, regulation and punishment are major challenges across jurisdictional borders. As will be discussed in Chapter 7, in many jurisdictions it is not a criminal offence to take, share or threaten to share, nude or sexual images, and even where it is a criminal offence, many jurisdictions include various thresholds and caveats that limit the scope of the offence.

Bandura (1986) also notes that the absence of punishment may communicate that such behaviours are socially acceptable and normative to individual users. In a study on men and pornography, Antevska and Gavey (2015) interviewed 21 men about their pornography consumption and their reflections on what they were watching. Their participants described their pornography use as normative among other men – so much that they failed to think about it and were untroubled by some of the content they consumed. Again, it is useful to draw on Bourdieu's philosophy about preconsciousness. According to Bourdieu, "social agents" internalise and accept as natural assumptions, postulates and axioms about the world "because *their mind is constructed according to cognitive structures that are issued out of the very structures of the world*" (Bourdieu & Wacquant, 2007: 168, emphasis original). In relation to gender and power, Bourdieu further argues that the "male order is so deeply grounded as to need no justification: it imposes itself as self-evident, universal..." (Bourdieu & Wacquant, 2007: 171). Indeed, Bourdieu demonstrates that gender domination is the clearest example of what he called *symbolic violence*, which accomplishes itself *"through an act of cognition and of misrecognition that lies beyond – or beneath – the controls of consciousness and will"* (Bourdieu & Wacquant, 2007: 171–172, emphasis original).

Dehumanisation

Dehumanisation is another cognitive mechanism that facilitates aggressive behaviour (Bandura, 1986) and is useful for thinking about in relation to image-based sexual abuse and other forms of online abuse. Dehumanisation refers to the attribution of subhuman qualities to others, serving to exonerate and justify offensive behaviour towards them. The divesting of human qualities to minority or marginalised groups is strikingly evident in the language used to abuse and humiliate victims online, as described with words such as "cunt", "whore" and "slut" (see also Jordan, 2018 for a discussion of "objectification"). This process enables individuals to overcome feelings of empathy and concern for others because the target is perceived as different and dissimilar; as something less than human. Once dehumanised, writes Bandura (1986: 382), the enemy is "no longer viewed as persons with feelings, hopes, and concerns, but as subhuman objects demeaningly stereotyped". Drawing on Bourdieu's theory of symbolic power, women are required to conform to a "masculine ideal of feminine virtue", treated as *objects of exchanges* between and among men for social capital; as "symbols for striking alliances" (Bourdieu & Wacquant, 2007: 173). As explained in detail above, this is illustrated in the online peer networks that see users exchanging non-consensual sexual imagery as a form of illicit trade – as a form of both compliance and competition (Henry & Flynn, 2019).

Attribution of blame

Finally, Bandura (1986) discussed the ways in which attribution of blame serves to deactivate self-regulatory mechanisms to produce the deviant behaviour. Blaming the victim has long been recognised in feminist literature on sexual and domestic violence. Feminist scholars have recognised that it is not just the perpetrator in social isolation who blames the victim-survivor, but the victim-survivor herself or himself also internalises those broader societal discourses. In relation to image-based sexual abuse, many scholars identify victim-blaming as a key issue, with significant implications for media reporting, educational programs, victim support services and law and policy responses. In particular, victim-survivors are routinely blamed for having taken and shared intimate photos of themselves. Burns (2015), for instance, argues that notions of "choice" are used to blame victim-survivors for the original sharing of nude or sexual images. She claims that this serves a dual purpose of facilitating sexual gratification, as well as serving to condemn and degrade women who choose to take images of themselves.

Understanding these disinhibiting cognitive factors and the *field* and *habitus* in which they are part, is not akin to justifying or excusing these behaviours. Rather, it helps us to understand why people behave in the ways that they do, as well as assisting in the design of more effective laws, policies and practices to both respond to and prevent image-based sexual abuse from occurring in the first place (see Chapters 7 and 8). As we have shown here, it is essential that in conceptualising the "causes" or "drivers" of image-based sexual abuse, we adopt a feminist ecological approach that positions the individual within multiple sociocultural contexts where certain norms, beliefs and behaviours have certain value over others. But, as we argue in the final section of the chapter below, it is important also to consider other aspects of culture which also serve to legitimate and normalise image-based abuse behaviours, alongside cultures of gender hierarchy, domination and inequality.

Voyeurism, pornification and the age of user-generated content

Image-based sexual abuse is not only a manifestation of gender inequality, domination and gender performance, it must also be contextualized within broader sociocultural contexts that are characterised by rapidly changing conceptualisations of privacy, new forms of pornography, voyeurism and exhibitionism, and a deep societal fixation with visuality and technological innovation. Of course, the *fields* associated with these trends (to use Bourdieu's language) are not devoid of the hierarchies and relations of symbolic power derived from the *broader field* of gender, race and class inequalities (Bourdieu & Wacquant, 2007). In this section, we briefly examine these trends in visual culture to understand the demand for user-generated sexual or pornographic content that is non-consensual.

Voyeurism and performative surveillance

Although the term "revenge porn" is problematised because (among other things) it likens the non-consensual taking or sharing of nude or sexual images to the production of commercial pornography (Henry & Powell, 2015), non-consensual nude or sexual images are nonetheless taken or shared in some cases for sexual gratification and social status building purposes (see Chapter 4). Given that there is so much commercial and amateur pornography available to users online for free, it is useful to reflect on why there is a demand (or indeed a marketplace of sorts) for nude or sexual images that have been produced or distributed *without consent*. In particular, how do such images come to have significant social capital?

To explain the "cultural appetite" for non-consensual nude or sexual imagery, we need to first turn our attention to voyeurism. According to the American Psychiatric Association's Diagnostic and Statistical Manual-V (APA DSM-V), a voyeuristic disorder is defined as "intentionally spying on unsuspecting people who are naked, getting undressed, or participating in sexual activities". This is narrowly restricted to psychopathology beyond the norm – where a person is over the age of 18 years, has persistent and intense sexual arousal from deliberately observing the unsuspecting person over a period of at least six months, and has either acted on these sexual urges or is significantly distressed or impaired by them (APA, 2013). The DSM (and psychiatry more broadly) is by and large focused on psychological, pathological and biological factors with little reference to the social and cultural contexts that shape and produce these affective states in individuals. For example, depression is often treated not as an illness that may in part be caused by social dislocation and disconnection, but by low serotonin levels. Similarly, in relation to voyeurism, the DSM treats voyeurism as a psychopathological deficit and fails to account for the complex manifestations of voyeurism within popular culture which are facilitated and normalised by reality television, pornography and social media, and in turn, are internalised by social agents. This is what Calvert (2000: 2) describes as the obsession with "the mass consumption of information about others' apparently real and unguarded lives". Thus, while voyeurism continues to be conceptualised as a form of mental illness in law and medical discourses, voyeurism trends in contemporary settings, particularly relating to non-consensual nude or sexual imagery, reflect a "more pervasive practice ... that informs, and perhaps infects, much of our modern world" (Green, 2018: 213). Indeed, the production and dissemination of non-consensual nude or sexual imagery in contemporary digital societies is part of the ever-encroaching external and voyeuristic gaze into people's private lives.

This is by no means divorced or separate from the pervasive influence and encroachment of digital surveillance. This is manifested in two ways. First, "surveillance capitalism" is what Zuboff (2019: 53) argues is an unprecedented form of capitalism where our "lives are plundered for behavioral data" by global technology companies, who use machine learning and algorithms to sell information about us to business customers, particularly advertisers for the purpose of economic profit. Second, those same technology companies, through their platforms and services, have created the norms and means through which individual users can themselves engage in "performative surveillance" in the form of tracking, monitoring and observing other users on social media, whether that be romantic partners, friends, acquaintances or strangers (e.g., Marshall, 2012; Westlake, 2008).

Combined with increasing surveillance (including the more voyeuristic forms), whether from above or below, digital culture is also increasingly marked by the democratisation of production, where ordinary internet users are not simply passive recipients of content but also producers of content. This is particularly evident within the online pornography economy where the diversification of pornography (e.g., "queer porn" or "women-friendly porn") (Attwood, 2018; McNair, 2017) has seen an exponential growth in user-generated pornographic content or "amateur pornography" online over the past few decades. McNair (2017: 29) describes this as "citizen porn" or "DIY porn" – pornography made by amateurs "armed with digital cameras and the facility to upload their video" within a globalised online network on social connectivity and interactivity.

And yet, it is not simply the capacity of digital technologies that enable individual users to produce their own content, but there is also a cultural yearning for authentic or "real" content, as strongly indicated by the popularity of, for example, reality television and amateur pornography. According to Paasonen (2010: 1305), amateur pornography's appeal lies in the "*fantasy of realness*, directness and authenticity, supported by low-fi aesthetic and lay performers" (emphasis added). Amateur pornography thus reflects a valorisation of the "real", alongside the rejection of commercially produced pornography. But as L'Hoiry (2019) explains in relation to reality television, it is perhaps more complicated than this. Although audiences are seeking to encounter the "real" in their consumption of visual content, L'Hoiry (2019: n.p.) argues that realism in digital media is attractive to audiences because of "the fluid nature of realism, performance and identity" and the pleasure that is derived from not knowing for sure what is real and what is fake.

While understanding these broader social trends in digital media (or pornography more specifically) helps to explain the exponential growth in user-generated content (including amateur pornography), it does not sufficiently explain why there is a particular demand or market for *non-consensual* nude or sexual imagery online. In Henry and Flynn's (2019) digital ethnography, they observed that *non-consensual material* (e.g., "hidden web cam", "deepfakes", "revenge porn") are popular genres in mainstream pornography (see also McGlynn & Vera-Gray, 2018). This includes stylised (fake) representations of non-consensual acts, as well as authentic intimate imagery created and shared without the knowledge or consent of the subject depicted in the image. On one site, for instance, there were 9,160 videos under the category "Leaked" (a colloquial term used to describe content that is shared without consent), 15,965 videos under "Hidden Cam" (secret cam recordings of upskirting or downblousing, women undressing or engaged in a sexual act), 16,619 videos under the category "Ex-girlfriend" and 17,358 videos under the "Revenge Porn" category (see Henry & Flynn, 2019).

These findings on the popularity of non-consensual pornographic genres support those of another study by the cybersecurity company, Deeptrace (Ajder et al., 2019), which discovered 14,678 deepfake videos on the internet, with 96% of those being deepfake pornography exclusively of women (mostly female actors and musicians). The authors note that deepfakes are growing in popularity, with an increase of 100% of videos being made available online between December 2018 and August 2019, and on the top four deepfake websites, more than 134 million views of videos targeting women celebrities.

It is again useful to ask about the appeal of deepfakes and other forms of image-based sexual abuse. In relation to pornographic texts more broadly,

Braidotti (2011: 200) suggests that such text discloses and reveals "actions and interactions that are commonly kept private". She notes that the pornographic text is a *"confessional genre that brings the intimate, the forbidden, and the shameful into full vision and representation"* (emphasis added). Although both commercially produced and amateur pornography can bring the taboo of sexuality into full view, non-consensually produced or shared content may be considered a more "authentic" representation imbued with ambiguity that certain audiences might find gratifying. As we have explored in this chapter, image-based sexual abuse must be understood within the broader cultures of visuality and voyeurism, as well as gender and identity practices of the "self" (as gendered). In this way, it is complex and cannot be explained by a single-factor theory.

Conclusion

Images are *embodied* because they have a "genesis in material production" (Kappeler, 1986: n.p.), and are identity-shaping because they represent that which we reject or disavow within ourselves; that is, the maternal object that created us (Kristeva, 1982), or the vulnerability (Gavey, 2019) that is inherently marked as "other", abject and feminine. Non-consensually produced or shared images are thus not merely representational, but function also as relational "objects of exchange" (Bourdieu & Wacquant, 2007) among producers, distributors and consumers, and can be understood as part of the performance of gender by subjects. As we have argued in this chapter, we must examine image-based sexual abuse in context – not exclusively as a gendered phenomenon but also, as a reflection of contemporary visual culture.

This chapter has drawn on feminist, criminological and philosophical perspectives to contextualise image-based sexual abuse within broader trends around digitisation, the over-saturation of visual imagery, online pornography and the existing structures of gendered power relations. We argue that the production and distribution of non-consensual intimate imagery online, through the invocation of broader norms and values around gender and sexuality, is a source of identity-negotiation for producers, traders and consumers of such images, which is achieved through the debasement, dispossession, reduction and commodification of those depicted in the images.

While some feminist criminological theories provide a useful starting point, it is important that feminist scholars continue to theorise the causes and consequences of online abuse and harassment. This will further help to inform best practice education, prevention and awareness of image-based sexual abuse that is designed to address gender inequality, foster respectful relationships and dismantle the problematic norms, values and attitudes around gender and sexuality.

Acknowledgements

With permission of Palgrave Macmillan, this chapter draws on a small number of excerpts from Henry, N., & Flynn, A. (2020). Image-based sexual abuse: A feminist criminological approach. In T. Holt & A. M. Bossler (eds.), *The Palgrave handbook of international cybercrime and cyberdeviance.* Cham: Palgrave Macmillan.

Notes

1 Note that in this chapter we do not engage with evolutionary perspectives on image-based sexual abuse, nor do we explore in detail psychological theories on individual psychopathology.
2 Several studies have empirically examined the applicability of routine activities theory to technology-facilitated victimisation. For instance, Reyns et al. (2011) found that the measures of each theoretical concept – proximity/exposure to offenders, absence of guardianship and target attractiveness – were significantly related to cyberstalking victimisation, with online deviance having the strongest effect on all forms of victimisation. Bossler et al. (2012), on the other hand, found that measures assessing proximity to motivated offenders were more significantly related to online victimisation compared with guardianship or target attractiveness.

References

Ajder, H., Patrini, G., Cavalli, F., & Cullen, L. (2019). *The state of deepfakes: Landscape, threats, and impact.* Amsterdam: Deeptrace.
American Psychiatric Association (APA). (2013). *Diagnostic and statistical manual of mental disorders* (5th edn). Arlington, VA: American Psychiatric Publishing.
Andrejevic, M. (2004). The work of watching one another: Lateral surveillance, risk, and governance. *Surveillance & Society, 2*, 479–497.
Antevska, A., & Gavey, N. (2015). "Out of sight and out of mind": Detachment and men's consumption of male sexual dominance and female submission in pornography. *Men and Masculinities, 18*(5), 605–629.
Arendt, H. (1963). *Eichmann in Jerusalem: A report on the banality of evil.* New York: Viking Press.
Attwood, F. (2018). Women's pornography. In K. Harrison & C. A. Ogden (eds.), *Pornographies: Critical positions* (pp. 49–69). Chester: University of Chester Press.
Bandura, A. (1971). *Social learning theory.* New York: General Learning Press.
Bandura, A. (1986). *Social foundations of thought and action: A social cognitive theory.* Englewood Cliffs, NJ: Prentice-Hall.
Baron, L., & Straus, M. A. (1987). Four theories of rape: A macrosocial analysis. *Social Problems, 34*(5), 467–489.
Belknap, J., & Holsinger, K. (2006). The gendered nature of risk factors for delinquency. *Feminist Criminology, 1*(1), 48–71.
Bossler, A. M., Holt, T. J., & May, D. C. (2012). Predicting online harassment victimization among a juvenile population. *Youth & Society, 44*(4), 500–523.
Bourdieu, P., & Wacquant, L. J. D. (2007). *An invitation to reflexive sociology.* Cambridge, UK: Polity Press.

Braidotti, R. (2011). *Nomadic subjects: Embodiment and sexual difference in contemporary theory.* New York: Columbia University Press.

Braithwaite, J. (1979). *Inequality, crime, and public policy.* London; Boston, MA: Routledge.

Broidy, L. M., & Agnew, A. (1997). Gender and crime: A general strain theory perspective. *Journal of Research in Crime and Delinquency, 34*(3), 275–306.

Brown, W. (1995). *States of injury: Power and freedom in late modernity.* Princeton, NJ: Princeton University Press.

Brownmiller, S. (1975). *Against our will: Men, women and rape.* London: Penguin Books.

Burgess-Proctor, A. (2006). Intersections of race, class, gender, and crime: Future directions for feminist criminology. *Feminist Criminology, 1*(1), 27–47.

Burns, A. (2015). In full view: Involuntary porn and the postfeminist rhetoric of choice. In C. Nally & A. Smith (eds.), *Twenty-first century feminism* (pp. 93–118). London: Palgrave Macmillan.

Calvert, C. (2000). *Voyeur nation: Media, privacy, and peering in modern culture.* Boulder, CO: Westview Press.

Carrington, K., McIntosh, A., & Scott, J. (2010). Globalization, frontier masculinities and violence: Booze, blokes and brawls. *British Journal of Criminology, 50,* 393–413.

Carrington, K., & Scott, J. (2008). Masculinity, rurality, and violence. *British Journal of Criminology, 48*(5), 641–666.

Chesney, R., & Citron, D. K. (2019). Deep fakes: A looming challenge for privacy, democracy, and national security. *California Law Review, 107,* 1753–1820.

Clark, L. M. G., & Lewis, D. J. (1977). *Rape: The price of coercive sexuality.* Toronto: Women's Press.

Cohen, A. K. (1955). *Delinquent boys: The culture of the gang.* New York: Free Press.

Cohen, L., & Felson, M. (1979). Social change and crime rate trends: A routine activity approach. *American Sociological Review, 44,* 588–608.

Connell, R. W. (1987). *Gender and power.* Oxford: Polity Press.

Connell, R. W., & Messerschmidt, J. W. (2005). Hegemonic masculinity: Rethinking the concept. *Gender & Society, 19*(6), 829–859.

DeKeseredy, W. S. (1988). Woman abuse in dating relationships: The relevance of social support theory. *Journal of Family Violence, 3,* 1–13.

DeKeseredy, W. S., & Schwartz, M. D. (1993). Male peer support and woman abuse: An expansion of DeKeseredy's model. *Sociological Spectrum, 13,* 393–413.

DeKeseredy, W. S., & Schwartz, M. D. (2010). Friedman economic policies, social exclusion, and crime: Toward a gendered left realist subcultural theory. *Crime, Law and Social Change, 54,* 159–170.

DeKeseredy, W. S., & Schwartz, M. D. (2016). Thinking sociologically about image-based sexual abuse: The contribution of male peer support theory. *Sexualization, Media, & Society, 2*(4). doi: 10.1177/2374623816684692.

Durkheim, É. (1984). *The division of labor in society* (W. D. Halls, trans.). New York: The Free Press. (Original work published 1893).

Dye, J. (2015, August 9). Revenge porn website operator claims "free speech" defence. *Sydney Morning Herald.* Retrieved from www.smh.com.au/entertainment/tv-and-radio/revenge-porn-website-operator-claims-free-speech-defence-20150809-giv74g.html.

Flood, M. (2008). Men, sex, and homosociality: How bonds between men shape their sexual relations with women. *Men and Masculinities, 10*(3), 339–359.

Garfinkel, H. (1967). *Studies in ethnomethodology.* Englewood Cliffs, NJ: Prentice-Hall.

Gavey, N. (2019). *Just sex? The cultural scaffolding of rape* (2nd edn). London; New York: Routledge.

Goffman, E. (1977). The arrangement between the sexes. *Theory and Society, 4*(3), 301–331.

Gorman, G. (2019). *Troll hunting.* Melbourne, VIC: Hardie Grant Publishing.

Grabosky, P. (2001). Virtual criminality: Old wine in new bottles? *Social & Legal Studies, 10,* 243–249.

Green, S. P. (2018). To see and be seen: Reconstructing the law of voyeurism and exhibitionism. *American Criminal Law Review, 55*(2), 203–258.

Heise, L. L. (1998). Violence against women: An integrated, ecological framework. *Violence Against Women, 4*(3), 262–290.

Henry, N., & Flynn, A. (2019). Image-based sexual abuse: Online distribution channels and illicit communities of support. *Violence Against Women, 25*(16), 1932–1955.

Henry, N., & Powell, A. (2015). Beyond the "sext": Technology-facilitated sexual violence and harassment against adult women. *Australian & New Zealand Journal of Criminology, 48*(1), 104–118.

Holt, T. J., & Bossler, A. M. (2008). Examining the applicability of lifestyle-routine activities theory for cybercrime victimization. *Deviant Behavior, 30*(1), 1–25.

Jane, E. A. (2014). "Your a ugly, whorish, slut": Understanding e-bile. *Feminist Media Studies, 14*(4), 531–546.

Jewkes, R. (2012). *Rape perpetration: A review.* Pretoria: Sexual Violence Research Initiative.

Jordan, J. (2018). Surveying the womanscape: Objectification, self-objectification and intimate partner violence. In K. Fitz-Gibbon, S. Walklate, J. McCulloch & J. Maher (eds.), *Intimate partner violence, risk and security: Securing women's lives in a global world* (pp. 88–106). New York: Routledge.

Kappeler, S. (1986). *The pornography of representation.* Cambridge, UK: Polity Press.

Kelly, L. (1988). *Surviving sexual violence.* Cambridge, UK: Polity Press.

Kristeva, J. (1982). *Powers of horror: An essay on abjection* (L. S. Roudiez, trans.). New York: Columbia University Press.

Lapidot-Lefler, N., & Barak, A. (2012). Effects of anonymity, invisibility, and lack of eye-contact on toxic online disinhibition. *Computers in Human Behavior, 28*(2), 434–443.

L'Hoiry, X. (2019). *Love Island,* social media, and sousveillance: New pathways of challenging realism in reality TV. *Frontiers in Sociology, 4,* article 59. doi: 10.3389/fsoc.2019.00059.

Malamuth, N. M., Sockloskie, R. J., Koss, M., & Tanaka, J. S. (1991). Characteristics of aggressors against women: Testing a model using a national sample of college students. *Journal of Consulting and Clinical Psychology, 59,* 670–681.

Marcum, C. D., Higgins, G. E., & Ricketts, M. L. (2014). Sexting behaviors among adolescents in rural North Carolina: A theoretical examination of low self-control and deviant peer association. *International Journal of Cyber Criminology, 8*(2), 68–78.

Marshall, T. C. (2012). Facebook surveillance of former romantic partners: Associations with postbreakup recovery and personal growth. *Cyberpsychology, Behavior, and Social Networking, 15*(10), 521–526.

Marshall, W. L., & Barbaree, H. E. (1990). An integrated theory of the etiology of sexual offending. In W. L. Marshall, D. R. Laws, & H. E. Barbaree (eds.), *Handbook of sexual assault: Issues, theories, and treatment of the offender* (pp. 257–275). New York: Plenum.

McGlynn, C., & Vera-Gray, F. (2018, November 23). No woman in a public place is free from the risk of upskirting – We must do more to tackle image-based sexual abuse. *Huffington Post.* Retrieved from www.huffingtonpost.co.uk/entry/upskirting-law-sexual-harassment_uk_5bf7c501e4b088e1a6888e47.

McNair, B. (2017). *Porno? Chic!: How pornography changed the world and made it a better place.* London; New York: Routledge.

Merton, R. (1938). Social structure and anomie. *American Sociological Review, 3*(5), 672–682.

Navarro, J. N., & Jasinski, J. L. (2012). Going cyber: Using routine activities theory to predict cyberbullying experiences. *Sociological Spectrum, 32*(1), 81–94.

Nietzsche, F. (1969). *On the genealogy of morals* (W. Kaufmann & R. J. Hollingdale, trans.). New York: Vintage. (Original work published 1887).

Nussbaum, M. C. (2010). Objectification and internet misogyny. In S. Levmore & M. C. Nussbaum (eds.), *The offensive internet: Speech, privacy, and reputation* (pp. 68–90). Cambridge, MA; London: Harvard University Press.

Office of the eSafety Commissioner (OeSC). (2019). *Understanding the attitudes and motivations of adults who engage in image-based abuse: Summary report.* Melbourne, VIC: Social Research Centre. Retrieved from www.esafety.gov.au/sites/default/files/2019-10/Research_Report_IBA_Perp_Motivations.pdf.

O'Sullivan, C. (1993). Fraternities and the rape culture. In E. Buchward, P. Fletcher, & M. Roth (eds.), *Transforming a rape culture* (pp. 23–30). Minneapolis: Milkweed Editions.

Paasonen, S. (2010). Labors of love: Netporn, Web 2.0, and the meanings of amateurism. *New Media & Society, 12*(8), 1297–1312.

Paris, B., & Donovan, J. (2019). *Deepfakes and cheap fakes: The manipulation of audio and visual evidence.* New York: Data & Society. Retrieved from https://datasociety.net/wp-content/uploads/2019/09/DS_Deepfakes_Cheap_FakesFinal-1.pdf.

Pinchevsky, G. M., & Wright, E. M. (2012). The impact of neighborhoods on intimate partner violence and victimization. *Trauma, Violence, and Abuse, 13*(2), 112–132.

Powell, A., & Henry, N. (2017). *Sexual violence in a digital age.* London: Palgrave Macmillan.

Renzetti, C. A. (2013). *Feminist criminology.* London: Routledge.

Reyns, B. W., Burek, M. W., Henson, B., & Fisher, B. S. (2013). The unintended consequences of digital technology: Exploring the relationship between sexting and cybervictimization. *Journal of Crime and Justice, 36*(1), 1–17.

Reyns, B. W., Henson, B., & Fisher, B. S. (2011). Being pursued online: Applying cyberlifestyle-routine activities theory to cyberstalking victimization. *Criminal Justice and Behavior, 38*(11), 1149–1169.

Ringrose, J., & Walkerdine, V. (2008). Regulating the abject: The TV make-over as site of neo-liberal reinvention toward bourgeois femininity. *Feminist Media Studies, 8*(3), 227–246.

Schwartz, M. D., & Pitts, V. L. (1995). Exploring a feminist routine activities approach to explaining sexual assault. *Justice Quarterly, 12*(1), 9–31.

Suler, J. (2004). The online disinhibition effect. *CyberPsychology & Behavior, 7*(3), 321–326.

Sutherland, E. H., & Cressey, D. R. (1974). *Criminology.* Philadelphia, PA: Lippincott.

Thornhill, R., & Palmer, C. T. (2000). *A natural history of rape: Biological bases of sexual coercion.* Cambridge, MA: MIT Press.

Van Ouytsel, J., Ponnet, K., & Walrave, M. (2018). Cyber dating abuse victimization among secondary school students from a lifestyle-routine activities theory perspective. *Journal of Interpersonal Violence, 33*(17), 2767–2776.

Walzer, M. (1992). *Just and unjust wars: A moral argument with historical illustrations* (2nd edn). New York: Basic Books.

Ward, T., & Siegert, R. J. (2002). Rape and evolutionary psychology: A critique of Thornhill and Palmer's theory. *Aggression and Violent Behaviour, 7*(2), 145–168.

West, C., & Zimmerman, D. H. (1987). Doing gender. *Gender & Society, 1*(2), 125–151.

Westlake, E. J. (2008). Friend me if you Facebook: Generation Y and performative surveillance. *The Drama Review, 52*(4), 21–40.

White, R., Haines, F., & Asquith, N. (2017). *Crime & criminology* (6th edn). South Melbourne, VIC: Oxford University Press.

Wolfe, S. E., Marcum, C. D., Higgins, G. E., & Ricketts, M. L. (2016). Routine cell phone activity and exposure to sext messages: Extending the generality of routine activity theory and exploring the etiology of a risky teenage behaviour. *Crime & Delinquency, 62*(5), 614–644.

Yar, M. (2005). The novelty of "cybercrime": An assessment in light of routine activity. *European Journal of Criminology, 2*(4), 407–427.

Zimbardo, P. (1970). The human choice. Individuation, reason, and order versus deindividuation, impulse, and chaos. In W. J. Arnold & D. Levine (eds.), *Nebraska symposium on motivation 1969* (pp. 237–307). Lincoln: University of Nebraska Press.

Zuboff, S. (2019). *The age of surveillance capitalism: The fight for a human future at the new frontier of power.* London: Profile Books.

Chapter 6

The missing culture of consent

Shifting social norms on image-sharing, sexual autonomy and harm

Introduction

Digital communications have not only influenced the commission of sexual harms, but also the negotiation of consensual sexual self-expression, intimacies and practices more broadly. The preceding chapters have clearly shown that image-based sexual abuse is not a single, universal type of abusive behaviour or experience. For some victim-survivors, the experience of a nude or sexual image being taken, shared or threatened to be shared without consent is unmistakably a traumatic one. The reality for many victim-survivors is that they experience image-based sexual abuse as a sexual violation, a tool for coercive control in domestic violence situations, and/or as a powerful threat that enables blackmail and sexual exploitation. Women are more likely to experience image-based sexual abuse in conjunction with other abusive behaviours from the perpetrator and are more likely to report experiencing harmful impacts as a result of these behaviours. Some perpetrators of image-based sexual abuse describe their malicious motivations, such as wanting to embarrass, control or "get back at" the victim-survivor. A substantial proportion of image-based sexual abuse also occurs within peer and friendship contexts, with equally harmful impacts, and can similarly be understood as a form of abuse or harassment.

Together, these findings tell us that image-based sexual abuse is being used as a tool or strategy by perpetrators to carry out harassment, sexual violence or intimate partner violence in ways which both facilitate and extend the harms of that abuse (see also Douglas, Harris, & Dragiewicz, 2019). Yet, not all image-based sexual abuse fits with broader and familiar patterns of gender-based interpersonal violence, harassment and abuse. The findings of our survey research suggest that the extent of image-based sexual abuse may be similar for men as it is for women (as outlined in Chapter 2). In some instances, men experience these behaviours at slightly higher rates. Moreover, a minority of survey respondents who had ever experienced a nude or sexual image being used in some way without their express permission, described their experience as "funny" or "flattering", and some further reported experiencing no harmful impacts at all. There is also an overlap between those who have experienced image-based sexual abuse victimisation, and those who have engaged in image-based sexual abuse perpetration. These findings sit alongside the reality that in Australia, New Zealand and the United Kingdom, women remain overwhelmingly the victim-survivors of sexual violence and domestic abuse (both physical and coercive controlling behaviours) and most often from men.

This chapter seeks to disentangle the complexity of image-based sexual abuse behaviours which are, in many instances, a tool of very serious and harmful forms of abuse, whilst in others, a behaviour which is not experienced as overtly harmful. Holding these two seemingly contradictory sets of experiences together and attempting to understand how they might represent shifting norms and practices of sexual harm on the one hand, and sexual expression on the other, is not a straightforward task. Yet it is important for researchers in this field to do justice to the significant harms experienced by many victim-survivors of image-based sexual abuse, while acknowledging the complexity of non-consensual behaviour that might not always be experienced as harmful, but which nonetheless speaks to a broader cultural context in which the importance of consent is often minimised.

In order to navigate the complex spectrum of behaviours that constitute image-based sexual abuse, this chapter examines the *shifting social norms* in relation to intimate image taking and sharing, and how these might be interacting with persistent problematic social norms regarding sexual autonomy and consent. In the first section, we provide a brief overview of the popular narratives regarding image-based sexual abuse, foremost focusing on the framing of victim-survivors and perpetrators in the news media and education resources. The second section moves on to discuss some of the normative shifts in nude and sexual imagery as a mode of empowerment, libertarianism, representation and democratisation in the digital age, and we contextualise these with survey data regarding consensual digital dating and sexual self-image behaviours. In the third section, we engage with critiques of empowerment framings and highlight the unequal ways in which social, cultural and individual pressures to express a sexually agentic self have been theorised to impact on the "sexualisation" of young women in particular. In the fourth section, we extend on earlier discussions of the cultural scaffolding of rape and a "non-consent" culture that has arguably been amplified, or at least made more visible, in the digital age. Here, we present key findings from our survey regarding levels of support for responding to image-based sexual abuse behaviours as a crime, as well as the willingness of respondents to intervene when witnessing image-based sexual abuse behaviours among their peers. We then discuss what these findings suggest about shifting normative expectations regarding the use and misuse of nude or sexual images in the digital age.

From "sex scandal" to "sex crime": public narratives of image-based sexual abuse

The non-consensual taking and/or sharing of nude and sexual images of women is not a new phenomenon. As discussed in Chapter 1, in 1980 the American pornographic magazine *Hustler* started a monthly contest featuring reader-submitted photographs of naked women (see Franks, 2017; Hall & Hearn, 2017; Levendowski, 2014; Powell & Henry, 2017). Named "Beaver Hunt", the submitted images "were often accompanied by details about the woman: her hobbies, her sexual fantasies, and sometimes her name. Some of the photos were stolen. Exes submitted many more" (Levendowski, 2014, n.p.).

Several women sued the magazine for using their images without permission. In one case, the judge ruled that the publication of a nude image without the victim-survivor's consent in a "coarse and sex-centred magazine" was not only an invasion of privacy, but that Hustler had shown "reckless disregard for her right to be free from publication of a matter that would be *highly offensive* to a reasonable person" (*Wood v. Hustler Magazine*, 1984 (emphasis added)). As Hall and Hearn (2017) point out, there have been many other examples of the non-consensual sharing of nude or sexual imagery from polaroids, to photocopies, to leaked "sex tapes" both prior to and since that time.

In 2004, the word "sext", referring to sexual text messages via SMS (see Vogels, 2004), was first used. By 2008, media reports began focusing on an "explosion" of sexual image-sharing – "sexting" – among young people (Battersby, 2008). Also, in 2008, an American report by The National Campaign to Prevent Teen and Unplanned Pregnancy, stated that 20% of teenagers had sent or posted nude or semi-nude photos of themselves. Referred to as "teen sexting", news reports rarely made a distinction between consensual and non-consensual sexual image sharing, with both behaviours seen as sexually risky and problematic for youth, particularly young girls (see Albury & Crawford, 2012; Dobson & Ringrose, 2016; McGovern, Crofts, Lee, & Milivojevic, 2016). Where the non-consensual sharing of a nude or sexual image was the focus, it was often presented within a "sexting gone wrong" narrative, in which much of the fault could be traced to the person depicted in the image. Indeed, scholarly analysis of news media and education campaigns of the time have highlighted the common victim-blaming approach adopted in societal discourse, and the ways in which young women and girls were held responsible and repeatedly advised to abstain from sexting as a means to prevent the non-consensual misuse of their sexual images (Albury & Crawford, 2012; Döring, 2014; Powell & Henry, 2014; see also Chapter 8).

By 2010 however, we began to see some key shifts in reporting and the discursive framing of non-consensual nude and sexual imagery. The most well-known of the early "revenge pornography" websites was launched by a (then) 25-year old man, Hunter Moore. His website, IsAnyoneUp.

com, published user-contributed content, as well as illegally obtained non-consensual sexual images of women which were often accompanied by identifying information of the victim (also known as "doxing"). By 2011, news media started reporting on whether the site should be taken down as women began making complaints that their nude images were being published online without their consent (Errett, 2011). By 2012, after Moore had sold the site, it was taken down.

Self-described as the "revenge porn king", but elsewhere as the "most hated man on the internet" (Morris, 2012), Moore was later investigated by the FBI, resulting in a prison sentence of two and half years, as well as a fine of $500,000 for unauthorised access to a computer and aggravated identity theft. The Moore case helped to shift public understandings and popularised the term "revenge porn" to refer to the non-consensual sharing of nude or sexual images, typically of women and typically by a "jilted ex".

Some public commentary has continued the victim-blaming narrative, framing the non-consensual sharing of nude or sexual images as a "sex scandal" in which the scandalous behaviour is typically that of a young woman who "should have known better" than to have taken nude or sexual "selfies" in the first place (Marwick, 2017). When in 2007, nude photos of actor Vanessa Hudgens (then 18 years old) were shared online, a Disney spokesperson told *People Magazine*: "Vanessa has apologized for what was obviously a lapse in judgment. We hope she's learned a valuable lesson" ("Vanessa Hudgens 'embarrassed'", 2007). Media coverage at the time blatantly blamed Hudgens for her "mistake" in taking the "saucy snapshot" ("Vanessa Hudgens apologizes", 2007), rather than problematising the crime committed by the hacker responsible (Giles, 2019; Sunderland, 2017). Further examples of this victim-blaming narrative include news headlines (e.g., "Want to stop revenge porn? Just keep your clothes on!", see Johnson, 2014); public statements by senior police ("People just have to grow up … if you go out in the snow without clothes on you'll catch a cold – if you go on to the computer without your clothes on, you'll catch a virus", see AAP, 2016); and politicians ("The safest way to be is not to be sharing intimate pictures", Smith, 2019). Implicit in such victim-blaming narratives is the simultaneous excusing of the perpetrator and displacement of responsibility. It is not *their* behaviour that is seen as scandalous or wrong, rather the sharing of another person's nude or sexual image is seen as unsurprising, or even expected. In short, much public discourse has presented image-based sexual abuse within an overtly gendered double standard – namely, normalising men's sexual entitlement to women's bodies, whilst shaming and denying sexual subjectivity to women victim-survivors (see Marwick, 2017).

Yet, as Marwick (2017) argues, something happened in 2014 that shifted the public discourse from that of *sex scandal* to one of *sex crime*. Hundreds of nude photographs and other private information were leaked publicly after the Apple iCloud accounts of some 240 people were illegally accessed.

Among them were images of several celebrities including Jennifer Lawrence, Kirsten Dunst, Kate Upton and Vanessa Hudgens. This event came to be known as "Celebgate" (or "The Fappening" on 4Chan and Reddit). Rather than apologising from the position of a "shamed starlet" (see Valenti, 2014), actor Jennifer Lawrence gave an interview featured in *Vanity Fair* magazine, saying that:

> I started to write an apology, but I don't have anything to say I'm sorry for. ... It is not a scandal. It is a sex crime. It is a violation. ... Just because I'm a public figure, just because I'm an actress, it does not mean I asked for this. It is my body and it should be my choice. The fact it is not my choice is absolutely disgusting.
>
> ("Jennifer Lawrence calls", 2014)

Lawrence's palpable rage and powerful statement was widely praised and has arguably provided a clear alternative narrative for media engagement with the issue. Notably, the shift has come about at the same time as the introduction of specific legislation criminalising image-based sexual abuse in multiple jurisdictions globally, and as technology companies have started taking these harms more seriously (see Chapters 7 and 8).

More recently, some media reports have gone so far as to applaud the actions of victims, such as actress Bella Thorne, who "took the power back" by making her nudes public themselves in response to threats of blackmail (Abad-Santos, 2019). As columnist for *The Guardian* Eva Wiseman (2019) suggests, one way to remove the power of image-based sexual abuse is to proactively disclose your sexual images: "Everybody should post their nudes ... We need to inoculate ourselves against sexual shame" (Wiseman, 2019). It is an approach taken by other victims, celebrities and non-celebrities alike, who have received threats that their nude or sexual images would be posted online for all to see (e.g., Barrett-Ibarria, 2018). In 2017, Australian singer-songwriter Sia posted a nude image of herself on Twitter after a paparazzi company said that they had nude images which they were trying to sell for publication (Aswad, 2017). More recently, in August 2019, stand-up comedian Whitney Cummings posted a topless image of herself on Twitter after receiving threats that nude images would be released if she did not pay her blackmailers (Hosie, 2019). Thousands of users took to Twitter in support of Cummings posting their own "embarrassing" (and in some cases semi-nude images) with the trending hashtag #istandwithwhitney. In her original tweet Cummings (2019) said:

> They all must think I'm way more famous than I am, but they also must think I'm way more easily intimidated than I am. If anyone is gonna make money or likes off my nipple, it's gonna be me. So here it all is, you foolish dorks.

A further shift in media narratives has been the visibility of a broader range of victim-survivors of image-based sexual abuse. Despite the more common focus in media reports on women victim-survivors, some media articles are now recognising the extent and impacts of image-based sexual abuse on men and on sexual minorities. In 2016, YouTuber Davey Wavey, who has made a career speaking openly about his homosexuality, dating and sexual experiences, was alerted by fans that nude pictures of him had appeared online without his consent (Donovan, 2018). In an in-depth interview about his experiences, Davey talked about feeling sexy and proud when he first took the images and sent them to several different men. However, not only did the non-consensual publication of the images cause Davey anger, but he also faced a wave of online shaming and abuse from people who saw them (Donovan, 2018). It is an experience documented elsewhere, such that gay men in particular may face an additional risk of image-based sexual abuse, as well as others participating in harassment and hate online (Hall & Hearn, 2017; Waldman, 2019). For sexual minorities, there is a further implication of image-based sexual abuse which can be used to cause further abuse, harassment and harms by "outing" people, something media reports appear to be increasingly recognising (Reigstad, 2018). Yet as argued by Jessica Valenti (2014), columnist for *The Guardian:* "A culture of consent demands that both women and men ask for and receive it, and not proceed without it".

In summary, there is arguably a positive shift in public discourses away from victim-blaming and shaming, towards recognising the seriousness of image-based sexual abuse, albeit these are still largely focused on the victim-survivor, as opposed to the perpetrators. In media reports, there is an observable shift towards discourses that validate the rights to sexual autonomy and expression of particularly women and LGBTQI people, as discussed above. Increasingly, media reports emphasise that there is nothing inherently wrong with someone choosing to take and exchange nude or sexual images; that to do so is an expression of sexual liberty, and that the harms come from the violation of autonomy when those images are used without consent. In our previous research, we have likewise sought to recognise that much of the harm that perpetrators are able to cause through image-based sexual abuse is due to the social and cultural sexual taboos attached to those images (Powell, Henry, & Flynn, 2018). These social and cultural taboos are not, however, experienced evenly among society.

There is a long-established body of research demonstrating that powerful social norms regarding both women's and men's sexual expression and conduct continue to persist. For example, the sexual double standard by which women continue to be viewed as "sluts" for expressions of sexual agency and desire, whilst men are viewed as "studs" for demonstrating sexual promiscuity, conquest and domination (see e.g., Powell, 2010), is arguably evident in the differential impacts of image-based sexual abuse according to gender (see Chapter 3). At the same time, women's resistance to these traditional sexual taboos is arguably evident in the shifting victimisation narratives emerging that seek to emphasise women's sexual autonomy and empowerment through taking and choosing to share sexual images. Such resistance and agency in regaining sexual autonomy and empowerment through sexual self-imagery is also recognised in research on digital dating, particularly among sexual minority men and women.

For many LGBTQI identifying people, expression of their sexuality and/or gender identity in public spaces can too often result in harmful experiences from perpetrators of violence, harassment and/or discrimination (Konik & Cortina, 2008), and in many countries and local contexts has been (and continues to be) subject to social stigma and criminalisation (Arreola et al., 2015; Roberts, 2019). In this context, digital spaces have long provided a relatively safe environment in which to engage in sexual self-expression for many LGBTQI people, and the higher uptake of many digital platforms in the negotiation of sexual encounters by LGBTQI people can be understood within this historical and current cultural context (Albury & Byron, 2016; Waldman, 2019). It is our contention that in order to develop a more nuanced understanding of the differential prevalence and harms of image-based sexual abuse, it is vital to understand the shifting social norms on sexual image sharing itself as a form of empowerment and sexual expression.

Sexual empowerment, libertarianism and digital democratisation

Victim-blaming narratives in response to image-based sexual abuse are arguably an extension of victim-blaming narratives in response to other forms of sexual violence, harassment and abuse which predate the digital age. The "advice" typically offered to women – don't go out at night, don't wear short skirts, and don't get too drunk – have been translated in the digital realm into "don't date online" in the 1990s, and "don't take sexual selfies" in the 2000s (Powell & Henry, 2017). In other words, victim-blaming narratives rely on shaming and chastising women and girls for engaging in "dangerous" or "deviant" behaviours and environments in which they "should have known better", and therefore must bear some responsibility for the risk. Feminist scholars have long critiqued "crime prevention" approaches, arguing that women's liberty and participation in society should not be curtailed in order to manage men's violence towards them (Flynn, 2015). In a related vein, casting online dating and consensual sexual image-sharing as sexually "deviant" behaviour arguably extends heterosexist and homophobic narratives that are overlaid with victim-blaming in LGBTQI people's experiences of non-consensual sexual behaviours.

In addition to problematic tendencies towards victim-blaming and responsibilisation, the framing of digital dating and image-sharing behaviours as inherently deviant, dangerous or risky is arguably at odds with broader social changes in people's everyday sexual practices. As will be discussed further below, there are historically persistent cultural anxieties about particularly public forms and representations of sex and sexuality which have for many societies been seen as both private and taboo. Yet, as Mulholland (2015: 321) argues, "in profound ways, the historical function of the illicit to be secreted away is experiencing a serious revision". Drawing on a Foucauldian understanding of normalised sexual knowledge and practices being culturally and historically (re)produced through dominant discourses, she argues that constructions of normal and acceptable sexuality in many Western societies rely on "notions of respectability, adulthood, heteronormativity and the private, and establish normal as respectable, restrained and moral, based on a series of raced, classed and gendered assumptions" (Mulholland, 2015: 322).

Many scholars have argued that contemporary (and particularly Western) societies have experienced an observable shift towards more permissive sexual attitudes, including more public forms of sexual expression and representation, greater acceptance of a diversity of sexualities and sexual tastes, as well as new forms of online sexual encounters and practices (see e.g., Attwood, 2006; Kalms, 2016; Mulholland, 2018; Page Jeffery, 2018).

Contemporary opportunities for technology-facilitated sexual practice and expression, in particular, represent a disruption to traditional sexual norms, as they enable the experience of "intimate acts in 'public' space" (Attwood, 2006: 81), as well as blurring the experience of sexual "reality" and "representation" (see Wiley, 1999). Within technofeminist theorising more broadly, there have been optimistic accounts of the capacity of technology-facilitated sexual practices and representations to enable a greater democratisation of sexual experience (Bauman, 2003; Giddens, 1992; Hobbs, Owen, & Gerber, 2017; Wiley, 1999). In short, as human sexuality is no longer tied to the embodied norms, sexuality discourses and gender inequalities that are automatically at work in physical sexual encounters, a proliferation of creativity, diversity and equality in sexual practices are enabled online that can influence and transform embodied sexual practices. Within such frameworks, digital dating and sexual experiences are not only increasingly normalised, they also represent new opportunities for sexual expression and empowerment particularly for marginalised and/or minoritised groups, in a similar way to other arguments about technologies as a "democratising force" (see e.g., Castells, 2015).

There does appear to be evidence that digital dating and sexual practices are increasingly commonplace and "normal". For instance, international research into digital dating, as well as the consensual production and exchange of sexual images online or via digital technologies, repeatedly finds that these are normalised, "ordinary and unremarkable practice[s], for both men and women" (Albury & Byron, 2014: 142). For example, an Australian study (Smith et al., 2018) based on a 2012–2013 representative survey of sexual behaviour found that overall 12% of participants (14% men; 11% women) had ever engaged in online or smartphone app dating, with higher rates among younger people (14% for those aged 16–29 years; 16% for those aged 30–39 years) compared to older people (12% for those aged 40–49 years; 10% for those aged 50–59 years; and 6% for those aged 60–69 years), and among LGB respondents (43%) compared to heterosexuals (11%). A similar rate (15%) of participation in online dating was also reported in the Pew Research Center (2016) study in the United States, again with higher rates for younger populations (27% for those aged 18–24 years; 22% for those aged 25–34 years, 21% for those aged 35–44 years) compared to older people (13% for those aged 45–54 years; 12% for those aged 55–64 years; and 3% for those aged 65+ years).

In our 2019 survey of 6,109 Australian, New Zealand and United Kingdom respondents, we found that engagement in online dating behaviours was an extremely common experience. Overall, 4,537 (74.3%) had participated in one or more online dating behaviours, including via websites, email, text or mobile messaging and mobile dating applications. Behaviours included flirting, asking someone out for a date, asking someone to meet up for sex, and sending "sexy" messages. We found that participation in these digital dating behaviours was slightly higher for respondents in the United Kingdom (77.2%, n=1,565), followed by New Zealand (74.6%, n=1,512), and Australia (71.1%, n=1,460). There was no difference in behaviours according to gender, with males (73.4%, n=2,335) and females (75.2%, n=2,202) equally likely to report participating in one or more of the digital dating behaviours we asked about. Overall, we found that engagement in online dating behaviours was an extremely common experience.

There were, however, significant and large differences according to age, with younger people (particularly those aged 20–29 years, 89.5%, n=1,263) more likely than older people (particularly those aged 50–64 years, 49.8%, n=800) to have ever engaged in digital dating behaviour. This trend across age is not unexpected in light of both the higher technology uptake among young and middle adulthood, as well as the life-stage of active dating and sexual behaviour among these same cohorts. Our survey also found that LGB+ people (84.7%, n=575) were more likely to have engaged in digital dating behaviours as compared with heterosexuals (73%, n=3,962). This trend is consistent with the international literature which has highlighted the uptake of digital dating technologies among LGBTQI communities, largely as a tool for sexual safety, sexual self-expression, as well as for the negotiation and set-up of sexual encounters (Pew Research Center, 2016; Smith et al., 2018).

Of more direct relevance to the contextualisation of image-based sexual abuse is an understanding of the extent to which sexual self-image taking and sharing might be understood as increasingly normalised behaviours. Studies into the prevalence of sexual self-image behaviours have overwhelmingly focused on the experiences and practices of adolescents and young people; and problematically, some of this literature fails to make a distinction between consensual and non-consensual "sexting" behaviours or between text-based and image-based sexually explicit content (see Klettke, Hallford, & Mellor, 2014 for a review). However, there are some studies which provide an indication of the scale of young people's and adult engagement in consensual sexual self-image taking and exchange practices. For example, the oft-cited Associated Press and MTV (2009) youth survey found that 33% of young adults aged 18–24 years had sent a nude or semi-nude photo of themselves. Other studies have found as many as 51% of adults (aged 18+ years) who had sent nude photos of themselves (Wysocki & Childers, 2011), with one study of US undergraduate students (aged 18–30 years) finding that 60% reported having sent a nude image of themselves to someone else (Henderson & Morgan, 2011).

Our survey asked respondents about six consensual sexual self-image taking and/or exchange behaviours in a range of relational contexts. We asked people if they had ever sent someone a nude or sexual image, whether a photo or video, including people they had just met online, sexual partners or dates; whether they had made a nude or sexy video with a partner; whether they had asked someone to send them a nude or sexy image. Overall, we found that 47.1% (n=2,875) of respondents had engaged in one or more sexual self-image behaviours, with no significant differences by gender. There were slightly higher levels in the United Kingdom (50.4%, n=1,023), followed by New Zealand (45.9%, n=931) and Australia (44.8%, n=921). However, again, it was young adults aged 20–29 years who were most likely to have engaged in these sexual self-image behaviours (65.8%, n=928), as compared with those aged 30–39 years (57.9%, n=916), 16–19 years (46.9%, n=175), 40–49 years (43.9%, n=498) and 50–64 years (22.3%, n=358).

Our survey also found that LGB+ respondents (63.5%, n=431) were significantly more likely to have engaged in consensual sexual self-image behaviours than heterosexuals (45%, n=2,444). This finding is consistent with the international research cited above which similarly suggests a higher use of consensual sexual self-image behaviours among gay men in particular, and furthermore situates this uptake with both the relative safety of online spaces for sexual minorities, as well as the political and social meanings of sexual self-expression for groups whose sexuality has been traditionally marginalised and silenced (Albury & Byron, 2016; Phillips, 2015; Waldman, 2019).

Overall, there may be evidence of both a sexual libertarianism and digital democratisation effect in terms of which individuals and groups may be most likely to engage in both digital dating and sexual self-image behaviours. Importantly, this was also evident in our qualitative interviews with victim-survivors who had experienced the non-consensual taking, sharing, or threats to share, their nude or sexual images. In our interviews, for instance, some participants expressed positive views towards consensual sexual self-imagery. Indeed, the taking or sharing of sexual selfies was described by some participants as a pleasurable experience. For example, Chelsea (Aus) said "I think one of the little joys in life is sending cheeky photos. ... I don't think that should be taken away from people". This was also mentioned by Nicole (Aus), who said "I'd still send naked photos to my boyfriend. ... It's my right to do that and it's something that I like to do with intimate partners and it makes me feel sexy, it makes me feel good". Similarly, Esther (NZ) was very clear in making a distinction between her choice to express herself sexually, and the non-consensual behaviour of a perpetrator:

> The pictures weren't the problem. The problem was he's doing it without my consent. ... My mentality towards that is I'm not going to let a possibility [that the images could be shared without consent] change how I feel and how I express myself, because that's all it is. It's a possibility, and if that possibility happens I deal with it.

For some of our interview participants, actively resisting the bodily and sexual shaming that can often be directed at victim-survivors, and refusing to let the perpetrator of the abuse have a lasting impact on their sexual self-expression in other sexual relationships, was really important. As Maya (Aus) describes:

> It's so unfair that women are told ... 'Go be private, don't post this'. It's just so unfair. ... It's basically quite sexist. ... We need a more nuanced debate about this situation because I'm not going to change my social media presence and my online interactions, my online stuff, and I don't believe anyone should.

Far from inherently "risky" or "deviant", consensual sexual self-image behaviours are increasingly common and normalised across young and middle-aged adults from a range of backgrounds and experiences. The commonality of these online dating and consensual sexual self-image behaviours is vital to contextualising image-based sexual abuse and our policy responses to it. It is impractical to suggest that image-based sexual abuse can be prevented through discouraging individuals to engage in online dating and/or sexual self-image behaviours. Our research suggests that consensual engagement in these practices form an important and often positive experience in contemporary sexual negotiations and interactions. In other words, greater emphasis needs to be placed on the harms of non-consensual taking, sharing or threats to share nude or sexual images, rather than an abstinence approach to consensual sexual self-imagery (see also Chapter 8).

At the same time, there have been concerns raised in the international literature (Agostinone-Wilson, 2020; Dobson, 2015; Gill, 2011), that sexual libertarianism, empowerment and sexual self-expression is itself further overlaid with subtle pressures, and in some instances, unequal power relations. This theme was also evident in our interviews with victim-survivors of image-based sexual abuse both for the many women we spoke to, and some men. For example, Kyle (Aus) described contradictory feelings about exchanging sexual imagery with potential male partners, after his account was hacked and his nudes had been shared. On the one hand, Kyle spoke about the inherent pressures to "compete" in the dating/sexual marketplace:

> I was sick of I guess feeling like I have to compete with others for their attention through nude pictures. … I find that most people just really like receiving pictures and collecting pictures. … I know that even if I send nude pictures, it's not going to mean anything, like it's not going to go anywhere. It doesn't have the outcome that I thought it would once have led to, which is sustained attention or that it would lead to us meeting in person or anything like that.

On the other hand, Kyle spoke about "trying to resist the feeling of shame" through continuing to share nude pictures with selected recipients. It is a contradictory tension that many women interview participants also described, where there was simultaneously widespread acceptance of consensual sexual self-image behaviours as a common practice, and yet blaming and shaming of victim-survivors as if they have done something wrong when someone else shares that image without permission. Kerry (NZ) observed: "[The other students at my school] … called me a slut and it was just, it was, yeah, it was pretty much like, 'oh that's so gross', but it was really stupid because everyone did it".

There is a long-standing scholarly debate over what is often referred to as the "sexualisation" or "pornification" of culture thesis, in which girls and young women (in particular) are widely acknowledged to face unique pressures to represent themselves in accordance with narrow and objectified sexual identities. Though there are certainly limitations and justifiable critiques of overly simplified accounts of pornification (see Dobson, 2015), there are some parallels between this concept and the pressures experienced by some of our image-based sexual abuse victim-survivors to represent their sexual selves visually, as we discuss in the section below.

Gender, "sexualisation" and sexual pressure

There is a tension within current scholarly debates regarding consensual sexual self-images which has implications for how we might frame the nature of the problem when those images are shared without consent. In one way, it appears that digital sexual practices are broadening and that these practices, including sexual self-image taking and sharing, can be experienced as a pleasurable, empowering and a free expression of sexual tastes and identities. This first framing is arguably vital to understanding the uptake of such practices, particularly for those who have been traditionally marginalised, regulated and silenced. Taking and exchanging sexual self-images is also an expression of sexual agency for some in defiance of traditional cultures that have positioned both young women and sexual minorities as passive or deviant, rather than agentic and desiring.

However, it is also important to recognise that "developments in sexual taste, representation and practice may be related to positions of power, particularly in terms of class and gender relations" (Attwood, 2006: 82–83). This second framing draws attention to the ways that gendered power differentials may be at play not only in the impacts of image-based sexual abuse (see Chapter 3), but that the very nature of sexual selfies as a form of sexual experience and representation might already be unequal. There is a long-standing feminist critique of the "sexualisation" of contemporary Western societies, which is, on the one hand, lauded as a positive sign of libertarianism through public and explicit representations of sex and sexuality in our culture, yet on the other hand is obscuring persistent sexism and a continuing denial of women's sexual agency and pleasure (Allen & Carmody, 2012; Attwood, 2006; Gill, 2003). Gill (2003: 105), for instance, has warned that what appears to be a repertoire of new liberating and empowering sexual subjectivities available for women and girls in contemporary Western cultures, have "turned out to be objectification in new and even more pernicious guise". Likewise, Attwood (2006: 83) suggests that "women are offered a limited and commodified vision of active female sexuality in place of the new languages and practices of eroticism demanded by feminism".

The continuing uneven sexual objectification of women and girls has particular implications for their experiences of both consensual and non-consensual sexual image behaviours, or rather, a continuum of such behaviours with shades of pressure and coercion in between. For example, as Summers (2018: 104–105) argues, sexual self-images might be understood "less as empowering freedom and more as an emerging compulsive duty; a growing submission to a forced choice ... [that] perpetuates a brutally patriarchal and misogynistic 'exchange of women'". Meanwhile, Ringrose, Tolman and Ragonese's (2019) research with young racially diverse women regarding their consensual sexual imagery suggests this might be seen through a lens of socially and culturally pressured behaviours that reinforce both traditional gender norms and racialised norms valuing young women primarily as sexual objects.

Similarly, though young heterosexual men's engagement with the sexual self-imagery of women might be understood partly through feminist analyses of unequal power and feelings of sexual entitlement, young men too arguably face a continuum of sexual pressure to engage with sexual imagery in particular ways consistent with normative masculinities (further discussed below). Such social and cultural norms also interact with sexism, heterosexism and homophobia, such that young men can experience bullying and harassment in relation to their sexuality for *not* engaging in the exchange of sexual imagery of women (see Powell, 2010). Meanwhile for LGB+ young people there may be distinct, though not unrelated, pressures to engage in sexual self-imagery as a form of sexual empowerment and resistance against heteronormative power structures. There is a notable lack of research into these experiences, particularly for young LGB+ women.

Our survey asked participants about four pressured or unwanted sexual self-image behaviours, including whether they had ever: Sent someone a nude or sexual image when they didn't really want to; felt pressured to send someone a nude or sexual image when they didn't really want to; received a nude or sexual image of someone when they had not requested it; and/or received an image of someone's genitals when they had not requested it. Overall, we found that 47.2% (n=2,882) of our respondents had experienced one or more of these unwanted behaviours, with similar rates in Australia (45.3%, n=930), New Zealand (47.4%, n=960) and the United Kingdom (48.9%, n=992), as well as for women (46.8%, n=1,489) and men (47.6%, n=1,393). This is a very comparable figure to those who had also reported engaging in *consensual* sexual self-image behaviours (47.1%, n=2,875), and when these two groups of experiences are combined, over half of our whole survey sample (56.2%, n=3,436) had experienced one or more sexual self-image behaviours (whether consensual or unwanted). Individuals who were most likely to report experiencing unwanted sexual self-image behaviours were: Those aged 20–29 years (67.7%, n=955), compared to 16–19 year olds (58.4%, n=218), 30–39 year olds (54.4%, n=861); 40–49 year olds (41.7%, n=473); and 50–64 year olds (23.3%, n=375). LGB+ respondents (67.6%, n=459) were also more likely to report experiencing unwanted sexual self-image behaviours, compared to heterosexuals (44.6%, n=2,423). There were no significant differences by gender, either for those respondents identifying as heterosexual or for LGB+ respondents.

It is important to note that in our survey, we did not ask whether respondents had received persistent requests (in other words pressure or coercion) from someone else to send or share a sexual self-image, but rather we asked about unwanted sexual self-image behaviours. However, there is research suggesting that pressure and coercion to take and send a nude or sexual self-image is a significant issue, and one that may differ in nature according to gender. For instance, in an American study, Drouin, Ross and Tobin (2015) found that one fifth of their sample (undergraduate students (n=480)) were coerced into taking explicit images in the context of an intimate partner relationship. They found that while more women than men engaged in unwanted sexting, "sexting coercion victimization" was common among both men and women, and these individuals were more likely to experience traditional forms of intimate partner violence. In another study, Wood, Barter, Stanley, Aghtaie, and Larkins (2015) found that over a quarter of girls in England who had sent a sexual image had been pressured by a partner to do so, and almost half had sent the image to prove their commitment.

The commonality of these experiences among younger adults and LGB+ respondents may reflect a combination of pressure from others, as well as social and cultural pressure to represent oneself. The research literature provides a stronger basis for understanding young women's experiences in this context, where pressures may be subtle rather than received directly from someone else. For instance, young women may feel that it is expected that they send sexual self-images even if they do not really want to; they may feel that they will not be liked by others unless they choose to represent themselves as sexually desirable in particular image-based representations; and they may feel that they will be judged as "frigid" for not representing themselves in accordance with the libertarian empowerment discourses of contemporary femininity (see Gill, 2003). There is less research into the social and cultural pressures, or the "will to represent" one's sexually agentic self for sexual minorities (to paraphrase Foucault, see also Yar, 2012). In other words, little is known about the social and cultural normative expectations to display one's sexual identity, self-expression and tastes in digital environments that may, in turn, form a kind of pressured experience for individuals. Nonetheless, some research is suggestive of related, though differential, social and cultural power structures at play. Young men, for example, are also impacted by cultural pressures to represent themselves in accordance with particular normative expectations of masculinity and sexual conquest (Lasén & Garcia, 2015), though with arguably different effects, such as contributing to women's differential receipt of unsolicited genital images for instance.

A key finding of our research (discussed in Chapter 3) is that when a perpetrator uses a nude or sexual image in the context of sexual assault, harassment, bullying, stalking or domestic violence, there are extensive harms to victim-survivors. At the same time, sexuality, sexual agency and identity are important aspects of people's self-representation and experience – it would be too simplistic to suggest that all sexual imagery is pressured, or that every image that goes onto to be used in a way that was not explicitly agreed to is then experienced as sexual abuse.

Throughout this book, we have argued that although our survey found that the overall extent of image-based sexual abuse may not differ by gender, its nature and effects are experienced unevenly by different groups (see Chapter 2). For example, an image shared without consent might not immediately result in further harmful effects; it may take months or even years for an image to be shared in ways that then result in further harassment, harm and subsequent distress to a victim-survivor. Some image-based sexual abuse victim-survivors may not yet know what the negative impacts may be in the future. Similarly, just because a proportion of self-reported image-based sexual abuse perpetrators describe their motivations as being "funny" or "flirty", does not mean that victim-survivors experienced these behaviours in the same way.

The final section below seeks to further unpack contemporary social norms regarding the non-consensual sharing of nude or sexual images, through an exploration of our survey respondents' self-reported attitudes. In short, despite this range of different contexts and potential harmful impacts of image-based sexual abuse for victim-survivors, our research has sought to explore the levels of community support for taking image-based sexual abuse seriously as a harm.

Bystanders and cultural support for challenging image-based sexual abuse

One way to gauge the extent to which the community takes image-based sexual abuse seriously as a harm is to examine bystander intentions to intervene in image-based sexual abuse behaviours when they are observed. In our survey, we asked respondents a set of questions to gauge bystander intentions, peer support for taking action, as well as whether participants had actually taken some action when they had the opportunity to do so. We found that over two-thirds of the respondents (67.5%, n=4,124) across all three countries reported that they either *would* say or do something to express their disapproval, or *would like to* say or do something (but didn't know how), if someone showed or sent them a nude or sexual image of another person without that person's consent. Female respondents (77.9%, n=2,477) were more likely than males (56.3%, n=1,647) to say that they would, or would like to, take action. Perhaps unsurprisingly, we found that there were also differences between those who had experienced or engaged in image-based sexual abuse and those who had not. For instance, respondents who had no experience either as victims or perpetrators were most likely to report that they would, or would want to, say or do something (73.1%, n=2,624), followed by victims of image-based sexual abuse (70.1%, n=1,016). This is compared to those who had engaged in perpetration only (56.5%, n=121), or those who had mixed experiences as both perpetrators and victims (42.4%, n=363). Overall, what these bystander intentions data suggest is that most of the survey respondents believe that the sharing of a nude or sexual image without a person's consent is a serious enough harm that warrants taking action to intervene.

Decades of research into bystander action in response to other forms of sexual violence and harassment has found that in addition to intentions to intervene, individuals need to feel as though they would have the support of their peers in order to actually take action (see e.g., Brown, Banyard, & Moynihan, 2014). A majority of respondents (60.2%, n=3,679) reported that they believed they would have the support of most or all of their friends for saying or doing something to express disapproval, and a further 19.1% (n=1,164) reported that they would have the support of some or a few of their friends for taking such actions, if someone showed or sent them a nude or sexual image of another person without that person's permission. Once again, there were significant gender differences, with more female respondents (65.9%, n=2,096) than males (54.1%, n=1,583) reporting that they felt they would have the support of all or most of their friends for taking action as a bystander. Likewise, those who either had no experiences of image-based sexual abuse (59.8%, n=2,147), as well as those who only had victimisation experiences (60.3%, n=874), were more likely to say that they would have the support of their friends for intervening as bystanders, as compared with those who had engaged in perpetration only (54.2%, n=116), and those who had mixed experiences as both perpetrators and victims (63.3%, n=542).

In seeking to understand the opportunities for bystander intervention, we also asked respondents whether someone had ever actually shown or sent them a nude or sexual image of another person without that person's permission. Approximately one in four (26.4%, n=1,612) respondents reported this had happened to them at least once. This was somewhat higher for male respondents (29.9%, n=876) than for females (23.1%, n=736). It was highest among younger respondents (42.4%, n=158 of those aged 16–19 years, 39%, n=550 of those aged 20–29 years, and 31.6%, n=501 of those aged 30–39 years), as well as for LGB+ respondents (41.2%, n=280) as compared with heterosexuals (24.5%, n=1,332). Finally, of these respondents who had the opportunity to intervene as bystanders, we asked if they actually said or did something when this last happened. Just under half of those respondents (46.1%, n=742) who had the opportunity to intervene did so. Actual bystander action was much higher for female respondents (54.6%, n=402) than for males (38.9%, n=340), as well as among LGB+ respondents (50%, n=140) as compared to heterosexuals (45.3%, n=602). Given the higher observation of image-based sexual abuse sharing behaviour among male and younger respondents, these findings suggest that such groups are particularly important subpopulations to work with in education and prevention.

Overall, what these findings suggest is that despite a high prevalence of consensual sexual self-imagery, and sometimes mixed victim feelings and perpetrator motivations towards the non-consensual taking, sharing or threats to share nude or sexual images, there is nonetheless a normative expectation that nude or sexual imagery should remain private (as shown through the proxy measures of both individual and peer support for bystander intervention). Our survey data clearly demonstrate that these expectations are more commonly held by women compared to men, and by non-victims/victims of image-based sexual abuse compared to perpetrators and those who had experienced both victimisation and perpetration. Arguably then, there is some evidence to suggest that those who engage in image-based sexual abuse perpetration are lacking in both an understanding of, and regard for, the potential harms of their actions and the centrality of privacy and consent. There is some promise then, that incorporating image-based sexual abuse into sex education alongside other discussions of privacy and consent, could be an important avenue for prevention (see Chapter 8). There is furthermore some potential in empowering bystanders to be confident in intervening when they observe image-based sexual abuse in their peer groups, particularly for male peer groups. Importantly, what prevention measures should seek to address is the underlying missing culture of consent and the cultural scaffolding of sexual violence.

Conclusion

Despite consensual sexual selfie behaviours being extremely common, there is a missing culture of consent that contributes to image-based sexual abuse. In this chapter, we have sought to engage with the shifting and seemingly contradictory emerging social norms regarding sexual self-imagery as a form of sexuality expression and empowerment, as well as a site for the reproduction of gender inequalities, and as a tool in abuse. Importantly, we suggest that efforts to respond to victim-survivors and to work with perpetrators towards preventing image-based sexual abuse need to take account of this dual reality of victim-survivors' lives.

Sexual self-imagery represents an important practice in contemporary sexual experiences, as well as a site of vulnerability to misuse, with uneven effects for different members of the community. Legal and policy responses need then to protect individuals' enjoyment of visual forms of sexual self-expression and subjectivity and focus on problematising the *non-consensual* misuse of those nude or sexual images. Providing multiple responses for different image-based sexual abuse experiences is also important as these allow for every incident of image-based sexual abuse to be recognised as a violation of sexual choice and autonomy, whilst recognising that the consequential harms of image-based sexual abuse are uneven for different victim-survivors. In other words, while the impacts and consequential harms of image-based sexual abuse vary, each time a sexual image is taken and/or shared without consent it is a violation of that individual's rights to privacy and sexual autonomy. Thus, it is vital that we challenge all forms of image-based sexual abuse so that we do not sit by and allow a culture of non-consent to become the new norm.

References

Abad-Santos, A. (2019, June 21). Bella Thorne and Whoopi Goldberg's fight over nude photos is bigger than both of them. *Vox*. Retrieved from www.vox.com/culture/2019/6/21/18693604/bella-thorne-nude-photos-whoopi-goldberg.
Agostinone-Wilson, F. (2020). *Enough already! A socialist feminist response to the re-emergence of right wing populism and fascism in media*. Leiden: Brill Sense.

Albury, K., & Byron, P. (2014). Queering sexting and sexualisation. *Media International Australia, 153*(1), 138–147.

Albury, K., & Byron, P. (2016). Safe on my phone? Same-sex attracted young people's negotiations of intimacy, visibility, and risk on digital hook-up apps. *Social Media + Society, 2*(4), 1–10.

Albury, K., & Crawford, K. (2012). Sexting, consent and young people's ethics: Beyond Megan's Story. *Continuum, 26*(3), 463–473.

Allen, L., & Carmody, M. (2012). "Pleasure has no passport": Re-visiting the potential of pleasure in sexuality education. *Sex Education, 12*(4), 455–468.

Arreola, S., Santos, G. M., Beck, J., Sundararaj, M., Wilson, P. A., Hebert, P., ... & Ayala, G. (2015). Sexual stigma, criminalization, investment, and access to HIV services among men who have sex with men worldwide. *AIDS and Behavior, 19*(2), 227–234.

Aswad, J. (2017, November 7). Sia pokes paparazzi by posting nude photo they'd threatened to publish. *Variety*. Retrieved from https://variety.com/2017/music/news/sia-pokes-paparazzi-by-posting-nude-naked-photo-they-threatened-to-publish-1202608739/.

Attwood, F. (2006). Sexed up: Theorizing the sexualization of culture. *Sexualities, 9*(1), 77–94.

Australian Associated Press (AAP). (2016, February 18). "Grow up" and stop taking naked photos of yourself, police tell revenge porn inquiry. *The Guardian*. Retrieved from www.theguardian.com/australia-news/2016/feb/18/grow-up-and-stop-taking-naked-photos-of-yourself-says-senior-police-officer.

Barrett-Ibarria, S. (2018, July 25). I posted my own nudes on Instagram before my ex could. *Vice*. Retrieved from www.vice.com/en_au/article/d3e3my/i-posted-my-own-nudes-on-instagram-before-my-ex-could.

Battersby, L. (2008, July 10). Alarm at teenage "sexting" traffic. *The Age*. Retrieved from www.theage.com.au/national/alarm-at-teenage-sexting-traffic-20080709-3clg.html.

Bauman, Z. (2003). *Liquid love: On the frailty of human bonds.* Cambridge, UK: Polity Press.

Brown, A. L., Banyard, V. L., & Moynihan, M. M. (2014). College students as helpful bystanders against sexual violence: Gender, race, and year in college moderate the impact of perceived peer norms. *Psychology of Women Quarterly, 38*(3), 350–362.

Castells, M. (2015). *Networks of outrage and hope: Social movements in the internet age.* Cambridge, UK; Malden, MA: Polity Press.

Cummings, W. [@WhitneyCummings]. (2019, August 13). https://twitter.com/WhitneyCummings/status/1160937893059158016?ref_src=twsrc%5Etfw%7Ctwcamp%5Etweetembed%7Ctwterm%5E1160937893059158016 [Tweet]. https://twitter.com/WhitneyCummings.

Dobson, A. S. (2015). *Postfeminist digital cultures: Femininity, social media, and self-representation.* New York: Palgrave Macmillan.

Dobson, A. S., & Ringrose, J. (2016). Sext education: Pedagogies of sex, gender and shame in the schoolyards of *Tagged* and *Exposed*. *Sex Education, 16*(1), 8–21.

Donovan, F. (2018, May 7). Male revenge porn victim explains why he didn't go to the police. *Unilad*. Retrieved from www.unilad.co.uk/featured/male-revenge-porn-victim-police/.

Döring, N. (2014). Consensual sexting among adolescents: Risk prevention through abstinence education or safer sexting? *Cyberpsychology: Journal of Psychosocial Research on Cyberspace, 8*(1), article 9. http://dx.doi.org/10.5817/CP2014-1-9.

Douglas, H., Harris, B., & Dragiewicz, M. (2019). Technology-facilitated domestic and family violence: Women's experiences. *British Journal of Criminology, 59*(3), 551–570.

Drouin, M., Ross, J., & Tobin, E. (2015). Sexting: A new, digital vehicle for intimate partner aggression? *Computers in Human Behavior, 50,* 197–204.

Errett, J. (2011, December 8). Social nudeworking. *NOW.* Retrieved from https://nowtoronto.com/news/social-nudeworking/.

Flynn, A. (2015). Sexual violence and innovative responses to justice: Interrupting the recognisable narratives. In A. Powell, N. Henry, & A. Flynn (eds.), *Rape justice: Beyond the criminal law* (pp. 92–111). Basingstoke: Palgrave Macmillan.

Franks, M. A. (2017). "Revenge porn" reform: A view from the front lines. *Florida Law Review, 69,* 1251–1337.

Giddens, A. (1992). *The transformation of intimacy: Sexuality, love and eroticism in modern societies.* Cambridge, UK: Polity Press.

Giles, S. (2019, April 2). Never forget how horrible our reaction was to Vanessa Hudgens' 2007 leaked nudes. *GOAT.* Retrieved from https://goat.com.au/vanessa-hudgens/never-forget-how-horrible-our-reaction-was-to-vanessa-hudgens-2007-leaked-nudes/.

Gill, R. (2003). From sexual objectification to sexual subjectification: The resexualisation of women's bodies in the media. *Feminist Media Studies, 3*(1), 100–106.

Gill, R. (2011). Sexism reloaded, or, it's time to get angry again!. *Feminist Media Studies, 11*(1), 61–71.

Hall, M., & Hearn, J. (2017). *Revenge pornography: Gender, sexuality and motivations.* Abingdon, Oxon; New York: Routledge.

Henderson, L., & Morgan, E. (2011). Sexting and sexual relationships among teens and young adults. *McNair Scholars Research Journal, 7*(1), article 9. https://scholarworks.boisestate.edu/mcnair_journal/vol7/iss1/9.

Hobbs, M., Owen, S., & Gerber, L. (2017). Liquid love? Dating apps, sex, relationships and the digital transformation of intimacy. *Journal of Sociology, 53*(2), 271–284.

Hosie, R. (2019, August 13). A comedian with 1.3 million followers posted her own nude photo to Twitter after blackmailers allegedly tried to extort her. *Insider.* Retrieved from www.insider.com/comedian-whitney-cummings-posts-nude-photo-blackmail-response-2019-8.

Jennifer Lawrence calls photo hacking a "sex crime" (2014, October 7). *Vanity Fair.* Retrieved from www.vanityfair.com/hollywood/2014/10/jennifer-lawrence-cover.

Johnson, R. (2014, July 6). Want to stop revenge porn? Just keep your clothes on! *Daily Mail.* Retrieved from www.dailymail.co.uk/debate/article-2681951/Rachel-Johnson-Want-stop-revenge-porn-Just-clothes-on.html.

Kalms, N. (2016). Regulation and the tactics of soft-core urbanism. *Urbana, 17,* 32–48.

Klettke, B., Hallford, D. J., & Mellor, D. J. (2014). Sexting prevalence and correlates: A systematic literature review. *Clinical Psychology Review, 34*(1), 44–53.

Konik, J., & Cortina, L. M. (2008). Policing gender at work: Intersections of harassment based on sex and sexuality. *Social Justice Research, 21*(3), 313–337.

Lasén, A., & Garcia, A. (2015). "… but I haven't got a body to show": Self-pornification and male mixed feelings in digitally mediated seduction practices. *Sexualities, 18*(5–6), 714–730.

Levendowski, A. (2014, February 4). Our best weapon against revenge porn: Copyright law? *The Atlantic*. Retrieved from www.theatlantic.com/technology/archive/2014/02/our-best-weapon-against-revenge-porn-copyright-law/283564/.

Marwick, A. E. (2017). Scandal or sex crime? Gendered privacy and the celebrity nude photo leaks. *Ethics and Information Technology, 19*(3), 177–191.

McGovern, A., Crofts, T., Lee, M., & Milivojevic, S. (2016). Media, legal and young people's discourses around sexting. *Global Studies of Childhood, 6*(4), 428–441.

Morris, A. (2012, November 13). Hunter Moore: The most hated man on the internet. *Rolling Stone*. Retrieved from www.rollingstone.com/culture/culture-news/hunter-moore-the-most-hated-man-on-the-internet-184668/.

Mulholland, M. (2015). Is there a new normal? Young people negotiate pornification. In E. Renold, J. Ringrose, & R. D. Egan (eds.), *Children, sexuality and sexualization* (pp. 321–336). Basingstoke; New York: Palgrave Macmillan.

Mulholland, M. (2018). "Western sexy?": The West, the rest and sexualised media. *Feminist Media Studies, 18*(6), 1102–1116.

Page Jeffery, C. (2018). Too sexy too soon, or just another moral panic? Sexualization, children, and "technopanics" in the Australian media 2004–2015. *Feminist Media Studies, 18*(3), 366–380.

Pew Research Center. (2016, February 11). *15% of American adults have used online dating sites or mobile dating apps*. Retrieved from www.pewresearch.org/wp-content/uploads/sites/9/2016/02/PI_2016.02.11_Online-Dating_FINAL.pdf.

Phillips, C. (2015). Self-pornographic representations with Grindr. *Journal of Visual and Media Anthropology, 1*(1), 65–79.

Powell, A. (2010). *Sex, power and consent: Youth culture and the unwritten rules*. Melbourne, VIC: Cambridge University Press.

Powell, A., & Henry, N. (2014). Blurred lines? Responding to "sexting" and gender-based violence among young people. *Children Australia, 39*(2), 119–124.

Powell, A., & Henry, N. (2017). *Sexual violence in a digital age*. London: Palgrave Macmillan.

Powell, A., Henry, N., & Flynn, A. (2018). Image-based sexual abuse. In W. S. DeKeseredy & M. Dragiewicz (eds.), *Handbook of critical criminology* (pp. 305–315). Abingdon, Oxon; New York: Routledge.

Reigstad, L. (2018, October 31). Catfishing and conspiracy in groves. *Texas Monthly*. Retrieved from www.texasmonthly.com/articles/catfishing-and-conspiracy-in-groves/.

Ringrose, J., Tolman, D., & Ragonese, M. (2019). Hot right now: Diverse girls navigating technologies of racialized sexy femininity. *Feminism & Psychology, 29*(1), 76–95.

Roberts, L. L. (2019). Changing worldwide attitudes toward homosexuality: The influence of global and region-specific cultures, 1981–2012. *Social Science Research, 80*, 114–131.

Smith, L. W., Guy, R., Degenhardt, L., Yeung, A., Rissel, C., Richters, J., & Liu, B. (2018). Meeting sexual partners through internet sites and smartphone apps in Australia: National representative study. *Journal of Medical Internet Research, 20*(12), e10683. doi: 10.2196/10683.

Smith, M. (2019, June 26). Tory minister accused of "victim blaming" over revenge porn comments. *Mirror*. Retrieved from www.mirror.co.uk/news/politics/tory-minister-accused-victim-blaming-17259617.

Summers, F. (2018). What a body can do: From the frenzy of the communicative to the visual bond. In B. Burbridge & A. Pollen (eds.), *Photography reframed: New visions in contemporary photographic culture* (pp. 99–107). London: I. B. Tauris.

Sunderland, M. (2017, September 12). Vanessa Hudgens deserved better after her 2007 nude photo leak. *Vice*. Retrieved from www.vice.com/en_us/article/bjjw33/ vanessa-hudgens-deserved-better-after-her-2007-nude-photo-leak.

Valenti, J. (2014, June 26). It's still revenge porn when the victim is a man and the picture is of his penis. *The Guardian*. Retrieved from www.theguardian.com/ commentisfree/2014/jun/26/revenge-porn-victim-conservative-man-penis.

Vanessa Hudgens apologizes for nude picture. (2007, September 8). *Daily News*. Retrieved from www.nydailynews.com/entertainment/gossip/vanessa-hudgens-apologizes-nude-picture-article-1.244088.

Vanessa Hudgens "embarrassed", apologizes for nude photo. (2007, September 7). *People Magazine*. Retrieved from https://people.com/celebrity/vanessa-hudgens-embarrassed-apologizes-for-nude-photo/.

Vogels, J. (2004, May 3). Textual gratification: Quill or keypad, it's all about sex. *Globe and Mail*. Retrieved from www.theglobeandmail.com/technology/textual-gratification-quill-or-keypad-its-all-about-sex/article1136823/.

Waldman, A. E. (2019). Law, privacy, and online dating: "Revenge porn" in gay online communities. *Law & Social Inquiry, 44*(4), 987–1018.

Wiley, J. (1999). No body is "doing it": Cybersexuality. In J. Price & M. Shildrick (eds.), *Feminist theory and the body* (pp. 134–140). Edinburgh: Edinburgh University Press.

Wiseman, E. (2019, July 7). The key to avoiding sexual shame online: Reveal it all first. *The Guardian*. Retrieved from www.theguardian.com/lifeandstyle/2019/ jul/07/the-key-to-avoiding-sexual-shame-online-reveal-it-all-first.

Wood v. Hustler Magazine, 736 F.2d 1084 (5th Cir. 1984).

Wood, M., Barter, C., Stanley, N., Aghtaie, N., & Larkins, C. (2015). Images across Europe: The sending and receiving of sexual images and associations with interpersonal violence in young people's relationships. *Children and Youth Services Review, 59*, 149–160.

Wysocki, D. K., & Childers, C. D. (2011). "Let my fingers do the talking": Sexting and infidelity in cyberspace. *Sexuality & Culture, 15*, 217–239.

Yar, M. (2012). Crime, media and the will-to-representation: Reconsidering relationships in the new media age. *Crime, Media, Culture: An International Journal, 8*(3), 245–260.

Chapter 7

Seeking justice for victim-survivors of image-based sexual abuse (with Erika Rackley)

Introduction

Given the pervasiveness and impacts of image-based sexual abuse, governments around the world have introduced a range of new criminal and civil laws to provide victim-survivors with some form of justice and redress. In addition, there have been many examples of the imaginative use of "old" laws, often where existing or new laws have failed to address certain forms of image-based sexual abuse. While these new provisions are generally a welcome first step, they typically only cover some forms of image-based sexual abuse, predominantly non-consensual sharing, and often have various thresholds and motive requirements, meaning that not all forms of abuse are covered. In practice, therefore, victim-survivors are often faced with a bewildering array of legal provisions which apply in very specific circumstances depending, for example, on whether images were taken or shared without consent, whether they were taken in public or private, and the motives of the perpetrator. By way of example, in England and Wales alone, image-based sexual abuse could be prosecuted, depending on its manifestation, under at least 10 different criminal offences, as well as a number of separate civil offences.

Perhaps not surprisingly, therefore, despite the introduction of specific criminal offences and new civil penalties, our research has found that legal systems have failed to respond to the pervasiveness and significant harms of image-based sexual abuse. In other words, as in other areas of sexual violence, there remains a significant "justice gap" (see e.g., Jordan, 2004; Kelly, Lovett, & Regan, 2005; Lonsway & Archambault, 2012; McGlynn & Westmarland, 2019; Temkin & Krahé, 2008).

In this chapter, we examine what justice means to victim-survivors of image-based sexual abuse. We begin by exploring victim-survivors' experiences of the criminal justice system, before considering the extent to which justice for victim-survivors extends beyond the bounds of the (criminal) law. While many of the victim-survivors we spoke to had engaged (with varying degrees of success) with the criminal justice process, it is clear that few (if any) saw this as the only – or indeed best – avenue for support or redress. As with other survivors of sexual violence, victim-survivors of image-based sexual abuse perceive "justice" as "kaleidoscopic" – neither fixed nor linear, but rather a "continually shifting pattern ... constantly refracted through new circumstances, experiences and understandings ... [with] multiple beginnings and possible endings" (McGlynn & Westmarland, 2019: 186). Therefore, when considering what constitutes justice in cases of image-based sexual abuse, we need to look beyond the conventional criminal justice system and understand the varied, nuanced and often indeterminate nature of justice.

To this end, we explore a number of themes that have emerged from our survey and victim-survivor interviews, namely: Justice as criminal punishment; justice as enforcement; justice as recognition; and justice as regaining control. We found that while conceptions of justice vary from person to person, at every stage of the criminal justice process, victim-survivors are commonly being denied justice. The chapter further presents findings from our survey regarding community understanding and support for criminal laws addressing image-based sexual abuse, as well as implications for public legal education. We conclude by arguing for the importance of a multi-stranded, multi-institutional and multi-agency response to image-based sexual abuse. Such an approach would enable victim-survivors to "reclaim control" of their images, bodies, lives, careers and physical and mental health by utilising, concurrently or consecutively, one or more of a number of options within and beyond the criminal justice system, including more restorative and transformative approaches.

Justice as criminal punishment

While the enactment of specifically crafted laws in many jurisdictions has been the default political response to image-based sexual abuse, these have taken an array of different forms. "The Law", in both its criminal and civil guises, has been harnessed in political efforts to stem the tide and respond to the harms of image-based sexual abuse (see e.g., Haynes, 2018). Accordingly, many countries across the world have created or amended their criminal laws over the past decade (Haynes, 2018; Nigam, 2018; for a summary of laws in common law countries, see Henry, Flynn, & Powell, 2019). The exact nature of these laws varies considerably, with some jurisdictions only capturing the non-consensual sharing of nude or sexual images, while others neglect to cover digitally altered images or threats to share images.

In some countries, the criminal law is complex and piecemeal, with separate laws covering the distribution of sexual images, voyeurism and upskirting (McGlynn & Rackley, 2017; McGlynn et al., 2019). In other jurisdictions, the laws are more comprehensive, capturing the complexity and harms of image-based sexual abuse.[1] Below, we describe five key shortcomings with regard to image-based sexual abuse laws: The exclusion of digitally altered images and "fake porn"; the exclusion of threats to share nude or sexual images; the requirement of proof of harm or distress; the absence of anonymity provisions to protect the identity of the complainant; and the lack of awareness of new laws within the community more broadly.

"Fake porn" and "deepfakes"

First, the exclusion of so-called "fake porn" or "deepfakes" from the criminal law in many jurisdictions is a major problem (McGlynn et al., 2019). "Fake porn" involves the use of digital technology to alter videos or photographs to make them sexual; for example, taking a profile picture from Facebook and digitally altering it to make it pornographic. While "photoshopping" technology has now been available for two decades, the more recent developments in the use of artificial intelligence means that fake images (also known as "deepfakes") are becoming more sophisticated and increasingly difficult to discern as fake (see e.g., Chesney & Citron, 2019; Henry, Powell, & Flynn, 2018). While none of the victim-survivors we interviewed had "deepfake" experiences, some mentioned other techniques involving the creation of fake images. Sarah (UK), for example, told us about her experience:

> I got an email … saying … 'Are you sure you want this on the internet?' And it was a load of very explicit porn with my name attached and my face attached. But it was photoshopped … he'd clearly gone through my Facebook photos … and then photoshopped me into some very hardcore porn and had put it on the internet under my real name with my Facebook profile picture as the profile picture up there. So it was very identifiably me.

In some Australian jurisdictions (New South Wales and the Australian Capital Territory) and Scotland, wording makes it clear that "intimate images" include digitally altered or manipulated images that depict a person's private parts or a person engaged in a private act. However, in many other international jurisdictions, digitally altered images are either not covered at all, or in the case of English and Welsh and Northern Irish laws, are explicitly excluded.

The exclusion of digitally altered images is highly regrettable, particularly in the light of our survey findings that around one third of those whose images were taken without their consent (34.1%, n=691) had experienced their images being digitally altered (see further Chapter 2). To the untrained eye, it is very often difficult to tell the difference between fake and real images, and so the harm and harassment felt by victim-survivors can be just as significant. As one UK stakeholder who supports victim-survivors told us: "It's still a picture of you … it's still abuse".

Threats to share nude or sexual images

We have discussed at length the harms that can result when someone *threatens to share* nude or sexual images of another person (see Chapters 2 and 3). Victim support advocates have also expressed grave concern about the extent to which implicit or explicit threats to share nude or sexual images can have silencing and harmful impacts on victim-survivors of domestic violence, such as forcing them to stay in an abusive relationship or coercing them into unwanted acts. In all Australian jurisdictions that have introduced specific criminal offences on image-based sexual abuse, threats to share intimate images are covered, attracting a maximum penalty of between two to three years in prison. Significantly, Australian laws state that it is irrelevant whether or not the image or images actually exist. Threats to share intimate or sexual images are also covered in some US states and under Scots law.

By way of contrast, in other jurisdictions, making threats to share nude or sexual images is not captured, such as in England and Wales, and New Zealand. For example, the New Zealand Law Commission (2012) recommended against making the threat to publish intimate images a criminal offence under the New Zealand law, stating that it would "involve considering whether a threat to commit any offence should itself be criminal and as such it would "open the door too wide". The only recourse in these such countries is to use existing extortion or blackmail provisions (see Henry et al., 2019).

Proof of harm or intention to cause distress

A third key concern in countries such as the United Kingdom and New Zealand, as well as a number of US states, is the requirement that the perpetrator must have intended to cause distress (Gavey & Farley, in press; Henry et al., 2019; Kirchengast & Crofts, 2019; McGlynn & Rackley, 2017). In comparison, Australian and Canadian jurisdictions do not require the prosecution to prove the victim suffered distress or harm, or that the perpetrator intended to cause the victim distress or harm. Instead, it is accepted that this form of abuse would reasonably be expected to cause distress or harm to a person. The *mens rea* of the crime is the perpetrator's intention to create, share or threaten to create/share, an "intimate" or "invasive" image, without consent. For instance, in the Australian state of New South Wales, the law requires that the accused intentionally shares an intimate image of another person without their consent and they must either know that they did not consent, or they are reckless as to whether they consented.

As we have argued throughout this book, perpetrators of image-based sexual abuse have diverse motivations which are not always about revenge or causing harm. In Ruvalcaba and Eaton's (2019) survey in the United States, of the 159 people who self-reported image-based sexual abuse perpetration, 79% selected their main motivation as being to share with friends "without the intention to hurt". Only 12% identified that they were upset with the victim and/or wanted to harm them (Ruvalcaba & Eaton, 2019). Thus, while some perpetrators intend to cause the victim-survivor distress, others are motivated by other factors such as sexual gratification, monetary gain or social status building – or even to make others "laugh". The removal of an intent to cause distress requirement in various jurisdictions would allow for these diverse motivations to still be captured by the criminal law. Currently, victim-survivors in various countries face different levels of protection and redress depending on the perpetrator's motivations (McGlynn, 2018).

Furthermore, under the New Zealand legislation, as well as Californian law, not only must it be proven that the perpetrator intended to cause serious emotional distress to the complainant, but there must be proof of actual serious harm to the complainant resulting from the disclosure of such images (Gavey & Farley, in press). These provisions presume a particular response from victim-survivors and a particular motive of perpetrators. There is no requirement in many other jurisdictions of proof of harm to the complainant. Flynn and Henry (2019) have argued that the benefit of such an approach includes a clear recognition that distress is difficult to define or quantify, with people differing considerably within the community about what would and would not cause distress. This approach also accepts that people experience image-based sexual abuse differently; some may find it devastating and others less so (McGlynn et al., in press; Powell, Henry, & Flynn, 2018). Likewise, the harm may not be measurable or felt by the victim at the time the offence is dealt with by the criminal justice system.

Anonymity for victim-survivors of image-based sexual abuse

A fourth shortcoming with some new laws criminalising image-based sexual abuse concerns the lack of automatic anonymity for some victim-survivors, meaning that their personal details may be shared across the media with impunity. In Australia, although victim-survivors of image-based sexual abuse can be granted anonymity when reporting to police and through the court process, there are no mandatory suppression orders for complainants of rape, sexual assault or image-based sexual abuse. In England and Wales, victims of "upskirting" and voyeurism are granted lifelong anonymity in the same way as victims of other sexual offences, but those who have experienced the non-consensual sharing of their nude or sexual images are not granted this protection. This is similar to New Zealand, which provides automated suppression of the identity of the complainant in specified sexual offence cases, but not for offences relating to "intimate visual recordings". This means that for many victims of non-consensual sharing in multiple jurisdictions, their names can be – and are – published in news reports and elsewhere. This can have a significant impact on the lives of the victim-survivor and their friends and family, and may play a significant role in whether or not the victim-survivor reports to police or proceeds with a court trial. As one UK stakeholder told us:

> The saddening part is that they named her in the court ... her name was in the [news]papers, and then it went viral ... She's told me that was worse than the crime. ... the fact that everybody knew who she was and what had happened to her, it was quite bad really. ... And, of course, she'd got a young child as well.

Unsurprisingly then, and in line with other research in the United Kingdom (e.g., North Yorkshire Police, Fire & Crime Commissioner, 2018), we found that the absence of anonymity is a key barrier to victim-survivors reporting these crimes to the police. Many victim-survivors we spoke to expressed this concern, including Lucy (UK):

> Because there is no anonymity ... [reporting to the police is] not something I would do again. Even if you could guarantee me that the police would be very sympathetic and take it seriously and investigate, I still wouldn't do it because there's no anonymity.

What this means in practice is that despite significant policy and parliamentary rhetoric, many victim-survivors are left without an effective remedy.

Public understanding of and support for image-based sexual abuse laws

Despite the introduction of specific criminal offences in multiple international jurisdictions, our survey research suggests that there is a lack of understanding of the nature and scope of these recently adopted criminal laws within the general community. While in Australia, New Zealand and the United Kingdom, there are criminal laws covering the non-consensual taking or sharing of nude or sexual images, albeit with various thresholds and constraints, overall, we found that there was a lack of awareness among our respondents about whether image-based sexual abuse was currently a crime in their country. Less than half (45.7%, n=2,792) of our survey respondents (n=6, 109) believed that it is currently a crime to take images without consent in their country, 15.1% (n=922) said that they do not think it is a crime, and 39.2% (n=2,395) said that they do not know. Likewise, less than half (48.7%, n=2,974) of respondents believed that it is currently a crime to share images without consent in their country, 13.4% (n=816) do not think it is a crime, and 38% (n=2,319) do not know. This is particularly concerning in jurisdictions where the criminal law on non-consensual sharing has been in place for nearly a decade.

While there may be a lack of awareness as to the current law, we also asked in the survey whether respondents thought it *should* be a crime to take nude and/or sexual images without a person's consent, to share such images without consent, and/or to threaten to share nude or sexual images of a person. We found that there was overwhelming community support in all countries for each of these behaviours to be criminal offences: 80% (n=4,886) agreed (images taken without consent); 83.2% (n=5,081) agreed (images shared without consent); and 81.8% (n=4,997) agreed (threats made to share images). Overall, female respondents were significantly more likely to support criminal offences than males (85.6%, n=2,722 compared with 73.9%, n=2,164 for images taken; 88.1%, n=2,802 compared with 77.8%, n=2,279 for images shared, and 86.2%, n=2,742 compared with 77%, n=2,255 for threats to share). A similar trend was observed between heterosexual and LGB+ respondents, with higher levels of support for criminalisation among those identifying as heterosexual (81.1%, n=4,405 compared with 70.8%, n=481 for images taken; 84.1%, n=4,568 compared with 75.6%, n=513 for images shared; and 82.5%, n=4,482 compared with 75.8%, n=515 for threats to share). The highest levels of support for criminal offences, by key respondent demographics, were among those aged 50–64 years (87.7%, n=1,411 for images taken; 91.2%, n=1,467 for images shared; and 89.2%, n=1,434 for threats to share).

Our findings therefore suggest that there is overwhelming support for the criminalisation of image-based sexual abuse, but low awareness of existing laws. This, combined with what we know about the current limitations of the criminal law in many countries, should encourage legislatures to take further steps to improve and enhance awareness of the current law, as well as ensuring greater enforcement, as discussed in the next section.

Justice as enforcement

In our study, many of the victim-survivors we spoke to had reported the image-based sexual abuse to the police. Where victim-survivors chose not to report to the police, it was often because they were concerned the police would blame them or not take their case seriously. They were also worried about others finding out about the abuse, leading to them being publicly identified. Some were ashamed about what happened, felt they were in some way to blame or not enough of a "real" victim (see also Henry, Flynn, & Powell, 2018). For example:

> Q: So you didn't consider going to the police at any stage? A: No, I just would've assumed they would have laughed at me. Q: Oh, really? A: Yeah, they've got bigger things to deal with than that, so I just kind of thought it was pointless.

> (Sarah, Aus)

Some victim-survivors felt the police had taken them seriously and treated them with respect – often going beyond their formal role or remit. Xia (NZ) had had covert photos taken of her while she was in the shower by her then boyfriend. She was called to the police station when he was arrested for other offences:

> [The police officer] said to me why I was there, why they wanted to speak to me. And it was in the back of my mind like 'oh my God they've seen those photos. Oh my God. Oh my God, when's it going to come up?' And he said, 'Before we go any further, I just wanted to tell you that there were some intimate images … Don't be embarrassed. I've worked many cases and you're one of many. And you're not the first. You won't be the last'. He said, 'To put it politely it's nothing special. We've seen far worse'. He said, 'If you want to take a minute to digest that, if you want anybody else to come in with the interview, if you don't feel comfortable carrying on, just say so'.

In contrast, the majority of the victim-survivors we spoke to were dissatisfied with the police response. Those we spoke to described the police as "disinterested", "dismissive", "cruel" and "judgmental". One participant had reported their abuse four times before it was taken seriously by the police, while another gave an example of the lack of urgency of the police's response – something which is particularly egregious in circumstances of image-based sexual abuse where each minute the private sexual images could be spreading further:

> I'm at the police station at 7am saying, 'Look, no-one's called me, this is ridiculous, I want to make a statement. Now, let's get the ball rolling, let's get this phone. I need some reassurances as to how far this photo has gone. Has it been deleted? Because, I don't trust this woman, I don't trust someone who would do that. I wouldn't trust her word to say she had deleted it'.
>
> (Dee, Aus)

Nicole's (Aus) partner had taken pictures of her naked while she was sleeping and sent them to around 50 of his sporting teammates via SnapChat. She told us:

> I felt kind of belittled, like I was just this silly girl who was like 'this boy is being mean to me', when really I think it should be just as serious as like if somebody hits you, or if somebody rapes you, or if somebody mugs you or whatever. You should be able to say like 'hey, this crime was committed against me'.

Many said the police did not have a good enough understanding of the relevant legislation, or how to effectively investigate the offence:

> I've gone to my local police on the first day of school, and there was just that detective there, he was straight up actually; a bit rude. He goes,

'Oh, this is not a criminal offence, she'll never go to jail'. Well, he was right, but he had no idea what he was talking about.

(Dee, Aus)

Other victim-survivors were told that there were not enough resources, or it was "too difficult" to investigate their case and prove an offence had been committed. This left many of our participants feeling as if the police did not take their reports seriously. In Lucy's (UK) words:

[My] overall impression of the police is that they're just not interested in [the non-consensual sharing of images] as a crime at all. They just don't want to touch it. [The officer] was just trying to fob me off, telling me all of the reasons why there were no resources for it, it was impossible to tell who'd done it. She didn't know anything about technology, so she wouldn't be able to investigate. She really went to town on telling me exactly why she wouldn't take any action.

Additionally, many victim-survivors described feeling they were blamed for the abuse they experienced:

I felt like they just did think 'oh it's just a girl sending nudes out, what does she expect?' and I don't know, it didn't have a good feeling to it at all … It was almost like '… well, you should've been more careful. Why did you let him have this picture?' And obviously all that is important, but I did definitely feel like I was back in school and sat down by a teacher and getting told off or something.

(Vicky, UK)

These findings were echoed by our survey respondents. Only 14.1% (n=135) found the police response "helpful", varying between 11.4% (n=38) in the United Kingdom, 16.8% (n=57) in New Zealand and 14.1% (n=40) in Australia. As these findings across our survey respondents and interview participants demonstrate, law reform is not enough to secure justice. There needs to be effective enforcement. Police need to be trained both in the actual law, but also in how to respond to victim-survivors (see Henry et al., 2018; Bond & Tyrell, 2018). The victim-survivors and stakeholders we spoke to suggested the need for specific training, as it is clear that these negative reactions from police can have serious, life-threatening consequences. As Heather (UK) told us:

The case officer I was given came around two days after I reported it and they took my first statement. So I had to tell them everything that happened … and they instantly like victim blamed me for what had happened. She said 'well I guess you've learnt your lesson'. … It felt like if the police didn't have any sympathy or anything then nobody else probably would either. So it made me feel really bad. And I had to get my friend to come over that night because I felt really unsafe in myself, I thought I'd probably harm myself ... I dreaded every phone call from [the officer] because I just found her so unhelpful.

Interestingly, when victim-survivors considered that the police "responded as best they could" this was typically in cases where individual police officers had responded "informally", for example, by issuing informal requests that images be taken down or destroyed, giving the perpetrator an "informal caution", or warning the perpetrator that their ongoing behaviour could amount to a criminal offence. Such responses commonly took place in situations where the police believed the abuse did not amount to a crime, or where they felt there was not enough evidence to prosecute. Often this amounted to giving the (potential) perpetrator "a fright":

At the time I think I really wanted the police to go and talk to her, to give her a fright. That's really what I wanted. I didn't need to prosecute her. I just wanted them to go around and say, 'You've done something really bad to this person. And if you do anything like this again, yeah, you're going to go to jail'.

(Adele, NZ)

The police supporting Sarah (UK), who had had images of her photoshopped and shared on porn sites (which are not covered by English and Welsh law), took a similar line:

So the police officer and I agreed that I would get hold of [the perpetrator's] mobile number and the officer would call him and give him an informal caution and tell him to take [the sexual images] down immediately or they would come down and go through all his computers with a fine-toothed comb. Which worked ... I think the threat [the officer] made was ... a complete bluff, but it did seem to do the trick. [But it is] an informal caution so he had nothing on his record ... later when I felt a little bit more secure and confident I was a bit angry that he hadn't had anything more serious, but at least it meant that he knew that it was absolutely not on and I've never heard from him since.

A number of victim-survivors felt that this approach allowed them to distance themselves from the perpetrator's actions and that it acted as a warning or half-way between doing nothing and formally reporting the perpetrator. Others, however, saw these informal responses as another way of the police minimising the seriousness of the abuse, and letting the perpetrator – in the words of one of our participants – "get off scot free". For these victim-survivors, "justice" also requires some form of recognition of the wrong done and harm caused, not only on the part of the police or politicians through the enactment of new laws, but from the perpetrators themselves.

Justice as recognition

The criminal law is just one route among many to securing justice. For some victim-survivors, this is not an ideal option at all. Kimberly (UK), whose ex-boyfriend took naked photos of her while she was sleeping, told us:

> It was never really on my radar ... Because I think in my mind it was, he was what 20 at the time. And I thought I don't really know what could happen but I just thought he's very young and actually the person who is when he's 40 or 50 years old is probably not going to be that same person and is it worth ruining so much for him?

Others had not involved the police or turned to the criminal law out of concern for the perpetrator. Aroha (NZ), for example, who had images taken of her during a Skype call with her then long-distance partner, told us:

> He had so many problems just on his own, like even just him as a person, his gender dysphoria, depression, anxiety, he was a little bit schizophrenic I'm pretty sure as well and incredibly bi-polar. ... I thought it was just better to leave things where they are and just let him find his own way because if I can't help him, his friends can't help him, his family can't help him. He's the only one that can help himself. ... I felt like that was ... better than trying to call the police on him and make his life even worse.

Karly (Aus) had a similar response:

> Annoyingly, 50% of it was just, 'oh my God, if she's already tried to commit suicide in the last year ... I would rather [be embarrassed] than be the one responsible for her [hurt]'. Because, like, ... I don't want someone to die over it either ... if she's that unstable.

Alana (Aus) mentioned that the reason she did not go to the police was because of her feelings of solidarity with other victim-survivors.

> If I were to try to bring about some sort of restority [sic] of justice, this would bring scrutiny to this website and then all of the images of these young women would then be even further distributed and publicised ... because they always put sample ones that are freely available and I felt that it would be a betrayal to ... the hundreds upon hundreds of thousands of young women whose graphic images are out there, and that if I would have gone to any sort of authority and gone public about it,

then this massive whole other level of attention would be on them and their lives would – you know, there's already the risk that they would be exposed to their communities and vilified is massively high, but it would then just skyrocket and basically be a foregone conclusion, and that to me ... was an unacceptable trade-off.

Also, for some participants, their views over what should happen to the perpetrator had changed over time. Danielle (UK), who had had private sexual images posted on WhatsApp by someone she was seeing, told us:

Initially, I wanted to see him punished more severely but ... looking back on it now it's not so much that I'd want him to be punished, it's just I'd want to promote ... the realisation that it isn't normal to do that and it's not okay to do that.

What emerged from our interviews was a complex and varying picture at the heart of which was a desire to ensure greater recognition of the wrongfulness of the perpetrator's actions and harms of their experiences. Victim-survivors spoke of a desire for the harms of image-based sexual abuse to be "taken more seriously" but did not necessarily equate this to increased or indeed any jail time. Others spoke of wanting to convey to the perpetrator and others the full impact and harms of what had happened to them, often (but not always) with the hope that the perpetrator would take responsibility and say sorry for what they had done: "They need to know that what they're doing affects the person emotionally and mentally and it can even hurt people physically" (Kristy, NZ). Faith's (NZ) comment is indicative of others:

[I] want the people that have done this to me to understand that it's not okay ... I just want them to know that what they did was wrong. I want them to never do it to anybody else again.

Several victim-survivors had also contacted the perpetrator directly. For Kimberly (UK) this had helped her to gain "closure":

Maybe two years, three years [later], I sent him ... [a] WhatsApp message basically saying 'I know what you did. I want you to know that this is very wrong. ... This is the impact it's had on me since. ... I hope you haven't done it to anyone else, don't do it to anyone else in the future'. And then ... [I said] 'I have genuinely forgiven you'. And it actually was such a release for me to be able to say that as well, which felt really good. ... Within about five minutes, probably less than that, he'd sent me a response [in which he admitted he was in the wrong].

While forgiveness should never be an obligation placed on victim-survivors to either pursue or initiate, it is vital to have restorative and therapeutic justice options in place. Restorative approaches are not common in the context of sexual violence, though there are some examples, such as conferencing, mediation, compensation and reparations (McGlynn, Westmarland, & Godden, 2012; Zinsstag & Keenan, 2017). The possibility of more restorative and therapeutic approaches both within and outside of formal legal processes, therefore, would be welcomed by some victim-survivors. As Danielle (UK) suggested, she would have liked to:

> Confront [the perpetrator] about it and just tell him what he'd done and like how awful it made me feel and just make it clear to him like what he did was wrong and why it was wrong and what the consequences were of it … because I think that kind of makes you, when you are confronted with the actual victim, that makes it more realisable.

Kerry (NZ), whose high school boyfriend shared private sexual images with other students at school, had a similar view:

> All that he really saw was his friends tak[ing] the piss out of me when I walked past or he'd see groups of girls occasionally go up to me at morning tea and just start yelling at me for some reason, and it wouldn't be such a massive deal. Like, he wouldn't see me going to hospital because I had tried to take a whole bunch of Panadol [in a suicide attempt]. He didn't see how serious it actually was and how it had affected me.

Understandably, many of those we spoke to did not want to – or could not – speak to the perpetrator directly, or desired a response which extended beyond the individual perpetrator. Participants described the need for "cultural change", pointing to the need for widespread and tailored education on the impact and effects of image-based sexual abuse as the primary means through which to achieve this, in common with other survivors of sexual violence who identify education and prevention as an important form of "justice" (McGlynn & Westmarland, 2019; see Chapter 8 for a further discussion). Echoing the views of many participants in our study, Heather (UK) commented:

> They're sharing it because they think it's a cool thing to do and not realise the effect that it actually has on the person, and I think if they were more aware [that might change] … even if it was just one of them that changed their view.

Justice as reclaiming control

Another key theme to emerge from our study was the desire of victim-survivors to "reclaim control" – of their images, bodies, lives and careers, as well as their physical and mental health (see further McGlynn et al., 2019).

For many participants, reclaiming control, rather than retribution, was their primary concern. The victim-survivors we spoke to identified a number of different avenues this might take, both within and beyond the legal system, as well as identifying the existence and limitations of support systems.

Access to practical and technological support

Almost without exception, the key priority for victim-survivors of image-based sexual abuse was the removal or takedown of their images from the internet or personal devices. The first port of call for many victim-survivors looking for practical support had been the police, often believing them to have more powers and/or influence than they did to request or remove content from digital platforms and devices. Often victim-survivors attempted to navigate the processes of removing their images alone, or with the help of a trusted friend. As one UK stakeholder put it: "They have to look for their own abuse online, to find it, in order to report it".

Victim-survivors might not have the expertise to ensure all traces of the image are removed. Moreover, the constant viewing of the images can itself be a "trauma". Victim-survivors spoke of spending hours and hours looking for their images, likening it to disappearing down an unwelcome and dangerous "rabbit hole". Many of the images are posted on sites where victim-survivors are necessarily encountering the abuse of others (in the form of other images) which for some victim-survivors simply reinforced the enormity of what had happened to them.

While organisations and peer communities like the Revenge Porn Helpline or Victims of Internet Crime (VOIC) in the United Kingdom, Netsafe in New Zealand and the Office of the eSafety Commissioner in Australia, provide excellent technical, practical and (in some cases) emotional support, they do so often with little funding, particularly in the case of the United Kingdom. As one UK stakeholder told us:

> We've had cases where things have ... been online for years ... you do get that slight sinking feeling when you search one image ... and they say 'I've found it on 3 websites', and you do a reverse image search ... and you find it on 10 pages ... of Google search results. And then you go, 'Okay, this is going to take a while to go through'.

As well as offering practical help and support, for some victim-survivors, these organisations act as a "half-way house" between going to the police and doing nothing. Gina (NZ) told us about her experience with Netsafe (New Zealand's independent online safety organisation), who had contacted the perpetrator on her behalf, asking him to remove the images and warning him of the consequences if he failed to do so:

> I'm just really appreciative of Netsafe, that they were able to do that and they solved it really quickly and they were extremely supportive as

well ... for me, it seemed like a step down from the police ... I wanted to give him a chance to remove it just in case., like benefit of doubt, I guess. Maybe I'm just a really optimistic person where I see the best in people but I thought by getting someone to contact him, he would actually remove the photo ...

Without doubt, these organisations are performing a vital role in facilitating victim-survivors' pursuit of justice, yet they are often doing it on "shoe-string" budgets or with a minimal workforce. This can also limit the services they are able to offer to victim-survivors. Small organisations or those with broad "cyber harm" or "online harm" remits are understandably less able to provide holistic support to victim-survivors of image-based sexual abuse. This can mean that rather than there being a single point of contact, victim-survivors are involved in a time-consuming and at times disorientating process of moving between organisations.

In Australia, the Office of the eSafety Commissioner co-ordinates and leads the online safety efforts of government, industry and the not-for-profit community. The Commissioner has a broad remit which includes: A complaints service for young Australians who experience serious cyberbullying; identifying and removing illegal online content; tackling image-based sexual abuse; and research and education. In 2018, the Commissioner was given responsibility for a new federal, civil penalties scheme which prohibits the non-consensual sharing of intimate images, as well as threats to share intimate images. Under this scheme, any victim-survivor of image-based sexual abuse (or a person authorised to act on their behalf) can report their experience to the Commissioner, who can then issue a takedown notice to an individual or corporation requiring removal of the image within 48 hours. The Commissioner can also issue a formal warning, infringement notices and/or seek an injunction or civil penalties order.

In 2017, the Australian eSafety Commissioner also developed a comprehensive national online image-based sexual abuse portal to help counter the effects of sharing intimate material without consent. The portal provides assistance, support and advice for victim-survivors, such as helping them to get images removed from online sites; guidance on how to communicate with someone who has intimate images in their possession; advice on collecting evidence; and advice on the applicable laws in their jurisdiction. Victims are able to report directly through the portal, prompting the Commissioner to work directly with social media providers, websites and search engines to help facilitate the removal of those images. In approximately 80% of cases, the Commissioner has been successful in getting images removed from online sites (Henry, personal correspondence).

The Australian eSafety Commissioner is a good example of a coordinated, high-level national effort to provide victim-survivors of image-based sexual abuse with practical support and assistance. However, most Australian victim-survivors we spoke to had not heard about the Commissioner, the portal, the civil penalty scheme or indeed the new criminal laws across Australia applying to image-based sexual abuse.

Similarly, respondents in our survey had limited knowledge of where to go for help. For instance, we found that only one third (33.5%, n=2,046) of victim-survivor respondents were confident they knew where or how to access support. This varied by country, with only 29.5% (n=598) of UK respondents being confident, compared to 34.7% (n=713) in Australia and 36.2% (n=735) in New Zealand. Practically, this means that victim-survivors are left with few options other than to "Google" for help and support at a time when they may understandably reluctant to go online. It also leaves them at the mercy of well-meaning but perhaps underinformed strangers, of lawyers keen to "cash in" on a growing area of litigation and – at times – isolated from specific communities of support. As time goes on, awareness of the available supports for image-based sexual abuse will grow, yet it is important that this support be well-resourced, coordinated and informed. It is important that victim-survivors are empowered to make choices about what kind of justice they need and how that might be pursued and facilitated. Above all, they need and deserve well-informed technological, legal and emotional support to help them navigate this complex problem.

Holding digital platforms to account

Conventional criminal prosecutions require the identification of a perpetrator. Yet, in many cases, it is not possible to find out who originally hacked, stole and/or uploaded images to the internet. In such situations, victim-survivors often feel they are being denied justice. Maya (Aus) told us:

> I don't know who the perpetrators are and you're almost lucky to be – and I hate to say the word lucky – but you're more at an advantage to have a situation where you know the perpetrator because you can actually get justice. If you're someone who doesn't know the perpetrator there is no justice afforded to you, and there's no laws that can actually be handed down ... if you do not know the perpetrator you are ... powerless.

Often the victim-survivors' sense of powerlessness was reinforced by an inability to "get at" other key actors, most notably the digital platforms that promote, facilitate and profit from image-based sexual abuse. Victim-survivors spoke of certain websites being "riddled" with image-based sexual abuse or pornographic content and "nobody does anything. Nobody can do anything" (Dylan, Aus). Therefore, even where individual perpetrators cannot be identified, there are important questions around the accountability of websites which are hosting illegal content.

Victim-survivors spoke of their desire to hold the online platforms accountable – and in particular, for them to take responsibility. While most social media and internet companies do have processes in place to remove image-based sexual abuse content, our participants found that too often these were slow, complicated, and sometimes reliant on personal connections between organisations (see also Cole & Maiberg, 2020). Lucy (UK), whose ex-boyfriend had uploaded consensually taken images onto porn websites, commented that it feels as if "they can just wash their hands of it":

> For me it would be a way of ensuring that the websites themselves aren't able to publish these pictures, or that they're shut down … I'm not particularly vengeful … So I wouldn't even be that bothered about seeing my ex behind bars or anything like that. I would just prefer to be able to move forward and live my life normally. But I don't feel that I can do that if these pictures are constantly popping up, and people are sharing them and things.

A number of the victim-survivors spoke of "bringing claims against websites" who are making money from their images and there was a strong sense, particularly among the UK lawyers we spoke to, that this is the next frontier in the fight against image-based sexual abuse. According to a UK stakeholder:

> Our legal crusade, for want of a better word, is really to try and create precedent that will hold websites to account for posting these images. … The problem there that we face is pinning down a website, finding its jurisdictional locus as it were. Because they are often … owned through this extremely labyrinthine structure of offshore companies and shell companies and affiliate companies and subsidiaries. And it's very difficult to trace back who owns the actual website that's posted the image.

At present, such claims are expensive, complex and time-intensive, requiring a heady mix of cross-jurisdictional lawyers and technological expertise. And, of course, some platforms are likely to be "extremely aggressive" in defending perpetrators or their sites, as well as resisting regulation. According to a UK lawyer we spoke to: "I'm sure they would get out all their lobbying big guns to try and resist this as much as they possibly could". Despite these barriers, should this avenue prove to be successful (and thee is no reason why, once the right case arises, that it won't be), the technological landscape could change dramatically. Images would disappear far more quickly or not be posted at all, and victim-survivors would be eligible for significant financial compensation.

Long-term specialist emotional support

Another aspect of a victim-survivor's ability to reclaim control is being able to access appropriate emotional and psychological support to help come to terms with their experiences. Many participants we spoke to had withdrawn from social media, notwithstanding the significant adverse impact on their social and professional lives, cutting them off from friends, family, peers and other forms of civic engagement (see further Chapter 3). Karen's (Aus) comment is indicative of many others:

> I've got to do this on my own. I essentially thought that I created the mess, I've been a part of the mess being created and therefore it was my responsibility and that to tell anybody would make it unbearable. ... My coping strategy was to keep it all to myself.

Not all victim-survivors want to talk to others about their experiences. Amy (NZ), for example, was unsure about the value of talking to others:

> What are they going to tell me? That's the thing. What can you say or what can someone say to take away my situation or what I've dealt with? You telling me that you've been through the same situation just makes me upset that it's happening to more people. It doesn't make me feel better. It's not, 'My cat also died' – 'Great you understand'. It doesn't take away from the fact that there is a part of me that's been invaded that I will never get that part back. I will never not have to deal with the fact that someone has done that to me and that there are images of me out there.

However, for many victim-survivors, seeking emotional support is vital, yet in so doing they encounter a number of hurdles. As with other forms of sexual abuse, accessing such services can be difficult, with long waiting lists. In Anna's (UK) words:

> The support system for people who have had this happen to them, it needs to be more available to people, because if you're waiting on the NHS [National Health Service] to give you help with anything, any therapy or anything like that, you'll be off the bloody bridge and you'll be gone by the time they phone.

Finally, in developing long-term, holistic support, it is crucial that the intersectional risks and harms of image-based sexual abuse are properly recognised and addressed. For example, stakeholders we spoke to who work with indigenous, black and minoritised women highlighted the additional risks, barriers and impacts that women might face, due to interlocking structural inequalities and oppressions such as racism, migrant status, misogyny and so-called honour-based violence. Similarly, specialist advice and support must be provided for people living with a disability, as well as LGBTQI victim-survivors. It is essential that there are a range of well-resourced services equipped to support victim-survivors of image-based sexual abuse across these marginalised groups.

Conclusion

The introduction of new criminal offences specifically tackling forms of image-based sexual abuse represent an important first step in acknowledging the harms of these behaviours. Unfortunately, however, too often these laws are not being used as they were intended because law enforcement personnel are unaware of the provisions, or do not view the offences as "serious" enough to proceed with an investigation. Moreover, for many victim-survivors, criminal justice options are fraught owing to concerns about future relationships with the perpetrator, their friends and family members, as well as the stress and publicity that a court action might bring. Due to the limitations of the criminal law, there should be additional justice options available to victim-survivors of image-based sexual abuse, including more restorative and transformative approaches.

The introduction of a civil penalties scheme in Australia represents an example of an additional justice pathway for victim-survivors of image-based sexual abuse, and indeed greater use of the civil law more generally could provide valuable mechanisms for victim-survivor redress, if current financial constraints could be reduced.

Nonetheless, it is important to view the law as only part of the solution. Justice requires a multifaceted, multi-institutional and multi-layered approach. There is no "one-size-fits-all" response. Our research suggests that while a number of the components for securing justice are present, the picture is currently incomplete and inadequate. There are too many gaps – in legislation, in practical and emotional support, and in education and advice. Moreover, currently the lack of regulation and immunity for digital platforms that host illegal content means that image-based sexual abuse content continues to thrive online, and will only be removed on the majority of platforms (if at all) once a victim-survivor commences complex content removal requests that ultimately may do little to ensure their images are removed from the internet or personal devices.

In addition to formal and substantive legal and non-legal responses that can provide justice and practical support to victim-survivors of image-based sexual abuse, what is needed is school-, community- and university-based education that will prevent image-based sexual abuse from happening in the first place. This is the focus of the next and final chapter.

Note

1   Across common law jurisdictions, there are a range of provisions which come under the broad umbrella of image-based sexual abuse but which we have not been able to explore in this chapter. These include specific legislation on "up-skirting"; the empowerment of courts to make orders that the accused person takes reasonable steps to remove, delete or destroy images (with accompanying criminal penalties); measures designed to avoid prosecuting young people under the age of 16 years; and explicit recognition that intimate images can include breasts of a female, intersex or transgender person.

References

Bond, E., & Tyrell, E. (2018). Understanding revenge pornography: A national survey of police officers and staff in England and Wales. *Journal of Interpersonal Violence*. Advance online publication. doi: 10.1177/0866260518760011.

Chesney, R., & Citron, D. K. (2019). Deep fakes: A looming challenge for privacy, democracy, and national security. *California Law Review, 107*, 1753–1820.

Cole, S., & Maiberg, E. (2020, February 7). Pornhub doesn't care. *Vice*. Retrieved from www.vice.com/en_us/article/9393zp/how-pornhub-moderation-works-girls-do-porn.

Flynn, A., & Henry, N. (2019). Image-based sexual abuse: An Australian reflection. *Women and Criminal Justice*. Advance online publication. doi: 10.1080/08974454.2019.1646190.

Gavey, N., & Farley, J. (in press). Reframing sexual violence as "sexual harm" in New Zealand policy: A critique. In G. Torres & K. Yllo (eds.), *Conceptualizing sexual violence in marriage: Research and policy*. New York: Routledge.

Haynes, J. (2018). Legislative approaches to combating "revenge porn": A multi-jurisdictional perspective. *Statute Law Review, 39*(3), 319–336.

Henry, N., Flynn, A., & Powell, A. (2018). Policing image-based sexual abuse: Stakeholder perspectives. *Police Practice and Research: An International Journal, 19*(6), 565–581.

Henry, N., Flynn, A., & Powell, A. (2019). *Responding to "revenge pornography": Prevalence, nature and impacts*. Report to the Criminology Research Advisory Council. Canberra: Australian Institute of Criminology. Retrieved from http://crg.aic.gov.au/reports/1819/08-1516-FinalReport.pdf.

Henry, N., Powell, A., & Flynn, A. (2018, March 1). AI can now create fake porn, making revenge porn even more complicated. *The Conversation*. Retrieved from https://theconversation.com/ai-can-now-create-fake-porn-making-revenge-porn-even-more-complicated-92267.

Jordan, J. (2004). *The word of a woman? Police, rape and belief*. Basingstoke: Palgrave Macmillan.

Kelly, L., Lovett, J., & Regan, L. (2005). *A gap or a chasm? Attrition in reported rape cases* (Home Office research studies, issue 293). London: Home Office Research, Development and Statistics Directorate.

Kirchengast, T., & Crofts, T. (2019). A critical analysis of the conduct and fault elements in "revenge porn" criminalisation. *Criminal Law Journal, 43*(4), 274–292.

Lonsway, K. A., & Archambault, J. (2012). The "justice gap" for sexual assault cases: Future directions for research and reform. *Violence Against Women, 18*(2), 145–168.

McGlynn, C. (2018, July 11). "Revenge porn" and upskirting remind us sexual offending is not about sexual arousal. *Huffington Post.* Retrieved from www. huffingtonpost.co.uk/entry/revenge-porn-and-why-sexual-offending-is-not-about_uk_5b45c9e7e4b00db1492ffe9f?ncid=other_email_o63gt2jcad4&utm_campaign=share_email.

McGlynn, C., Johnson, K., Rackley, E., Henry, N., Gavey, N., Flynn, A., & Powell, A. (in press). "It's torture for the soul": The harms of image-based sexual abuse. *Social and Legal Studies.*

McGlynn, C., & Rackley, E. (2017). Image-based sexual abuse. *Oxford Journal of Legal Studies, 37*(3), 534–561.

McGlynn, C., et al. (2019) *Shattering lives and myths: A report on image-based sexual abuse.* Retrieved from https://claremcglynn.files.wordpress.com/2019/10/shattering-lives-and-myths-revised-aug-2019.pdf.

McGlynn, C., & Westmarland, N. (2019). Kaleidoscopic justice: Sexual violence and victim-survivors' perceptions of justice. *Social & Legal Studies, 28*(2), 179–201.

McGlynn, C., Westmarland, N., & Godden, N. (2012). "'I just wanted him to hear me': Sexual violence and the possibilities of restorative justice". *Journal of Law and Society, 39*(2), 213–240.

New Zealand Law Commission. (2012). *Harmful digital communications: The adequacy of the current sanctions and remedies.* Wellington, New Zealand. Retrieved from www.lawcom.govt.nz/sites/default/files/projectAvailableFormats/NZLC%20MB3.pdf.

Nigam, S. (2018, April 25). Revenge porn laws across the world. *The Centre for Internet and Society.* Retrieved from https://cis-india.org/internet-governance/blog/revenge-porn-laws-across-the-world.

North Yorkshire Police, Fire & Crime Commissioner. (2018). *Suffering in silence: Image-based sexual abuse report 2018.* Retrieved from www.nomorenaming.co.uk/wp-content/uploads/2018/11/Suffering-in-Silence-2018.pdf.

Powell, A., Henry, N., & Flynn, A. (2018). Image-based sexual abuse. In W. S. De-Keseredy & M. Dragiewicz (eds.), *Handbook of critical criminology* (pp. 305–315). Abingdon, Oxon; New York: Routledge.

Ruvalcaba, Y., & Eaton, A. A. (2019). Nonconsensual pornography among US adults: A sexual scripts framework on victimization, perpetration, and health correlates for women and men. *Psychology of Violence.* Advance online publication. https://doi.org/10.1037/vio0000233.

Temkin, J., & Krahé, B. (2008). *Sexual assault and the justice gap.* Oxford; Portland, OR: Hart.

Zinsstag, E., & Keenan, M. (2017). *Restorative responses to sexual violence: Legal, social and therapeutic dimensions.* Abingdon, Oxon: Routledge.

Chapter 8

Preventing image-based sexual abuse

Ethics, consent and respectful relationships

Introduction

As discussed in the previous chapter, the law plays an important role in addressing image-based sexual abuse. In many jurisdictions, there are penalties in place for the non-consensual taking or sharing of intimate images. In some jurisdictions, there are specific requirements that persons delete, remove or retract non-consensual nude or sexual images. Increasingly, governments around the world are turning to greater regulation of technology companies to ensure that they are held accountable for hosting illegal content on their platforms and such companies are slowly responding by taking greater steps to prohibit and respond to image-based sexual abuse on their platforms.

Although these diverse legal or regulatory responses to the problem of image-based sexual abuse are no doubt important, they are nonetheless largely reactive measures that are activated once non-consensual nude or sexual images have been taken or shared. Indeed, they can often do very little to prevent the further dissemination of such images, nor ensure that they are removed altogether from internet sites or digital devices. It is imperative, therefore, that resources are heavily invested in prevention measures to prevent image-based sexual abuse from happening in the first place.

This chapter aims to explore different interventions beyond the law to address image-based sexual abuse across three categories of "prevention": Primary, secondary and tertiary (see Our Watch, ANROWS, & VicHealth, 2015; VicHealth, 2007). In the context of interpersonal violence, "primary prevention" seeks to stop the violence *before it ever occurs* by addressing the underlying causes or "drivers" within an entire population. This can include changing structural inequalities, cultural attitudes and common behaviours or practices that are linked to violence (e.g., through educational programs, social marketing campaigns, anti-discrimination policies or localised community interventions that reduce risk factors and promote protective factors for violence). "Secondary prevention", or early intervention, is aimed at contexts or population subgroups that are *at greater risk* of becoming victims or perpetrators of violence. This may include programs that seek to support sub-populations at higher risk for victimisation or perpetration, as well as those that identify the behaviour early, in particular, before it escalates (e.g., through targeted programs for subgroups such young people, new parents, women with a disability or men identified as having multiple risk markers such as anger management or substance abuse). Tertiary prevention refers to interventions that respond to abuse *after it has occurred*, seeking to prevent its escalation and recurrence. This can include emergency accommodation and health services, therapeutic support and criminal justice responses (see Powell & Henry, 2014; Sutton, Cherney, & White, 2008). Although these distinctions are important in the formation of multilevel abuse prevention policy, programs and services, in practice there is often much overlap in prevention work.

In the first section of this chapter, we explore existing public education anti-sexting campaigns that have been rolled out in schools, universities and the community. Our focus here is not specifically on the range of responses given by educational or community institutions when intimate images are shared either consensually or non-consensually, but rather on the messaging within educational campaigns. In the second section, we describe the approaches taken by digital platforms to address and prevent image-based sexual abuse. We argue that prevention interventions across the different community and educational sectors should deliver content which: Identifies and challenges the gender- and sexuality-based social norms and cultural practices that drive gendered violence; redirects the responsibility onto perpetrators of image-based sexual abuse rather than victim-survivors; and encourages and provides tools for people to take action as bystanders to report content for removal and call-out victim-blaming and shaming where they encounter the image-based sexual abuse of others. We argue that prevention interventions must, above all, be guided by a sexual ethics approach (Carmody, 2009) that prioritises affirmative consent, reciprocity, bodily integrity and sexual freedom, recognising the inherent dignity and equality of digital citizens.

Education and image-based sexual abuse

According to many cybersecurity experts, law enforcement personnel, educational authorities, parents and others, the most pragmatic solution to preventing cybercriminal activity is to advise potential victims to avoid certain behaviours, disclosures or locations to ensure both their online and offline safety. Such advice is necessary to keep internet users safe, such as not clicking on links or attachments from suspicious emails, adopting complex passwords that are not easy-to-guess or warning people of the implications of intimate content being posted online (Powell & Henry, 2017). However, when it comes to sexting and the sharing of intimate images, the nature and content of this messaging is often highly gendered because it is directed predominantly at young women, resulting in the failure to either address the perpetrator's actions or the underlying sociocultural causes of these behaviours. It can also have the effect of blaming the victim. Moreover, the campaigns, as we discuss below, are framed as "anti-sexting"; that is, rather than being focused on preventing the *non-consensual* taking or sharing of nude or sexual images, they warn young people not to (consensually) share sexual "selfies".

Anti-sexting education

Public educational "anti-sexting campaigns" in many countries have tended to focus on the lifelong and disastrous consequences that will befall women, particularly young women, when they consensually share nude or sexual images with someone they trust. For example, *I Shared a Photo* is a Canadian public service announcement video that shows a young woman sitting on her bed holding a series of placards to explain that she shared an intimate photo with someone she trusted, leading to thousands of other people seeing the photo. The video ends with the following message: "There's no such thing as 'just one photo'. Protect yourself from sexual exploitation. Be safe online". As noted by other commentators, this video "is eerily similar" to the final video that was made by Canadian teenager Amanda Todd who took her own life after her images were posted online and she faced horrific online bullying (Strapagiel, 2013; see also Dobson, 2015; Penney, 2016).

In Australia, the governmental cybersafety campaign, *ThinkUKnow*, is another example of problematic "anti-sexting" messaging. As part of the campaign, a short video, called *Megan's Story,* was designed as an educational resource for teachers and high school students on the dangers of sexting. The video appeared on YouTube and has been widely viewed by Australian audiences, broadcast across television, cinema and shown in school-based educational programs. The video depicts "Megan" who takes a photograph down her top and sends it to a boy in her class. As she sits down at her desk, it becomes apparent that her classmates have also seen the image; the boys in the class smirk, wink and nod, while the females look disgusted and disappointed with Megan – not with the boy who non-consensually shared her image. At the end of the video, the male teacher receives the image via text message and gives Megan a disapproving look. Megan runs out of the classroom and the video then ends with a male voiceover saying: "Think you know what happens to your images? Who will see them? How they will affect you? Think again" (for a discussion, see Albury & Crawford, 2012).

Similarly, in the United Kingdom, *Exposed,* a short film on the dangers of sexting, shows the adverse consequences for a high school student who has sent her boyfriend nude images of herself, which are later shared online by one of the boy's friends. The video presents the girl's self-dialogue with her "more rational self" who urges her to go back home after she has run away. Her "other self" tells her that she made a "stupid mistake" and that she needs to "stop blaming everyone else" and to "always think before you share" (see also Dobson & Ringrose, 2016). Like the other anti-sexting campaigns described above, the persons who shared or received her images are "strangely absent" in this video (Albury & Crawford, 2012: 465).[1]

A review of ten online educational campaigns found that the majority of sexting campaigns rely on messages of abstinence and fear through reference to criminal prosecutions and disastrous social consequences for the victim (Döring, 2014). While anti-sexting videos may deter *some* young people from sharing intimate images of themselves consensually with others, decades of research on abstinence sex education has shown that this approach is "at best ineffective and at worst results in negative health outcomes" (Albury, Hasinoff, & Senft, 2017: 527). Indeed, research has repeatedly shown that abstinence-focused sex education leaves young people disempowered and lacking the information and confidence they need to make agentic decisions about their sexual health, safety and well-being (Allen, 2005). As suggested by Crofts, Lee, McGovern and Milivojevic (2015), often the initial motivation for engaging in consensual sexual image exchanges is sexual pleasure and desire, and as such, educational messages that deny this experience are less likely to be seen as authentic and will have little influence on young people (see also Lee & Crofts, 2015).

Moreover, these messages can be read as examples of "slut-shaming", a term used to describe the condemnation of those who transgress societal norms about sexuality, particularly female or non-hetero sexuality. For instance, these campaigns reinforce a sexual double standard because girls and women are chastised for engaging in sexually "promiscuous" behaviours (see Dobson, 2015; Gong & Hoffman, 2012; Ringrose & Renold, 2012), while the boys and men who are non-consensually sharing these images receive little, if any, negative attention. As Karaian (2014: 284) argues, these campaigns thereby "reify and mobilize a culture of sexual shame in order to responsibilize certain girls for their own, and others', safety" which in turn "reproduce[s] and reif[ies] gendered, racialized, classed and hetero-normative ideas of sexual value, propriety, privilege and blameworthiness ...". This parallels the problems identified within broader strategies to prevent sexual violence, which have been "focused primarily on women taking action to avoid their victimisation" (Carmody & Carrington, 2000: 346).

Furthermore, these educational packages ultimately fail to capture the complexity of image-based sexual abuse. They ignore situations where persons are coerced into sharing intimate images, or when images are stolen, secretly taken or created using artificial intelligence and other digital technologies without the knowledge or consent of the person depicted in them (Powell & Henry, 2017). They fail to account for the vitriolic abuse and harassment that often occurs after nude or sexual images are shared online which are then typically framed as a problem of "cyberbullying" rather than as gender-based harassment (Bailey, 2013, 2014). And they also fail to recognise the significant societal and interpersonal/relationship pressures that are placed on people, particularly young people, to engage in taking or sharing sexual selfies of themselves. Above all, these educational campaigns focus on the victim and as such fail to target the persons who are engaged in the wrongful act – that is, those who take, share or threaten to share nude or sexual images without consent. As a result, they may have very little deterrent effect.

The implications of such messaging should not be downplayed. The way in which a problem is represented shapes the development of policies and laws to respond to the problem (Bacchi, 1999). In some international jurisdictions, for instance, legal responses have embraced simplistic understandings of image-based sexual abuse. For example, in 2014, California was one of the first US states to criminalise the non-consensual sharing of intimate images, yet the original legislation (which has since been changed) was limited in its scope as it did not cover "selfies" where the victim took the image him/herself. In several international jurisdictions (e.g., the United States, England, Wales and New Zealand), the requirement that the perpetrator intended to cause distress or harm to the victim fails to take into account the harm done to victim-survivors when the images are shared without their consent and the perpetrator *did not intend to cause harm or distress* (see Chapter 7).

Like all phenomena, there are contradictory power effects within certain discourses that should be acknowledged. The widespread attention to the problem of image-based sexual abuse has in part been assisted by the salaciousness of the term "revenge pornography" itself, which has caught the attention of law and policymakers, as well as academics and journalists. However, as we have described earlier in the book (see Chapter 1), the problem is that this term is exclusionary and narrow in its scope, and more problematically, it hampers the implementation of appropriate strategies to adequately respond to and prevent image-based sexual abuse (Franks, 2015). Like rape and sexual assault, the injustice stems not exclusively from the act itself – as a sexual violation of bodily autonomy and a major breach of trust – but also from societal and community reactions to the victim-survivor and the act itself, including the lack of perpetrator accountability, as well as poor societal attitudes that blame the victim. It is important to note, for example, that Amanda Todd, Audrie Pott and Rehtaeh Parsons all took their own lives after their sexual assault images were shared widely online *and* they faced a brutal campaign of harassment and abuse. As we discussed in Chapter Three, much of the anxiety that victim-survivors of image-based sexual abuse experience relates to the fear of who might discover the images, where they might appear in the future, and how others will react. Much of the harassment and abuse experienced can often be due to attitudes directed at the victim-survivor for 'being *that kind of woman* who took and/ or shared a sexual image" (Powell & Henry, 2017: 242, emphasis original).

The problem of image-based sexual abuse has frequently been framed as "sexting gone wrong" – represented in educational campaigns as "morality tale" about foolish young women who should know better (Albury & Crawford, 2012: 465). But the problem can and should be represented differently. First, the problem should be framed as nude or sexual images being created and/or shared *without the consent of the person depicted in the image*. And second, educational interventions should be focused on dismantling stigma, victim-blaming and showing bystanders how to effectively challenge perpetrator behaviours and support victim-survivors. In other words, prevention education needs to focus on raising awareness within the community more broadly about the harms and wrongs of image-based sexual abuse. This cannot be done through the release of a single public education video alone, but rather should be part of a comprehensive and holistic package focusing on respectful relationships and ethical sexual practices.

Towards an affirmative consent model for image-based sexual abuse

A number of victim-survivor participants in our study mentioned the importance of ensuring what happened to them did not happen to others. Education was a key factor identified by those participants to help achieve this. For example, Julia (UK) told us "basically the outcome that I want from this is to stop it happening to others. I can't change what's happened to me". Others expressed similar sentiments, such as Kimberly (UK) who told us "the only justice would be that this just doesn't happen to [others]". This was echoed by Margaret (UK): "I just want to make sure that ... nobody has to go through this again". Several participants discussed the importance of young people being educated as to the risks of sharing intimate images to warn them not to take or share intimate images of themselves in the first place. For example, Georgia (Aus) suggested that education needed to be focused on the following message: "once you put stuff on the internet it [might never] be deleted or erased", noting that people need to be "more careful for [their] own well-being".

Yet other participants commented that there should be education on the social and legal repercussions for those who engage in image-based sexual abuse perpetration, including understanding the "gravity" of their actions and recognising that image-based sexual abuse is wrong. In the words of Heather (UK):

> I think there's still people who don't realise that if you receive a photo with consent, but then you share it, you're committing an offence. I think people still think, 'Well, it's you that's done it, it's you that set the

ball rolling, it's your fault', so I think people need to be educated that, actually, it is wrong and it is against the law, and I think there's a lot of people that still aren't totally aware.

Education on the legal ramifications was also mentioned by others, including Rachel (NZ), who said:

In New Zealand, they were trying to really bring it to light that revenge porn is actually an offence, like a chargeable offence, so they were making examples of a lot of people that were doing, and my story as well. They wanted to get it out there in the news, but it would just be to educate people that this sort of behaviour, these threats, are very illegal, and the effects that they can have on people, too. Like, it truly can suck a person's life up. You're going out there to try and ruin their life by putting naked photos of them out there, people just need to realise how, actually, life-ruining that can be for someone.

Some participants mentioned that image-based sexual abuse should be part of consent and respectful relationships education – that people should be taught that consent to one act does not equate to consent to another act. For instance, Megan (NZ) said:

They should be told that if someone sends you a photo you do not share it. Unless the person says that you can share that picture, you do not share it because that is for your eyes, that is personal for you. If someone says, 'don't touch me', don't touch them. If someone says, 'please do not do this', do not do that. It's simple shit that they should be teaching in schools.

The importance of gender and sexuality in developing educational programs was also mentioned, for example, addressing masculine entitlement and promoting the empowerment of women (as well as men). According to Alison (Aus), men and boys "just get taught that women are basically there for their sexual pleasure and they don't have agency and you don't need to listen to what they say".

Other participants reflected on the futility of telling young people not to take or share images of themselves, saying that the focus should instead be on harm-reduction or harm-minimisation. For example, when asked what a good approach to prevention might be, Annie (NZ) responded:

Just more education about how to deal with it, if it does happen, because it does. … You can tell people not to send [images], but I mean it's going to happen anyways, with just the age group, and the wide scale, like it does happen. So, I reckon the best thing to do would be to educate about how to deal with it the best way, because that can minimise how it is. I think just more awareness around that subject, and definitely resources that are more available to girls so they know that what's happening to them. ... it shouldn"t just be something that you try and deal with yourself. Like, they have a right to go and seek help and they need to know that they're going to be taken seriously, especially if they're young.

Support for victim-survivors was also mentioned as an important part of any educational program. For instance, Xia (NZ) summed this up in the following way:

Yes, I think there's an ambulance at the bottom of the cliff in the sense that if this happens – let's educate on all the things we can do to prevent it happening, but what about if it does happen? We have all these education programs to keep kids off drugs. Don't use drugs, this is what happens. But what if it does happen? Where is the education for what if it does happen? Where do we go for help? You can tell a kid they're going to get cancer, they're going to be addicted, they're going to get pimples all over their face – but there's very little about but if it does happen, this is where you can get help, this is who you speak to, this is who you go to. And it's the same with online images. We can tell everybody not to do it and how to prevent it, but what if it did happen? Where's the education there?

In response to the shortcomings of existing anti-sexting campaigns in various country contexts, scholars have recommended alternative framings. In a study on young people's view on sexting education (n=14), Rübner Jørgensen, Weckesser, Turner and Wade (2019: 35) found that study participants were concerned that schools and police "placed too much focus on the victim (the person whose nude had been leaked), and that the sender of the nude should also be held accountable and face reasonable consequences". The authors concluded that educational campaigns that are taught by cyber safety or community police officers "tend to construct schools as sites for the policing of sex and gender norms" and are problematically contingent on a criminalisation and abstinence model (Rübner Jørgensen et al., 2019: 35). They argue that education in schools needs to "focus as much on wider relationship issues such as consent, trust, gender, body image, bullying and sexual harassment, as they do on the particular apps (which rapidly change) or the dangers of being online" (Rübner Jørgensen et al., 2019: 35).

Sexting researchers further propose that the *consensual* sharing of nude or sexual imagery should be reframed in school education programs as a form of sexual expression and media production (Albury et al., 2017;

Döring, 2014; Hasinoff, 2013; Karaian & Van Meyl, 2015; Lloyd, 2018). They recommend that educational content differentiate between consensual and non-consensual image sharing, and suggest that the latter needs to be the focus of educational campaigns, not the former. For instance, Albury et al. (2017) recommend an alternative approach to sexting that moves away from shame and fear-based messages, towards affirmative consent models that have been adopted for other forms of sexual behaviour. An affirmative consent standard is based on an ongoing, active agreement of all parties. In the context of image-based sexual abuse, it places the focus on the person seeking to create or share the image to take active steps to ensure they have ongoing, active consent from the person depicted in the image, to create and/or share that image (see also Burgin & Flynn, 2019).

Albury et al. (2017) recommend that educational packages develop student skills in recognising and negotiating affirmative consent to receive, request and share intimate images. They recommend a harm-reduction approach that balances discussion about risk and pleasure, and dismantles and problematises the sexual double standard that amplifies the shame and harm for girls/women as opposed to boys/men. This model has also been rolled out in broader sexuality education to overcome the problems of abstinence and de-eroticised approaches to sex, sexuality and relationships (see e.g., Allen, 2004, 2005; Kearney, Gleeson, Leung, Ollis, & Joyce, 2016).

Education on image-based sexual abuse, whether in schools, universities or in the community more generally, also needs to be inclusive of social, cultural and gender diversity. Currently, there are few studies on the effectiveness of primary prevention programs, such as sexuality education, within culturally and linguistically diverse (CALD) communities, as well as sexuality- and gender-diverse youth. This reflects a further lack of development of inclusive prevention and education materials within mainstream sexuality education, where in countries such as Australia, New Zealand and the United Kingdom, for example, the cis-gender, heterosexual and White European context continues to shapes both the content and approach (Allen, 2018; Botfield, Zwi, Rutherford, & Newman, 2018; Bragg, Renold, Ringrose, & Jackson, 2018; Ezer, Kerr, Fisher, Heywood, & Lucke, 2019).

Prevention initiatives in educational contexts require more than isolated curriculum delivery and are less effective when "they occur in isolation, and broader community or social and cultural norms and practices do not support their message" (Our Watch et al., 2015: 47). In other words, prevention may well deliver messages to young people in sexuality education about the importance of consent and privacy in sexting contexts, but these can be undermined by counter-messages in the schoolyard, at home and in popular media that reinforce problematic gendered notions of victim-responsibility and male sexual entitlement. In turn, education messaging that seeks to engage young people needs to pay due attention to the social and normative influence of particular masculinities in relation to sexual pressure and sexual practice. For instance, as Lee and Crofts (2015: 469) suggest, "the dynamics of masculinities and masculinized youth cultures that normalize and/or celebrate such behaviours or produce pressures where young boys feel compelled to ask for such images under threat of otherwise being labelled as 'gay' or emasculated" need to be understood and engaged with in prevention messaging "in the same way we might seek to understand the pressures on girls".

Finally, young people are an important population group for targeting primary prevention education interventions to. Yet, as our research has suggested, many of the victims and perpetrators of image-based sexual abuse are adults in their 20s and 30s, and as such are out of reach for school primary prevention education. An alternative format for primary prevention might include a community-wide mass media campaign, which has been shown to be effective in changing sex-related behaviours (Wakefield, Loken, & Hornik, 2010). Such campaigns tend to work best when they are reinforced with community-based programs and adequately funded to achieve wide exposure within the general population (Wakefield et al., 2010). Digital platforms may be a further avenue through which prevention messages reach these hard-to-reach cohorts.

In summary, prevention education needs to shift away from an "abstinence" approach that responsibilises young women, and move towards a model of ethics, respect and consent. Such an approach should seek to strike a balance between risk and pleasure, and be premised on a model of sexual rights (IPPF, 2008; WHO, 2015). Above all, prevention strategies must recognise individuals' rights to dignity, sexual integrity and sexual freedom: "The conditions necessary to create the capacity for developing a sense of sexual self, sexual self-esteem, the opportunity for sexual exploration, and beneficial sexual interactions" (Craig, 2011: 72).

The prevention of image-based sexual abuse, however, is not the sole responsibility of schools and universities. Other organisations within the community also play an important role. In the section below, we focus on the role of digital platforms in terms of responding to and preventing image-based sexual abuse, examining the extent to which such measures achieve primary prevention (preventing abuse before it occurs by addressing structural inequalities, cultural attitudes and behaviours), secondary prevention (targeting sub-groups that are at greater risk of becoming victims or perpetrators) or tertiary prevention (responding to abuse after it has occurred).

Digital platforms

In the wake of high-profile events such as the live-streaming of the mass shootings in Christchurch in March 2019 and Cambridge Analytica scandal, there has been growing pressure on governments to introduce greater regulatory oversight of internet intermediaries that host or facilitate illegal content and to hold them to account (see Gillespie, 2018a, 2018b; Kreimer, 2006; MacKinnon, Hickok, Bar, & Lim, 2014; Pasquale, 2010; Suzor, 2019).[2] Even Facebook founder and Chief Executive, Mark Zuckerberg, has called for more active governmental regulation of digital platforms that host harmful online content (Zuckerberg, 2019).

While technology companies continue to exert "unprecedented power" over "what we can see or share" (Suzor, 2019: 8), the past five years have seen a radical shift in terms of specifically crafted community standards, policies and practices on online abuse, including on child sexual abuse material, hate speech and image-based sexual abuse (see e.g., Citron & Norton, 2011; Gagliardone, Gal, Alves, & Martinez, 2015). The technology companies have, for example, introduced a range of different measures to tackle image-based sexual abuse, such as disabling or suspending accounts, providing victims the means to report their experiences, and ensuring that harmful content is taken down or content involving them excluded from internet searches. Facebook, for example, prohibits the sharing of image-based sexual abuse content according to three conditions: The image is non-commercial or produced in a private setting; the person is nude, nearly nude or engaged in a sexual act or posing in a sexual way; there is a lack of consent as indicated by captions, comments, the title of the page, independent sources (e.g., from law enforcement or media) or reporting from victims (Facebook, 2020). Deepfakes (digitally altered images) are also explicitly prohibited on several different platforms.

In addition to formal prohibition, digital platforms have also introduced technological tools to detect image-based sexual abuse content. For example, several platforms use photo-matching, digital-fingerprinting tools to prevent the further sharing of non-consensual nude or sexual images of their platform. These tools are based on the revolutionary PhotoDNA technology developed in 2009 by Microsoft and Professor Hany Farid from Dartmouth College, which enables the creation of a unique digital signature or a "hash" of child abuse images which can then be compared against images stored in a database to assist platforms to remove and block content, and assist law enforcement to make arrests and prosecute perpetrators (Langston, 2018).

One innovative, albeit controversial, "prevention" pilot program using "digital fingerprinting" methods was introduced in November 2017 by Facebook. The trial, currently operating in partnership with government and non-governmental partner organisations in Australia, Canada, the United States and the United Kingdom, seeks to prevent image-based sexual abuse from occurring on the platform. The program enables users who are concerned that *someone might* share a nude or sexual image of them to contact the relevant partner agency and complete an online form, leading to the creation of a unique hash that will block any future images from appearing on Facebook and Facebook-owned platforms.

In 2019, Facebook introduced a new artificial intelligence (AI) tool that can detect non-consensually shared "nearly nude" images. It does this by training the algorithm to recognise, using a database of previously flagged non-consensual intimate images, language patterns and key words that would suggest those images are non-consensual. After the content is flagged, a member of Facebook's Community Operations Team then reviews the content to decide whether or not the user has violated their community standards, leading to a range of possible outcomes, such as the removal of the image, account suspension or a warning issued to the offending user (see Davis, 2019; Salinas, 2019).

Although the explicit prohibition of image-based sexual abuse content on digital platforms and the use of automated technology (like artificial intelligence and photo-matching technologies) are welcome developments, the companies ultimately reserve the right to make decisions on what content has violated their terms of services and many companies are non-transparent around those decisions (see Suzor, 2019). US lawyer Carrie Goldberg (2019) starkly illustrates the gap between the rhetoric and reality of corporate responsibility in relation to image-based sexual abuse content. She notes that her clients' number one priority is always "their horrific Google results!", yet her repeated requests to Google's Legal Removals team to request they remove the links to pornographic videos of women who were "embroiled in a conspiracy to perform porn" and sexually assaulted, were ignored:

> The current policy says Google may remove nude or sexually explicit images that were shared without consent, but the company maintains sole discretion about when to remove non-consensual pornography. If Google decides it will keep linking to a website that contains your nude images, victims are just out of luck. And there's no appellate body. There is no law, only corporate policy, that protects (or fails to protect) victims' most private information.
>
> (Goldberg, 2019).

Goldberg tells the story of "Anna", an 18-year-old client who was filmed by three older men having violent sex with her:

> It wasn't long before the videos began to populate the first five pages of her search-engine results. Over the next several years, the stalking, harassment and death threats from her 'fans' became unbearable. My client moved and everybody in her family changed their names, yet somebody found her new name and posted that online. The video follower her because of Google. Initially, Google refused to remove the video because they said she didn't own the copyright and their revenge-porn policy, they say, doesn't apply to what they call 'regret porn'.
>
> (Goldberg, 2019)

In the United States, section 230 of the *Communications Decency Act of 1996* gives corporations immunity for defamatory or injurious content published by third party users (Tushnet, 2008). This means that digital platforms cannot be held legally liable for illegal content hosted on their platforms, with the exception of copyrighted material. Many companies thus make it clear, in their Terms of Service, that they do not have the obligation to review or moderate content and many in fact do not do so. Even those companies that do engage in regular content moderation practices, it is important to note that this is a highly complex process (see Gillespie, 2018a). First, it may be difficult to differentiate between consensual and non-consensual nude or sexual content in the absence of any accompanying information to indicate that the persons depicted in the image did not consent to its distribution (Henry & Flynn, 2019). Second, what constitutes a "nude" or "sexual" image is subject to differing cultural standards. For instance, an image of a Muslim woman in her bikini or without her hijab may have very different consequences compared to an image of a non-Muslim woman under similar circumstances. Third, content moderators are often contract workers who "work in stressful conditions, with little job security on health insurance and suffer psychological damage from having to confront – and make decisions about – the horrific stuff that people post on social media platforms" (Naughton, 2019; see also Roberts, 2019). And fourth, although artificial intelligence provides much-needed assistance in terms of flagging image-based sexual abuse content, it is difficult to imagine a computer being able to discern intent when humans universally struggle to do so (Dickson, 2019).

Moreover, while technology companies may be able to remove the content before a victim even discovers it is there, the reality is that once an image is shared, there is little anyone can do to prevent the further sharing on other platforms, particularly those platforms that take little action to respond to or prevent the posting of illegal online content. As Franks (cited in Kelly, 2019), has noted:

> You can encourage these companies to do the right thing and to have policies in place and resources dedicated to taking down those kind of materials. But what we know about the viral nature of especially salacious material is that by the time you take it down three days, four days, five days after the fact, it's too late. So it may come down from a certain platform, but it's not going to come down from the internet.

Finally, these mechanisms do little to address broader structural inequalities or problematic cultural attitudes that drive the behaviours in the first place. Platforms that are proactive and committed to addressing image-based sexual abuse can issue pop-up warnings to users or suspend or disable accounts, yet in reality, users face very little real consequences for engaging in these behaviours since they can easily open up a new account or upload and share images on other platforms that facilitate or encourage such behaviour. Essentially, users hide behind the veil of anonymity. They experience very little social condemnation for their activities online as compared to criminal proceedings which are designed as "status degradation ceremonies" to transform the public identity of the individual and to publicly denounce their character (Garfinkel, 1967). The limitations of these various corporate and technological measures are a reminder of the importance of a whole-of-community multifaceted approach to addressing the problem of image-based sexual abuse in education, law, policy, therapeutic support and corporate social responsibility.

Conclusion

Educational and community responses that seek to prevent image-based sexual abuse must identify and challenge gender- and sexuality-based social norms and cultural practices that drive the behaviour, as well as seek to dismantle social stigma and victim-blaming. Responsibility must be redirected onto the perpetrators of image-based sexual abuse and more broadly the digital society which to a great extent normalises and encourages the non-consensual sharing of all images (including intimate images). Collective responsibility also lies with government and non-government organisations to empower bystanders to intervene to prevent image-based abuse and support victim-survivors, and for robust structures to provide the support and resources needed for victim-survivors.

Educational, therapeutic, legal and corporate responses must be guided by a model of digital and sexual ethics that not only recognises image-based sexual abuse as a societal and community responsibility, but fundamentally values rights to dignity, equality, privacy, bodily integrity and sexual freedom. This must be the starting point for all interventions on image-based sexual abuse. It is the only way, we believe, to achieve genuine cultural change and a substantial reduction in image-based sexual abuse behaviours.

Acknowledgements

With permission of Palgrave Macmillan, this chapter draws on a small number of excerpts from Powell, A., & Henry, N. (2017). *Sexual violence in a digital age*. London: Palgrave Macmillan.

Notes

1 The accompanying educational resource to *Megan's Story*, which is not widely available, suggests that the video be used as a talking point for classroom discussions to highlight the role of peers and bystanders in the non-consensual sharing of nude or sexual images. However, in isolation, the video serves predominantly as a warning to young girls about the dangers of sexting (Albury & Crawford, 2012).

2 An "internet intermediary" is broadly defined as a non-state organisation or entity which facilitates transactions, information exchange or communications between third parties on the internet (see Cotter, 2006). An internet intermediary can be further classified as either a technical provider – a carriage service or internet service provider (ISP) – or a content host or "digital platform", including social media, cloud computing and search engines. We thus refer to "digital platforms" throughout this chapter using Gillespie's (2018b: 254) definition:

> ... sites and services that host public expression, store it on and serve it up from the cloud, organize access to it through search and recommendation, or install it onto mobile devices. ... What unites them all is their central offer: to host and organize user content for public circulation, without having produced or commissioned it.

References

Albury, K., & Crawford, K. (2012). Sexting, consent and young people's ethics: Beyond Megan's Story. *Continuum, 26*(3), 463–473.

Albury, K., Hasinoff, A. A., & Senft, T. (2017). From media abstinence to media production: Sexting, young people and education. In L. Allen & M. L. Rasmussen (eds.), *The Palgrave handbook of sexuality education* (pp. 527–546). London: Palgrave Macmillan.

Allen, L. (2004). Beyond the birds and the bees: Constituting a discourse of erotics in sexuality education. *Gender and Education, 16*(2), 151–167.

Allen, L. (2005). *Sexual subjects: Young people, sexuality and education.* Basingstoke; New York: Palgrave Macmillan.

Allen, L. (2018). *Sexuality education and new materialism: Queer things.* New York: Palgrave Macmillan.

Bacchi, C. L. (1999). *Women, policy and politics: The construction of policy problems.* London; Thousand Oaks, CA: Sage Publications.

Bailey, J. (2013). "Sexualized online bullying" through an equality lens: Missed opportunity in AB v. Bragg? *McGill Law Journal, 59*(3), 709–737.

Bailey, J. (2014). Time to unpack the juggernaut?: Reflections on the Canadian federal parliamentary debates on "cyberbullying". *Dalhousie Law Journal, 37*(2), 661–707.

Botfield, J. R., Zwi, A. B., Rutherford, A., & Newman, C. E. (2018). Learning about sex and relationships among migrant and refugee young people in Sydney, Australia: "I never got the talk about the birds and the bees". *Sex Education, 18*(6), 705–720.

Bragg, S., Renold, E., Ringrose, J., & Jackson, C. (2018). "More than boy, girl, male, female": Exploring young people's views on gender diversity within and beyond school contexts. *Sex Education, 18*(4), 420–434.

Burgin, R., & Flynn, A. (2019). Women's behaviour as implied consent: Male "reasonableness" in Australian rape law. *Criminology & Criminal Justice.* Advance online publication. doi: 10.1177/1748895819880953.

Carmody, M. (2009). *Sex and ethics: Young people and ethical sex.* South Yarra, VIC: Palgrave Macmillan.

Carmody, M., & Carrington, K. (2000). Preventing sexual violence? *Australian & New Zealand Journal of Criminology, 33*(3), 341–361.

Citron, D. K., & Norton, H. L. (2011). Intermediaries and hate speech: Fostering digital citizenship for our information age. *Boston University Law Review, 91*, 1435–1484.

Cotter, T. F. (2006). Some observations on the law and economics of intermediaries. *Michigan State Law Review, 1*, 67–82.

Craig, E. (2011). *Troubling sex: Towards a legal theory of sexual integrity.* Toronto, Canada: UBC Press.

Crofts, T., Lee, M., McGovern, A., & Milivojevic, S. (2015). *Sexting and young people.* Basingstoke: Palgrave Macmillan.

Davis, A. (2019, March 15). Detecting non-consensual intimate images and supporting victims. *Facebook News.* Retrieved from https://about.fb.com/news/2019/03/detecting-non-consensual-intimate-images/

Dickson, E. J. (2019, March 15). Facebook says it's putting an end to revenge porn once and for all: But like… how? *RollingStone.* Retrieved from www.rollingstone.com/culture/culture-news/facebook-revenge-porn-ai-software-808867

Dobson, A. (2015). Girls' "pain memes" on YouTube: The production of pain and femininity in a digital network. In S. Baker, B. Robards, & B. Buttigieg (eds.), *Youth cultures and subcultures: Australian perspectives* (pp. 173–182). Farnham, Surrey, UK: Ashgate.

Dobson, A. S., & Ringrose, J. (2016). Sext education: Pedagogies of sex, gender and shame in the schoolyards of *Tagged* and *Exposed. Sex Education, 16*(1), 8–21.

Döring, N. (2014). Consensual sexting among adolescents: Risk prevention through abstinence education or safer sexting?. *Cyberpsychology: Journal of Psychosocial Research on Cyberspace, 8*(1), article 9. http://dx.doi.org/10.5817/CP2014-1-9.

Ezer, P., Kerr, L., Fisher, C. M., Heywood, W., & Lucke, J. (2019). Australian students' experiences of sexuality education at school. *Sex Education, 19*(5), 597–613.

Facebook. (2020). *Community standards: 9. Sexual exploitation of adults.* Retrieved from www.facebook.com/communitystandards/sexual_exploitation_adults.

Franks, M. A. (2015, June 22). How to defeat "revenge porn": First, recognize it's about privacy, not revenge. *Huffington Post.* Retrieved from www.huffingtonpost.com/mary-anne-franks/how-to-defeat-revenge-porn_b_7624900.html.

Gagliardone, I., Gal, D., Alves, T., & Martinez, G. (2015). *Countering online hate speech.* Paris: UNESCO.

Garfinkel, H. (1967). *Studies in ethnomethodology.* Englewood Cliffs, NJ: Prentice-Hall.

Gillespie, T. (2018a). Platforms are not intermediaries. *Georgetown Law Technology Review, 2*(2), 198–216.

Gillespie, T. (2018b). Governance of and by platforms. In J. Burgess, A. E. Marwick, & T. Poell (eds.), *The SAGE handbook of social media* (pp. 254–278). London; Thousand Oaks, CA: Sage Publications.

Goldberg, C. (2019, August 17). How Google has destroyed the lives of revenge porn victims. *New York Post.* Retrieved from https://nypost.com/2019/08/17/how-google-has-destroyed-the-lives-of-revenge-porn-victims/.

Gong, L., & Hoffman, A. (2012). Sexting and slut-shaming: Why prosecution of teen self-sexters harms women. *The Georgetown Journal of Gender and the Law, 13*, 577–589.

Hasinoff, A. A. (2013). Sexting as media production: Rethinking social media and sexuality. *New Media & Society, 15*(4), 449–465.

Henry, N., & Flynn, A. (2019). Image-based sexual abuse: Online distribution channels and illicit communities of support. *Violence Against Women, 25*(16), 1932–1955.

International Planned Parenthood Federation (IPPF). (2008). *Sexual rights: An IPPF declaration*. London: IPPF.

Karaian, L. (2014). Policing "sexting": Responsibilization, respectability and sexual subjectivity in child protection/crime prevention responses to teenagers' digital sexual expression. *Theoretical Criminology, 18*(3), 282–299.

Karaian, L., & Van Meyl, K. (2015). Reframing risqué/risky: Queer temporalities, teenage sexting, and freedom of expression. *Laws, 4,* 18–36.

Kearney, S., Gleeson, C., Leung, L., Ollis, D., & Joyce, A. (2016). *Respectful relationships education in schools: The beginnings of change*. Melbourne, VIC: Our Watch.

Kelly, C. (2019, November 18). Facebook's anti-revenge porn tools failed to protect Katie Hill. *WIRED*. Retrieved from www.wired.com/story/katie-hill-revenge-porn-facebook/.

Kreimer, S. F. (2006). Censorship by proxy: The first amendment, internet intermediaries, and the problem of the weakest link. *University of Pennsylvania Law Review, 155,* 11–101.

Langston, J. (2018, September 12). How PhotoDNA for video is being used to fight online child exploitation. *Microsoft News*. Retrieved from https://news.microsoft.com/on-the-issues/2018/09/12/how-photodna-for-video-is-being-used-to-fight-online-child-exploitation/

Lee, M., & Crofts, T. (2015). Gender, pressure, coercion and pleasure: Untangling motivations for sexting between young people. *British Journal of Criminology, 55*(3), 454–473.

Lloyd, J. (2018). Abuse through sexual image sharing in schools: Response and responsibility. *Gender and Education*. doi: 10.1080/09540253.2018.1513456.

MacKinnon, R., Hickok, E., Bar, A., & Lim, H. (2014). *Fostering freedom online: The role of internet intermediaries*. Paris; Reston, VA: UNESCO and the Internet Society.

Naughton, J. (2019, August 18). Behind the screen review – inside the social media sweatshops. *The Guardian*. Retrieved from www.theguardian.com/books/2019/aug/18/behind-the-screen-sarah-t-roberts-review.

Our Watch, ANROWS, & VicHealth (2015). *Change the story: A shared framework for the primary prevention of violence against women and their children in Australia*. Melbourne, VIC: Our Watch. Retrieved from www.ourwatch.org.au/getmedia/0aa0109b-6b03-43f2-85fe-a9f5ec92ae4e/Change-the-story-framework-prevent-violence-women-children-AA-new.pdf.aspx.

Pasquale, F. (2010). Beyond innovation and competition: The need for qualified transparency in internet intermediaries. *Northwestern University Law Review, 104*(1), 105–174.

Penney, R. (2016). The rhetoric of the mistake in adult narratives of youth sexuality: The case of Amanda Todd. *Feminist Media Studies, 16*(4), 710–725.

Powell, A., & Henry, N. (eds.). (2014). *Preventing sexual violence: Interdisciplinary approaches to overcoming a rape culture*. Basingstoke: Palgrave Macmillan.

Powell, A., & Henry, N. (2017). *Sexual violence in a digital age*. London: Palgrave Macmillan.

Roberts, S. T. (2019). *Behind the screen: Content moderation in the shadows of social media*. New Haven, CT: Yale University Press.
Ringrose, J., & Renold, E. (2012). Slut-shaming, girl power and "sexualisation": Thinking through the politics of the international SlutWalks with teen girls. *Gender and Education, 24*(3), 333–343.
Rübner Jørgensen, C., Weckesser, A., Turner, J., & Wade, A. (2019). Young people's views on sexting education and support needs: Findings and recommendations from a UK-based study. *Sex Education, 19*(1), 25–40.
Salinas, S. (2019, March 15). Facebook says it made an A.I. tool that can detect revenge porn before it's reported. *CNBC*. Retrieved from www.cnbc.com/2019/03/15/facebook-ai-tool-detects-revenge-porn-before-its-reported.html.
Strapagiel, L. (2013, March 26). Amanda Todd video channelled in "I shared a photo" anti-sexting PSA (VIDEO). *Huffington Post*. Retrieved from www.huffingtonpost.ca/2013/03/26/amanda-todd-video-i-shared-a-photo-sexting-psa_n_2957971.html.
Sutton, A., Cherney, A., & White, R. (2008). *Crime prevention: Principles, perspectives and practices*. Port Melbourne, VIC: Cambridge University Press.
Suzor, N. P. (2019). *Lawless: The secret rules that govern our digital lives*. Cambridge, UK: Cambridge University Press.
Tushnet. R. (2008). Power without responsibility: Intermediaries and the First Amendment. *George Washington Law Review, 76*(4), 986–1016.
VicHealth. (2007). *Preventing violence before it occurs: A framework and background paper to guide the primary prevention of violence against women in Victoria*. Melbourne, VIC: Victorian Health Promotion Foundation.
Wakefield, M. A., Loken, B., & Hornik, R. C. (2010). Use of mass media campaigns to change health behaviour. *The Lancet, 376*(9748), 1261–1271.
World Health Organization (WHO). (2015). *Sexual health, human rights and the law*. Geneva: World Health Organization. Retrieved from
Zuckerberg, M. (2019, March 31). The internet needs new rules. Let's start in these four areas. *The Washington Post*. Retrieved from www.washingtonpost.com/opinions/mark-zuckerberg-the-internet-needs-new-rules-lets-start-in-these-four-areas/2019/03/29/9e6f0504-521a-11e9-a3f7-78b7525a8d5f_story.html.

Chapter 9

Conclusion

Introduction

Despite significant social and technological shifts in the past two decades, research has been somewhat slow to fully elucidate and conceptualise the pervasiveness, nature and impacts of image-based sexual abuse. Much scholarship has instead focused either narrowly on the "sexting" behaviours of adolescents, or on criminal law reform responses to "revenge porn". Very few empirical studies have investigated the experiences of victims directly and even fewer have examined the motivations of perpetrators who engage in image-based sexual abuse behaviours. In this book, we have sought to contribute both empirically, through our multi-country and multi-methods study, as well as conceptually, through theory-knitting from across criminological, sociological, legal and psychological disciplines, to build a holistic and in-depth examination of the complexity of the phenomenon we call image-based sexual abuse.

In this final chapter, we draw together some of the key themes, concepts and findings that are examined throughout the book. We also suggest future directions for the continued development of this field. If there is one thing we can know for certain, it is that technology will continue to develop, change and adapt. But so too will perpetrators continue to use digital technology as a tool for coercion, harassment, abuse and violence. Ultimately, we argue that while the behaviours and impacts of image-based sexual abuse are diverse and vary across different contexts, we must not allow the violation of sexual autonomy, consent and privacy to become the "new normal" in the digital era.

Overarching themes

The diverse experiences of image-based sexual abuse that we describe throughout this book demonstrate the ubiquity of digital devices and platforms for the taking and sharing of non-consensual nude or sexual images in the digital era. They also demonstrate the extent to which image-based

sexual abuse goes well beyond the paradigmatic malicious ex-partner scenario (colloquially known as "revenge porn"), with perpetrators – both
known and unknown to the victim-survivor – being motivated by many differing and overlapping factors, such as power and control, financial gain,
amusement, sexual gratification and social status building. This book has
sought to demonstrate that image-based sexual abuse is not solely concerned with the non-consensual sharing of such images, but also includes
the non-consensual *taking* of nude or sexual images, including digitally altered images, as well as *threats to share* images. While some victim-survivors
of image-based sexual abuse have tragically ended their lives as a result of
their images going viral or have faced horrific forms of bullying, abuse and
harassment, there are other devastating harms that victim-survivors experience, such as social rupture, isolation, constrained liberty, constant hy-
pervigilance and existential threats. And yet for others, there may be few
discernible impacts, further pointing to the complexity of this phenomenon.

We have identified several overarching themes and key findings regarding
the pervasiveness and nature of image-based sexual abuse harms, including:
How relations of power and control shape and drive perpetration behaviours; the centrality of gender and misogyny for understanding the causes
and consequences of image-based sexual abuse, and its relationship with
other intersecting systems of power, such as colonialism, racism, ableism
and heterosexism; and the importance of comprehensive, coordinated and
holistic justice and educational packages that seek to provide much-needed
support and recognition to victim-survivors, and prevent image-based sexual abuse from happening in the first place. We briefly summarise each of
these key themes in turn below, before outlining the need for further research in this field.

Power and control

Public, media and legal discourses on image-based sexual abuse have all
too commonly focused on the paradigmatic malicious ex-partner seeking
"revenge" in the aftermath of a relationship breakdown. This focus has
thwarted policy, educational and legislative initiatives, meaning that the
full nature, extent and impacts of image-based sexual abuse have not been
properly understood. This focus has also hindered an understanding of the
complex nature of perpetration, both in terms of who the perpetrators are
and why they act in the ways they do.

Our research found that perpetrators of image-based sexual abuse are
more commonly men than women, and that perpetration is higher among
some groups, including younger men and sexual minority men. The gendered
nature of the abuse means that image-based sexual abuse is best understood
as being on a "continuum of sexual violence", with women often experiencing abuse as part of a broader pattern of gendered harassment and abuse.

In addition, the sexual double standards all too evident in many societies continue to shape women's experience of image-based sexual abuse, with harassment and abuse often targeting their sexual expression and perceived transgression of feminine norms. For sexual minority men, there appears to be a tension linked to perpetration behaviours, where on the one hand, consensual sexual imagery has been an important means through which to express and explore sexuality, which has arguably shaped the greater uptake of digital dating and sexual imagery among sexual minority men. On the other hand, this also appears to be associated with a greater opportunity for image-based sexual abuse perpetration among gay men. The specific nature of this association, however, is an area that requires further research and contextualisation.

We also investigated the range of motives for perpetrating image-based sexual abuse, as identified by the respondents in our survey who self-reported having engaged in image-based sexual abuse behaviour. The research confirms that there is an extensive range of often overlapping motivations, including malice, financial gain, sexual gratification, status building and control. Therefore, while "revenge" does motivate some perpetrators of image-based sexual abuse, it is by no means the dominant motive and, even where present, it is often interwoven with the desire for power and control. Indeed, it was power and control that dominated the responses of victim-survivors when asked why they thought the perpetrators had acted as they did. This was not only in the context of an abusive relationship, but across all types of relationships.

Our research emphasises the need for robust and effective educational, regulatory and legal interventions to be based on the evidence that motivations are multifarious, with power and control being a dominant theme. Education, for example, must target those individuals most likely to perpetrate image-based sexual abuse, particularly young men. Specialist work with LGBTQI groups is also necessary to understand the nature of both victimisation and perpetration within these communities.

In terms of legal regulation, our research also highlights the inadequacy of privileging certain perpetrator motivations in law. There is no evidence to suggest that the motivation of "revenge" with the intention to cause harm or distress is either more common or causes more harm to victim-survivors. Similarly, the requirement of many laws to prove the motive of sexual gratification for voyeurism and other forms of non-consensual image-taking, such as "upskirting", demonstrates the outdated nature of those laws, as well as a lack of understanding of the current-day manifestation of different forms of abuse in the digital era.

Gender, misogyny and entitlement

To understand image-based sexual abuse is to recognise that we continue to live in deeply gendered societies which are characterised by misogyny, male entitlement and sexual double standards. While our survey suggests similarities in victimisation rates between women and men, we recognise that the nature and extent of women's image-based sexual abuse victimisation cannot be easily captured by survey research. This may be because many victims are simply unaware that their nude or sexual images have been taken or shared without their consent, and survey research is thus most likely to underestimate the true prevalence of image-based sexual abuse. Furthermore, in light of emerging research analysing the online websites that facilitate and host non-consensual nude or sexual images, it is highly likely that there are uneven gendered patterns in the unknown victimisation of image-based sexual abuse, as the vast majority of websites, online communities and image-sharing platforms specifically trade in the images of women and girls without their knowledge or consent (see Henry & Flynn, 2019).

Gender is also significant in relation to perpetration. Our research found that men are more likely to perpetrate image-based sexual abuse, and gender is relevant in terms of why they engage in those behaviours. We have argued that for some perpetrators image-based sexual abuse is about "impression management" and performing their gender and masculinity to build their status and bond with other men through objectifying and harassing women.

Gendered power relations shape the nature of the harms of image-based sexual abuse. Many of the women victim-survivors who shared their stories with us have experienced significant, often all-encompassing harms – in large part because of the social stigma and shame around women's sexuality. Victim-survivors, for example, talked about how the harms are often constant, leaving them feeling isolated and under threat. Some experience image-based sexual abuse as a "social rupture", where their lives become demarcated between "before" and "after" the abuse. Others experience these harms alongside further experiences of domestic and sexual violence. There is no common pattern, no "worst" case scenario, no predictability about how victim-survivors may respond. Indeed, for many victim-survivors, their experiences were not properly understood and the harms not sufficiently recognised. We suggest, therefore, that a better understanding of the harms of image-based sexual abuse comes through a phenomenological approach which considers the experience and harms as a whole and in context. The common separation of harms into different categories, such as psychological, physical, economic, social and familial, may not adequately capture the interconnected, overlapping and often all-encompassing nature of the harms (see McGlynn et al., in press).

Furthermore, our survey found that particular groups were more significantly affected by image-based sexual abuse, with women, LGB+ respondents and those from minority racial and ethnic communities experiencing greater adverse impacts. Although we endeavoured to recruit a diversity of participants for our victim-survivor interviews to explore experiences beyond that of gender alone, the majority of self-selected participants were young, white heterosexual women. Further research is needed to examine image-based sexual abuse within marginalised groups to better understand the intersectionality of overlapping systems of power beyond the mono-categorical thinking of gender (Collins, 2019; Crenshaw, 1991).

Justice and redress within and beyond the criminal law

In recent years, specific criminal laws have been enacted in many international jurisdictions to address the problem of image-based sexual abuse. Despite the existence of these laws, victim-survivors continue to experience a significant "justice gap". Police responses are often victim-blaming or trivialising; existing laws do not capture certain behaviours; criminal justice processes are slow and arduous for complainants; and victim-survivors run the risk of being identified when anonymity provisions are not applied. For many victim-survivors, the criminal justice pathway is not necessarily the most conducive to achieving "justice".

While it is crucial that criminal laws are comprehensive, encompassing all forms of image-based sexual abuse, much more needs to be done to address this justice gap. For example, it is important that police, prosecutors and other personnel receive appropriate training and resourcing to take cases forward. Mandatory anonymity for complainants would also help to encourage victim-survivors to report to the police and proceed to trial. In addition to criminal justice avenues, civil law options are increasingly providing additional forms of redress for victim-survivors, including new statutory civil claims and remedies.

Beyond the substantive law, transformative and restorative justice options may help to bridge the justice gap. Ultimately, our research demonstrates that there is no "one-size-fits-all" response to image-based sexual abuse. What is needed is a multifaceted approach which encompasses comprehensive criminal and civil laws, as well as additional approaches and options focused more on recognition, restoration and prevention. Finally, far greater support is required to assist victim-survivors in removing images from the internet and digital devices. While there are examples of good practice in this regard in some countries, access remains limited by resources, as well as insufficient awareness of the support mechanisms that are available.

Prevention and education

Education and community responses to image-based sexual abuse are an important means of challenging gender- and sexuality-based social norms and cultural practices that underlie image-based sexual abuse and providing practical support to victims, perpetrators and bystanders. These responses should seek to dismantle the blaming of victim-survivors and place responsibility onto the perpetrators of the abuse. Prevention should also focus on the empowerment of bystanders to safely intervene to prevent abuse and support victim-survivors. Given the overlap between perpetration and victimisation reported in this book, it is important to address referral and support information in ways that does not blame or minimise the harms experienced by victims, while at the same time not excusing the behaviours of perpetrators. While no causal relationship can be attributed to the relationship between image-based sexual abuse perpetration and victimisation as reported in this book, it is possible that one may be a response or reaction to the other. In the Australian legal context in which redress options for image-based sexual abuse are variable across jurisdictions and are not always effectively utilised, it may well be the case that neither victims nor perpetrators of image-based sexual abuse are fully aware of the potential legal consequences of the non-consensual taking, sharing, and/or making of threats to share, nude or sexual images. This was certainly reflected in our study, where we found a widespread lack of knowledge about the laws in specific jurisdictions among survey respondents.

There is a clear need to continue to examine and understand the varied contexts and subgroups engaged in, and affected by, image-based sexual abuse. As countries globally continue to grapple with the extent, nature, impacts and legal ramifications of image-based sexual abuse, it is crucial that education and support are targeted appropriately to those who need them most. These efforts must be guided by a sexual ethics approach that prioritises affirmative consent, reciprocity, bodily integrity and sexual freedom.

Conclusion

This book presents new insights into the phenomenon of image-based sexual abuse, drawing on data from the first multi-jurisdictional project to use mixed methods to examine experiences of victimisation and perpetration in Australia, New Zealand and the United Kingdom. The analysis presented in this book draws on a substantive dataset, but further research is needed to respond to legal and societal changes, particularly if we are to better support and address the challenges facing those from minority racial and ethnic communities, as well as those identifying as LGBTQI.

Digital technologies and their misuse for abuse and harassment are continuing to evolve, and so too must our understandings of these harms and how to address them. In relation to our understanding of victimisation, further research is needed to recognise, centralise and respond to the experiences of indigenous, black and minoritised women experiencing image-based sexual abuse, as well as other individuals and groups facing interlocking oppressions in society, inclusive of racism, xenophobia, ableism, heterosexism and ageism.

Further research, particularly qualitative work, is also needed with perpetrators to explore motivations and understandings to inform prevention and education in this space, as well as improving responses (see OeSC, 2019).

Relatedly, it is important to engage in research on bystander prevention in relation to image-based sexual abuse to safely empower those who witness instances of abuse in supporting the victim-survivors and/or seeking ways to respond to perpetrators, especially given the results of our survey, which suggest a majority of respondents *want* to say or do something when they witness or become aware of image-based sexual abuse.

Finally, digital platforms play an important role in addressing image-based sexual abuse. More recently, there has been growing pressure on governments to develop regulatory regimes to hold the platforms more accountable for content posted by their users. In the past few years, some digital platforms have developed comprehensive tools, practices and policies designed to address image-based sexual abuse. Little is currently known about the effectiveness of these measures, and as such more research is needed.

While technology is quickly developing, and therefore methods of perpetration and experiences of abuse will continue to evolve, we hope that this book provides a valuable evidence base from which scholars and practitioners can continue to develop targeted, nuanced and effective educational and prevention initiatives, as well as comprehensive legal reforms and justice initiatives and properly resourced forms of support. As our lives are increasingly embedded in the digital realm, it is a sober reminder that harassment and abuse are likely to not only continue, but to adapt, develop and shift in new and potentially unanticipated ways. Though law and policy may always be playing catch-up, it is up to scholars, advocates and practitioners to continue to advocate for reform to address the harms of image-based sexual abuse.

References

Collins, P. H. (2019). *Intersectionality as critical social theory.* Durham; London: Duke University Press.

Crenshaw, K. (1991). Mapping the margins: Intersectionality, identity politics, and violence against women of color. *Stanford Law Review, 43*(6), 1241–1299.

Henry, N., & Flynn, A. (2019). Image-based sexual abuse: Online distribution channels and illicit communities of support. *Violence Against Women, 25*(16), 1932–1955.

McGlynn, C., Johnson, K., Rackley, E., Henry, N., Gavey, N., Flynn, A., & Powell, A. (in press). "It's torture for the soul": The harms of image-based sexual abuse. *Social and Legal Studies.*

Office of the eSafety Commissioner (OeSC). (2019). *Understanding the attitudes and motivations of adults who engage in image-based abuse: Summary report.* Melbourne, VIC: Social Research Centre. Retrieved from www.esafety.gov.au/sites/default/files/2019-10/Research_Report_IBA_Perp_Motivations.pdf.

Index